A Pictorial History of Western Art

PAUL V. SPADE

1044

ERWIN O. CHRISTENSEN
is Director of Publications of
the American Association
of Museums in Washington, D.C.
Formerly he was the Curator
of Decorative Arts and The Index
of American Design at The National
Gallery of Art. He is the author
of *Early American Wood Carving,*
The Index of American Design,
Primitive Art, and *Popular Art*
in the United States.

A PICTORIAL HISTORY OF

WESTERN ART

Erwin O. Christensen

A MENTOR BOOK

PUBLISHED BY THE NEW AMERICAN LIBRARY

For a fuller understanding of the history of Western art, this book should be used together with Mentor Book MQ357, entitled *The History of Western Art*. One book parallels the other without duplication in text or illustrations; together they contain 768 illustrations.

Contents

Preface

THIS BOOK takes the reader on a tour through about five thousand years of Western art. It begins with the origins of art in the prehistoric period and ends with the art of today. Those works of art discussed in some detail are also illustrated; all important periods and leading countries are included. Architecture, sculpture, and painting are emphasized, but the decorative arts and the graphic arts are also represented.

Much care was spent on the selection of illustrations. With a wealth of art to choose from, each work had to be representative of its own period and to contribute in style and subject matter to the total panorama as well. Well-known masterpieces were included, even though they have been often reproduced. There are also works by unknown artists that have never been illustrated in this kind of book. Most of the works here discussed or illustrated are by outstanding artists, but there are many others of equal merit that had to be omitted.

To condense the history of art into a given number of pages is an agonizing task. Much one would like to include has to be left out; otherwise it would be difficult to say much about anything. The history of art would become a string of names and dates connected by generalities and unsupported by interpretations or illustrations. In this volume most of the text deals with the illustrations. The best photographs obtainable were used; at times the one photograph that would result in the best reproduction was selected from several.

To cover the history of art in a book of this size may be compared to a trip on a plane. As the plane in approaching its goal descends at reduced speed, you begin to see individual houses and the people on the streets. Much the same is true of our flight through time as we approach the art of our own period. Turn the pages of this book. When you are less than halfway through, you have covered, of the five thousand years, all but the last five hundred. Thereafter the pace becomes more leisurely. The works of art often belong to the same century or decade, and some are contemporary. More pages are given to the art that begins with the Renaissance than to the earlier periods. It is modern art and its origins in the Renaissance with which we are chiefly concerned.

For a more detailed account of the pre-Renaissance periods, the reader should turn to *The History of Western Art* (Mentor MQ 357), which deals more fully with the earlier centuries; it too brings the history of art up to date and supplies background information for all periods.

Introduction

MAN OWES his gradual rise to civilization in a large measure to the development of his hand and eye. The two used together in complex tasks produced tools and weapons; with their aid man learned to cope with a hostile environment. At an early stage in his development man's basic dissatisfaction with his lot drove him on to ever greater efforts.

He took pride in his upright posture, which gave him a sense of the significance of verticals as denoting firmness and domination, horizontals suggesting repose. The ascending curve of the rising sun gave him joy; its descent brought on despair. Man's preference for symmetry was based on his body, which is symmetrical throughout.

Thus art became related to the human body; its basic lines and forms are imbedded in experience and have become part of our human heritage. In a world invested with myth and magic, man's life was only beginning to be controlled by reason. His lack of experience set limits to what was within his realm. Other basic elements of experience, like conceptions of space and preferences for colors, were gradually developed and eventually used for purposes of art.

What sustains the artist beyond the necessity of earning a livelihood is important. The medieval artist worked in a spirit of self-denial and humility. The Renaissance artist gloried in art as an expression of his own personality. To elevate himself through art drives the modern artist to explore the possibilities of discovering new beauty. This means strife and often frustration but also joy and release from tension.

Creativity in any field reconciles man with his fate and gives him a sense of dignity.

In addition to the personality of the artist, the kind of society of which he is a part determines the general character of his art. We learn from the history of art what affected art, such as myth, religion, the growth of the nation, and the struggle of the artist in society.

Art begins in the prehistoric period, and its most spectacular achievements are in the cave paintings of western France and northeastern Spain.

The real origins of a world art tradition are found in countries of a warm climate and broad river valleys, in Egypt with the Nile and Mesopotamia (modern Iraq) with the Tigris and Euphrates.

The Western art we speak of here begins its development only after it had come in contact with the countries of the Near East. With the Greeks, we arrive at a truly human art in the sense that the individual artist emerges as a free creator. As in Egypt, art continues to deal with religion; though tinged with human frailty, divinity is now represented as human, reflecting man at his best.

This humanizing trend in making the supernatural concrete was never abandoned in Western art. God the Father, as represented in Christian art, perpetuates a Father image that the Greeks in the Phidian Zeus had passed on to the Roman Jupiter (Ill. 49). Greek art had laid a foundation for Roman art after the Romans had gained control of the Mediterranean world.

Early medieval art north of the Mediterranean is based in its essential development on the styles that emerged in the wake of Roman provincial styles. With the Romans the first major chapter of ancient art comes to a close.

During the following Middle Ages the modern nations of Europe, outside of Italy, developed. They had in common a new religion, Christianity. Religion then became the dominant content and reason for art, as is evidenced by the great cathedrals of the time.

Panel painting—though known in antiquity—and oil painting on canvas appeared only at the end of the Middle Ages, and thereafter painting became the essence of Western art. During the same period sculpture developed along parallel lines, achieved its own triumphs, but assumed no position of leadership. Architecture, from Renaissance to contemporary, remained in basic conflict for the greater part of this period. Aesthetics obscured trends toward slowly emerging structural advances.

The twentieth century has witnessed the triumph of a modern style based on science and technology; architecture and painting are leading the arts today.

In this sweep from east to west, South and Central Europe receive most attention. The countries to the north and east, removed from the metropolitan centers to the south, also participated in the development of Western art and on occasion played a leading part.

I

Prehistoric Art in Europe

PREHISTORIC ART of the late Paleolithic period made its greatest advance in the cave paintings of the Ice Age [pp. 11–12].* They represent animals, often those of the hunt like reindeer and bison, painted on the bare stone walls. Just under life size, these paintings are of striking realism. The caves themselves were uninhabited and difficult of access. Man himself is represented rarely and then as sorcerer.

Prehistoric man held to beliefs in sympathetic magic, that like attracts like. Thus painted animals on cave walls, concealed in the bowels of the earth, could attract living animals. The earth, as the seat of life, symbolized fertility, and the cave served as a sanctuary for the performance of rites. Fertility magic was believed to ensure the survival of the herds on which the life of man depended. Through death magic the hunter increased the accuracy of his aim and through propitiation magic he appeased the animals killed [pp. 16–18].

What we know of the beliefs of primitive men of more recent periods suggests how magic may have functioned in prehistoric times. Through magic man sustained his sense of security in his struggle for subsistence. But this was achieved through art, which means that the artist must have held an important place in prehistory. A late stage of this Paleolithic hunting-culture art survived in animal engravings on open rock ledges in the Scandinavian countries.

* Bracketed material throughout the book refers to background information in *The History of Western Art* (Mentor MQ357).

During the New Stone Age, the Neolithic period, painting gradually disappeared in northern Europe. Where painting survived, in Spain and North Africa, it is small in scale, without the monumental vigor of the Ice Age style.

Lines now sufficed to mark the passing of the seasons on which the crops depended. Realistic pictures of animals were no longer needed after man had learned to grow crops and was no longer exclusively dependent on the hunt. What man made with his own hands became important, like the ships of the Swedish rock engravings of the Bronze period (Ill. 6). When this north European culture finally came into contact with the more advanced civilization of the Mediterranean world, art reflected this influence, as illustrated in a bronze pail (Ill. 7). Here prehistory is in contact with historic art.

Altamira cave drawing, Spain (Ill. 1)

The same cave walls were painted over many times so that the paintings on the bottom layers must be earlier than those superimposed. From this we know that lines, like the above found on lower layers, came before representation of animals. Though they suggest no meaning, they do not seem to be accidental, but could have been drawn playfully.

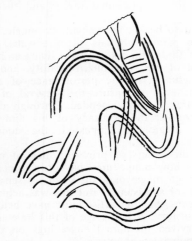

Ill. 1 Lines drawn in clay with a toothed implement, Altamira cave, Spain. *Breuil-Boyle-Windels,* Four Hundred Centuries of Cave Art *(1955)*

III. 2 Engraving on bone from Thaingen (Switzerland)

Engraving on bone, Switzerland (Ill. 2)

The earliest engravings of animals, on cave walls, are rigid profile views, drawn in outline with only two legs showing. As the style developed, the animals became more lifelike. We see an elk calmly grazing, slowly advancing step by step. Details are correctly drawn by an experienced artist who had mastered his subject. This small piece of bone might have been carried by a hunter as a good-luck talisman.

Bison Standing, Altamira cave (Ill. 3)

The developed Paleolithic style in painting appears in this standing bison. Delicately drawn horns, tufts of hair, and hoofs contrast with the fleshy mass subdivided by interior drawing. In outline and proportions the animal is wholly convincing. No ground is shown, so the legs seem suspended. Actually, each animal at Altamira is painted on a projecting part of the uneven cave ceiling, rather than on a flat surface. The hummock added relief to the painting, which looks flat only in reproduction. This deliberate search for effects of bulk was probably based on beliefs in magic [p. 17].

Ill. 3 Bison Standing, Altamira cave, Spain. L. c. 5 ft. *Archives Photographiques*

Two Elk, rock engravings, Sweden (Ill. 4)

Two elk engraved on a rock ledge in Sweden are without the full-bodied realism of the Altamira bison. This is an abbreviated, impoverished style that shows something of its realistic heritage. In the lowered heads, the bent legs, and the loosely drawn contour, we still sense the animal's forward stride.

Ill. 4 Two Elk, rock engravings, Jämtland, Sweden. *Frobenius Collection, Frankfurt-am-Main, Germany*

Ill. 5 Rock painting from Cueva del Civil, Valtorta Gorge, (Castellón), Spain. *After H. Obermaier and P. Wernert,* Humphrey Milford, *Oxford University Press* (1930)

Rock painting, Spain (Ill. 5)

Neolithic painting speaks a new language. Man appears in his own right with an increased sense of self-importance. In hunting scenes men are represented in groups in lively postures in pursuit of the fleeing herd. This new style seems to be associated with other remains that point to an agricultural economy after the crafts had made their appearance.

Bronze Age rock engravings, Sweden (Ill. 6)

This late stage of a decline in realism becomes abstract in the Bronze Age. In the rows of parallel vertical strokes lined up in the upper ship, presumably its crew, a pictorial style has become geometric. The recognizable figures of men or gods vary in height from one to several feet. Earlier death and fertility cults may have changed in meaning and become memorials with the passage of time. We are here close to a pictorial language rather than to an expression of art in a modern sense.

During the northern Neolithic and Bronze periods, monumental architecture that enclosed space was nonexistent. Sculpture may be as old as painting but most Paleolithic sculpture is modest in size, consisting of carvings that were easily carried, "mobile" art. During the Neolithic period pottery was widely distributed. Styles vary geographically but have in common a basic geometric character.

Before the end of the European Neolithic period, copper came into use, first in small ornamental pieces. The Mediterranean countries seem to have used copper earlier than northern Europe. The spread of metals, as used in tools and implements, is the special province of prehistoric archaeology. Such terms as Neolithic period, Copper, Bronze, and Iron ages do not imply that all countries passed from one to the other at the same time. Northern Europe was still using polished stone (before 1800 B.C.), long after Egypt (around 3000 B.C.) had been using tools of bronze, an alloy of copper and tin. During the Paleolithic Ice Age, Western Europe was leading in art, as shown by the cave paintings. Central Europe became artistically dominant during the Neolithic period. With the use of bronze (2000–1600 B.C.) southeastern Europe took a leading position in art, and in Egypt and the Near East writing appeared and history began.

Wherever individual finds from the preliterate northern countries reveal the characteristics of historic styles, like Egyptian, Greek, or Roman, we know the artists must have been familiar with the historic works they tried to imitate or modify in their own way. In that way the contents of an Iron Age tomb in Britain (Aylesford, Kent) have been attributed (Sir Arthur Evans) to the first century B.C.

Ill. 6 Bronze Age rock engravings (1000–500 B.C.) from Bohuslän, Island of Gotland, Sweden. Lars Jeybratt, Göteborg Art Museum, Sweden

Bronze-mounted bucket, England (Ill. 7)

Among the contents of this tomb was this bronze-mounted bucket, ten inches high. The embossed frieze suggests in the scroll ends a native Celtic adaptation of classical motifs.

Prehistoric north European art from east to west had developed in metal ornamental art styles before contact with Roman civilization. This bronze bucket belongs to the second part (La Tène period, 500–100 B.C.) of the Early Iron Age (1000–100 B.C.). It has been dated about the time of Caesar's invasion (55 B.C.) and may be taken as representing the end of prehistoric European art.

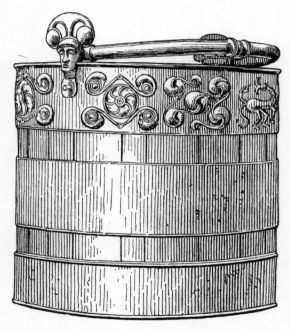

Ill. 7 Bronze-mounted bucket, Aylesford, England. *British Museum,* Guide to Iron Age Antiquities (*1925*)

II

Egyptian Art

ARCHITECTURE AS a major art originated in Egypt. The rectangular plan of the house was also used for tomb [mastaba] and temple [Karnak]. A simple utilitarian structure of four walls and a flat roof developed into an art form by repeating the basic rectangle on a central axis. Here, for the first time in history, we have architectural forms combined for purposes of artistic effect. Tomb and temple had developed their basic form by the time of the pyramids, around 2600 B.C. (Chephren), and were only elaborated in later temples of the XVIII Dynasty (Karnak and Luxor). Unlike an accumulation of structures, where one was added to another, as houses in city streets or lots in a cemetery, the sequence of entrance gate [pylon], forecourt, hall, and sanctuary was planned for an emotional effect.

The temple is essentially the house of man aggrandized to make it impressive as the house of a god. It was meant to inspire awe, a feeling all religions seek to arouse. The human figure looks small when set against the huge expanse of surface of the temple wall [Ill. 26]. The contrast was impressive, and man responded with a feeling of humility. As he entered the temple through a narrow passageway he was caught up between massive walls, overwhelmed by the towering pylons [Ill. 17]. Leaving the confining passageway, he was received, with a sense of exhilaration, by a large court, open to the sky and flanked by columns [Karnak and Luxor]. Narrow passageways and open courts, varied by columned halls, are repeated in an orderly fashion until the almost-dark sanctuary was reached. [Ill. 25, p. 37].

Massive architecture, gigantic in its bulk, is equaled by a

seemingly limitless expanse of painted surfaces. These represent a perpetual tribute to the great god of the temple, and were supplemented by an elaborate system of rituals administered by priests in the form of prayers, aspersions, and sacrifices.

Temples and tombs were often combined. The tomb of man was his eternal home, paralleling the temple, the house of the god. The tomb received the sarcophagus with the embalmed body of the deceased, his mummy. To ensure man a life after death, his body had to be preserved, but a statue could serve as an extra precaution, to replace the body. Statues and the power of magic formulas became a necessity for survival, but they received support from pictorial representation.

For a continuation of life in the hereafter, man had to have food and all the labor necessary to maintain a constant supply of the necessities and luxuries of life. To provide food and other things that made life comfortable, the tomb walls were painted to represent what was needed; through magic the paintings became real.

Paleolithic man had to spend his energy as hunter and artist to ward off starvation, but the Egyptian felt secure with regard to his needs on earth. A developed agriculture in the fertile Nile valley had solved that problem. Hemmed in by deserts, Egypt was protected against foreign invasions. Egyptian history is one of long periods of peace, only rarely interrupted by war. Stability and continuity were part of the Egyptian way of life. No period in Western history again experienced a comparable permanence. This image of an enduring culture in ancient Egypt has been preserved for us almost solely through her art. But the enduring style of Egyptian art did not lead to stagnation. Even in the late Ptolemaic period Egyptian art had elegance and vitality and produced variations within a basic pattern.

Palette of King Narmer, slate (Ill. 8)

This palette was not for domestic use, but a votive tablet dedicated to a god. A depression between the intertwined necks of the monsters was for grinding malachite for face paint. Two cow-headed goddesses (Hathor) enframe the coat of arms. In the uppermost row, the king wears the crown of Lower Egypt; on the other side he wears the white crown of Upper Egypt, as Narmer was the king of a united Egypt. In both royal images the king is represented as taller than other figures, as size denoted royalty.

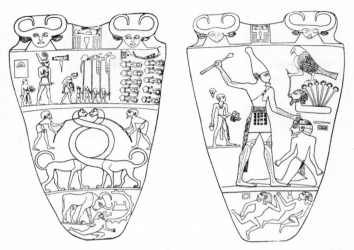

Ill. 8 Palette of King Narmer (Menes, or Mena), slate, carved in low relief, finished with a metal scraper; I Dynasty. H. c. 20 in. Cairo Museum. *After Forrer,* Reallexicon, *W. Spemann (1908)*

The palette is an early historic work, one of the few works known from the early dynastic period, before Egyptian art had achieved the maturity of the Old Kingdom period (IV Dynasty). It has been variously dated 3315 B.C. (Meyer), 3240 B.C. (Breasted), and 5500 B.C., just before I Dynasty (Petrie). Paleolithic painting [Altamira ceiling] shows no awareness of composition, and Neolithic painting [hunting scene, Ill. 10] does not relate figure to background. Figures, once scattered in lively action, are here placed in rows. A king, in form of a bull, is destroying the enemy's city as one defender is trampled beneath the bull and two others are running away. With a club in one hand and a whip in the other, the king follows a procession of standard bearers, differing in height presumably to indicate rank. A small sandal- and vase-bearer follows. Two rows of decapitated enemies have their heads placed before their feet, probably meant as a gesture of gratitude to the god for having granted victory. The king, with raised club, about to slay his adversary, is a symbol of victory. The hawk with a human hand holding a rope tied to the nose of a horse's head refers to the successful war. Six papyrus buds symbolize the number of captives made (6,000); hieroglyphic inscriptions are spaced in between.

The Egyptian relief style in its concentration on essential facts is here in its near-final form. The profile figure in its apparent distortion was not due to any lack of skill, but was a deliberate choice to retain for the image all basic aspects of the human personality. A few remaining archaic traits, flabby feet and small hands, were improved as the style gained maturity.

Ill. 9 Relief, Man and Wife, Memphis tombs, IV Dynasty, c. 2600 B.C. *After Schäfer (1932)*

Man and Wife, relief, Memphis tombs (Ill. 9)

Here the figure is firmly placed, contours are subtly varied to suggest correct anatomy, feet are strong, and fingers and fingernails are differentiated. The man, to denote male dominance, stands in front of the woman. His strength is contrasted with her delicacy; both conform to the Egyptian ideal of the lithe slenderness of youth. The relief is shallow, close to drawing, and enhanced by color, brown for the man and lighter for the woman.

Men Plowing, relief, Memphis (Ill. 10)

In representations of action the strict frontal shoulders are modified in the man guiding the plow. Hands and feet lack the precision of the preceding example. Animals are often drawn with skill, as in the joints and hooves of the oxen. The ground is indicated by a base line, but not the field itself. This is one section of a larger scene depicting agricultural labors to ensure a plentiful supply of food for the deceased. Compared to the realism of the Altamira bison, these oxen are but faint shadows. We sense here a relaxation of the naïvely primitive belief of Paleolithic man, who placed complete reliance on the persuasiveness of the realistic painting imbued with its magic power. The Egyptian had developed further; he had his gods to whom he could address his wishes through prayers and rituals, though much was still left to faith and magic. As far as his own person was concerned, the ancient Egyptian depended on his double (Ka) to recognize him in the accurately produced statue of himself.

In its totality, Egyptian art of 2500 B.C. has advanced immeasurably compared to Paleolithic art of 25,000 B.C.; civilization made the basic advance. The Egyptians' trust in magic concerned immortality, not survival on earth. The difference in art suggests that man has taken magic in his stride; to an extent beliefs are expressed in rituals; they have lost the frightful urgency they once had when man was still in his infancy.

Paleolithic man dealt with living animals, which paintings were believed to attract and serve in connection with the hunt [pp. 16–17]. The fact that the hunter did kill the bison could be taken as a proof that magic worked. Such proof of the power of magic the Egyptian no longer required, as he could support himself without the benefit of magic. It was where man dealt with the unknown that magic retained its potency.

Ill. 10 Relief from a tomb of ancient Memphis, Men Plowing. *After Lübke (1871)*

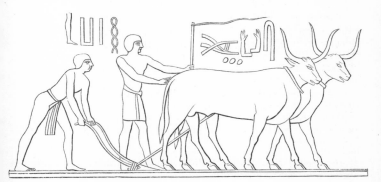

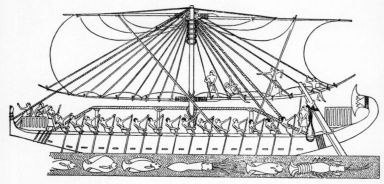

Ill. 11 Egyptian relief, galley with fifteen rowers, Queen Hatshepsut's Naval Expedition to the Land of Punt, temple of Deir-el-Bahri, XVIII Dynasty, Tuthmosis III, 1501–1447 B.C.; coregency with Queen Hatshepsut. *After Forrer,* Reallexicon, W. Spemann *(1908)*

Queen Hatshepsut's Naval Expedition, section, relief (Ill. 11)

This commercial trading expedition was an important event in Queen Hatshepsut's reign. Punt was the land of perfumes, incense, myrrh, and cinnamon, which Egyptians favored and used in their rituals. Punt has been identified as being inland off the coast of the Red Sea (Naville, Maspero). This relief shows one of the galleys in which the journey was made. The sailors on the spar are represented in free postures. One seated man (second from the mast) shows no longer the front-view shoulders. Sails, masts, and ropes are drawn with the accuracy of a technical drawing, whereas water and various fish are stylized.

Statuette of a Hooded Man, predynastic (Ill. 12)

The painted relief was the preferred medium for representing the activities of Egyptian life. Sculpture in the round developed only a few motifs, mainly the standing and seated figure. In both, immobility was more pronounced than action. An early stage of stylistic development for the standing figure is here illustrated, comparable to the stage represented for reliefs by Narmer's palette (Ill. 8). Arms and legs, cylindrical and softly rounded, compress the torso, which is slighted. Anatomical structure exists for the total figure but not in its subdivisions. The curve of the skullcap across the

Ill. 12 Statuette of a Hooded Man, basalt, predynastic, c. 3000 B.C. *Ashmolean Museum, Oxford*

24

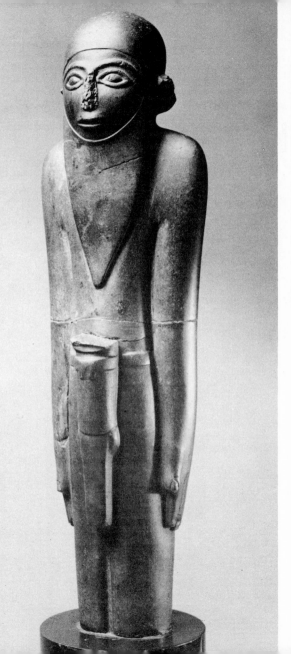

forehead is opposed by the edge of the (probably false) beard; elliptical brows and lids enframe the eyes and the semispherical head.

One may ask why the sculptor carved this statuette in the way he did. It may be that he imitated in stone a form already existing in ivory, or else he was unable to carve an anatomically correct figure. Perhaps the artist so much desired a replica of a man that any style would have sufficed. The content, man, was all-important; the art, its particular style, just happened. Such explanations fail to account for its artistic qualities; works of art are not created wholly accidentally, experimentation is also involved. If this statuette with its bulging planes that add up to a stark and severe simplicity is of an arresting interest today, it is difficult to believe that the carver was indifferent to its effect. Even though later Egyptian artists infused this type with suggestions taken from observation, that fact in no way detracts from the artistic value of this more formal rendering.

Goose, limestone relief (Ill. 13)

An accurate record of the visual facts, based on a study of living forms, distinguished the art of the Old Kingdom.

Ill. 13 Goose, relief carved in soft limestone, Old Kingdom period, IV Dynasty. *Freer Gallery of Art, Washington, D.C.*

The profile follows the undulating shape of the bird and accounts for every important detail. Each kind of feather is outlined as to shape and is given its own texture. Some portions are smooth; others show a slightly roughened surface brought out by using parallel lines to give the feeling of each part. In its perfection of craftsmanship, this relief compares with the best in any period of world art.

Mummy mask of King Tutankhamen (Ill. 14)

This royal tomb of the New Empire period is of the end of the XVIII dynasty to the beginning of which Queen Hatshepsut belongs. Tutankhamen was married to Ikhnaton's daughter, both mere children. This boy king died young after a short reign. He was probably not favored by the powerful priesthood that had returned to the traditional religion after Ikhnaton's monotheistic sun worship.

The sarcophagus contained three coffins, one inside the other. The outer two are of wood covered with thin sheets of gold. The third coffin, with the mummy, is of gold about one fourth of an inch thick, over six feet long, and weighs over 220 pounds. But its bullion value, though considerable, is the least of it. This golden mask was placed within his golden coffin over the king's head and shoulders. Compared with other known portraits, this mask is a carefully studied portrait, showing a likeness to Ikhnaton, indicating a family relationship. Eyelids and eyebrows are inlaid with blue stripes of lapis lazuli. The broad collar beneath the headcloth is inlaid with glass and semiprecious stones (cloisonné work). An ornament of the uraeus serpent and vulture is placed over his forehead. Superior performances in art are end results that depend on long periods of preparation. Where such treasures as the tomb furnishings of Tutankhamen come to light through a fortunate excavation, there were probably others. Either the missing links have been lost or they still await discovery.

Royal throne, back panel (Ill. 15)

The king is seated upon the upholstered chair in a relaxed posture; standing before him, the queen applies ointment to his shoulder. The sun disk symbolizes the supreme being, who is no longer represented in human form with a hawk's head. The sun's red rays end in hands that give life and receive offerings, as on Ikhnaton's reliefs [Ill. 29]. Basic conventions, front-view shoulder and eye, are retained; the queen, though standing, is no taller than the king. His footstool compensates for this discrepancy required by court etiquette, as the queen could not be represented as rising above the king. The action is one of graceful ease, a new trend toward naturalism in art, introduced by Ikhnaton's revolt against traditionalists in religion. Sumptuous materials and brilliant color enhance the lively action and contribute to the splendor of the throne.

Ill. 14 Mummy mask of King Tutankhamen, 1359–1350 B.C., gold and inlay. H. 21 1/2 in. *Ashmolean Museum, Oxford*

Ill. 15 Royal throne, back panel, wood carved in relief, overlaid with gold and inlaid with silver, stone, and faience. *Ashmolean Museum, Oxford*

Ramesses II, black granite (Ill. 16)

Egyptian sculpture in large statues often represented kings, nobles, priests, and occasionally gods. Cult statues of gods, placed in temple sanctuaries, were small. Like reliefs, statues were meant as portraits for tombs or temples. The soul, in the form of a bird (*ba,* or soul bird), descended from heaven to "animate" the statue.

Statues were painted over stucco, white, black, yellow, dark red, or turquoise green, even if made of the hardest

29

Ill. 16 Ramesses II (1300–1233 B.C.), black granite, XIX Dynasty. H. c. 6 ft. *Turin Museum*

kind of stone. The cubical character is here retained in a posture that expresses dignity and everlasting repose. There is even a trace of the early predynastic style in the slenderness of the torso, the broad shoulders, and powerful arms. But interior form is now revealed by subtle modeling that shows through pleated linen folds. In his right hand he holds the scepter, attribute of royal power; the uraeus serpent is placed above his forehead. The features—arched nose, delicate cheeks, and smiling lips—are individual; the king is represented at his best, youthful and benevolent.

Ramesses II was the great builder king; his name is identified with numerous temples [Luxor, Karnak] and particularly with Abu Simbel.[1] His wars brought him prisoners who were employed on public buildings. He reigned 67 years and had 170 children, or 119 according to another source. Under his thirteenth son and successor, Meneptah, Moses led the Israelites out of Egypt (Mariette).

[1] Superior numbers throughout refer to notes on pp. 465–67.

Facade of temple, with four statues of Ramesses II (Ill. 17)

The interior of the temple, cut into the rock, has halls and carved figures [Osiris] in the manner of the temple at Luxor. The king, seated, appears in two pairs on either side of the entrance, in imitation of the pylon [Edfu] of the temple erected in the plain. Smaller statues (not visible in illustration) of members of the royal family stand between the legs and on the sides of the statues; two Nile gods stand behind the entrance. The head of the southern Colossus (left one) shows the king's aquiline nose intact (compare Ill. 18). From an inscription in the temple, the date of completion was probably about 1257 B.C. (Baikie, 1932). Statues that were intended for eternity had to be patched up after fifty years, as in the case of the one to the right of the entrance. The second statue, of which only the legs remain, could not have lasted longer than 669 years. The mutilated leg bears an inscription in Greek from the XXVI Dynasty (c. 593–588 B.C.).

Ill. 17 Facade of rock-cut temple of Abu Simbel, sandstone, with four seated statues (colossi) of Ramesses II. H. of facade, over 100 ft.; of figures, 65 ft. *Services des Antiquités, Cairo*

Head of Ramesses II, statue to right of enetrance (Ill. 18)

A man standing on the shoulder of Pharaoh would about reach to the top of his ear, which measures 3 1/2 feet in height. Breadth and a simplification of form, necessary for rough sandstone, does not permit the delicate modeling found in the black granite statue of Ramesses (Ill. 16). For outdoor architectural sculpture, massive monumentality was the only reasonable treatment. As was common in sculpture, the heads were more carefully worked than the rest of the figure. The cheek is rounded, the lips arched, the corners of the mouth depressed. The total impression of the four seated statues is one of great power and dignity. When Europeans saw them in the early part of the nineteenth century, they were buried in the sand up to their heads. When finally cleared, their overpowering effect silenced criticism, though they were more abused than praised by nineteenth-century writers. Unfortunately they have not received the same critical appraisal that came to more accessible works.

Tomb of Ramose, painting (Ill. 19)

During the XVIII and XIX dynasties painting replaced reliefs in tombs. Individual figures [Ill. 31, Tomb of Nakht] and groups [Ill. 30, Tomb of Rekhmire] show easy, graceful postures and a beauty of line that place these paintings among the masterpieces of ancient painting. In this one section of the procession, men carry to the tomb furniture, jars, sandals, and papyrus bouquets to serve Ramose in afterlife. Professional mourning women raise their arms as they look toward the sarcophagus above, resting on the sacred boat that is being pulled on a sled. Inscriptions fill in the space between the figures. The dark-brown men are drawn with precision, there is emphasis on several figures detached from the group, and the manner in which they hold the objects is varied. The basic conventions are adhered to: left leg advanced and front-view shoulder and eye with heads in profile. The women stand feet together, according to convention, and are represented as a group.

Ill. 18 Head of Ramesses II, of statue to right of entrance. *Black Star and Dr. Geo. G. Gerster, Zurich*

Ill. 19 Painting, Tomb of Ramose; funeral procession from Thebes, tombs of the nobles, XVIII Dynasty, period of Ikhnaton. *Copy by Mr. and Mrs. Norman de Garis Davies after the originals. Metropolitan Museum of Art*

Funerary papyrus, Thebes (Ill. 20)

According to Egyptian belief the deceased had to pass judgment by Osiris, king of the netherworld, before he was granted entrance and immortality. If he did not pass the test his soul had to roam the earth forever. This drawing on a

Ill. 20 Funerary papyrus of the Princess Entin-ny from Deir el-Bahri, XXI Dynasty, Thebes. *Metropolitan Museum of Art, Rogers Fund*

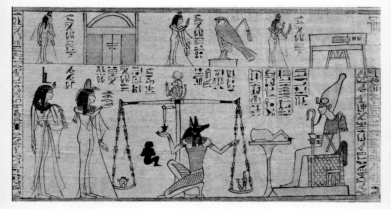

papyrus records the trial. The heart (left) is placed on the scales and weighed against a feather, symbol of truth. The weighing is performed by Anubis, the jackal-headed god of embalming. Papyri represent the oldest kind of book illustration. The text (hieroglyphics) is placed between the illustrations, in red or black line executed with the reed pen or brush. A papyrus roll was placed in the coffin to facilitate admission to an immortal life.

Ill. 21 Pectoral, gold and inlay, with name of Senusrit II, XII Dynasty, 2115–2099 B.C. W. at base, 3 1/4 in. *Metropolitan Museum of Art*

Pectoral, gold and inlay (Ill. 21)

The perforated gold plate is inlaid with dark-blue lapis lazuli, light-green turquoise, and red carnelian. The effect of brilliant color and glistening gold is enhanced by design. Solid areas on the side enframe open spaces by means of a pattern of gold bars. Solidity is pleasantly contrasted with well-defined shapes, and all parts have symbolic meanings. The flanking falcons were the sacred symbols of the sun god Horus. The beaks of the falcons continue into the curved lines of the uraeus serpent [p. 34, myths]. Between them is the name of the king, the cartouche of Senusrit, consisting of the scarab, the sacred beetle, and the sun disk. On either side of the scarab is a sign of life. A kneeling figure supports the king's name, aided on either side by a falcon foot pressed against the palm branch. The king, represented by his cartouche, is surrounded and protected by symbols of divinity.

Ancient Near Eastern Art

A NEAR EASTERN country that made a contribution to European art, ancient and medieval, was Mesopotamia. What has been preserved of Mesopotamian art does not compare in quantity or variety with the many monuments of Egyptian art. However, Mesopotamian sculpture compares favorably with Egyptian art, and such small reliefs as seal impressions (Ill. 24) achieve a vigor unknown in Egypt.

Before continuing with Mesopotamian and concluding with Aegean art, we should account for the peripheral regions of Asia Minor and Syria. The most important country was the empire of the Hittites (c. 1400–1200 B.C.) in Asia Minor, which ranked politically with Egypt and Mesopotamia. Hittite sculpture never developed a freedom comparable to that of the sculpture of the more stable empires.

Among the several sites that are important for archaeology in north Syria is Zinjirli (modern name), the most complete fortress among those excavated. Perhaps the most famous of Hittite works of sculpture are three stone lions (Ill. 22) that belonged to the inner gates of Zinjirli and show some Assyrian influence.

A narrow strip of Syrian coastline north of Palestine was occupied by the Phoenicians with their ancient cities of Sidon and Tyre. The Phoenicians, known as the seafaring traders who founded Carthage (845 B.C.), were the exporters of Eastern crafts to Greece. Politically and artistically they became dependent on Egypt and Mesopotamia. Ivory and engraving on metal were old established Phoenician crafts, and craftsmanship rather than originality seems to characterize Phoenician art, which was a conglomerate style fusing many borrowed motifs. Sumerian and Egyptian documents pointing to the invention of writing are older than Phoenician ones, and Egypt rather than Phoenicia made the earliest glass.

Guardian lions from citadel gates, North Syria (Ill. 22)

The lion on the left (c. 830 B.C.; formed part of the gate to the court of the palace. The one on the right (c. 730 B.C.) is from a colonnade and shows Assyrian influence. Only the heads are carved freely in the round; the sides are in relief as part of the wall. Wherever the Assyrian influence prevailed, the sculptural decoration gained in refinement. Zinjirli is but one of several mounds of North Syria that have been excavated. Recent scholars (Frankfort) have discontinued applying the label "Hittite" to this school that depended on Assyrian art.

Ill. 22 Guardian lions from different gates on citadel at Zinjirli, North Syria, ninth to eighth century B.C., Berlin and Istanbul. *Courtesy Penguin Books, Inc., Baltimore (1958)*

Head of Gudea, Neo-Sumerian period (Ill. 23)

Mesopotamian art is best represented by its sculpture. Of sculpture in the round, the most representative works are about a dozen statues, with heads broken off, and single heads. This head fits a seated statue representing Gudea, the king priest of Lagash. It was originally placed in a temple as a votive offering to the personal god of Gudea. Inscriptions on the side of the seated statue indicate that Gudea is holding on his knees a plan for a temple for the god. With folded hands, devout but confident, Gudea is making his offering. What Gudea most fervently desired was continued domination to prevent drought brought on by the failure of the Tigris River to rise. The god must be appeased by offerings, by presents and prayers. Statues are among these offerings. They do not refer to the hereafter as in Egypt, but are intended to avert disaster to the king's own city of Lagash. When floods and storms bring destruction, it must be due to the displeasure of the gods. To retain the benevolence of the gods, a well-stocked temple for the god—his house— was considered a wise investment. Art served the needs of religion in a practical way.

Gods, the personified forces of nature, still required the same conveniences as man, but at a high level of subsistence befitting their divine status. A statue of Gudea thus becomes a perpetual appeal to the god as well as a reminder of service rendered. The gods "delight in gifts"; they must be propitiated. This left the artist with the task of presenting the facts; a true likeness of the king, an expression of respect in a prayerful, devotional posture.

Mesopotamian history is beset with invasions, conquests, reconquests, and the destruction that followed. Architecture was possible by the use of only perishable materials, chiefly sun-dried brick. Huge structures, palaces and temples, eventually disintegrated into heaps of rubbish. Sculpture is remarkably conservative, one reason being its religious character. Free-standing statues were placed in the temples dedicated to the gods who were eternal; hence no change of style was imperative. Religious sculpture tends to be conservative. In all periods, regardless of which nation was in control, statues look much alike. They are cylindrical, wrapped in long robes that reach to the feet in a broad expanse showing occasional folds but no real drapery. The Mesopotamian style of costume, like a close-fitting bathrobe, offered the artist no opportunity to develop variety in the manner of the looser and more informal Greek dress. When arms and legs are exposed, muscles are exaggerated, necks are thick, and in seated postures the figure appears almost stunted. The massive proportions contrast with the slenderness of Egyptian figures, which are individualized and often retain a sense of life. Mesopotamian religion did not encourage the artist to experiment. Individual heads often

Ill. 23 Head of Gudea, diorite, Neo-Sumerian period, 2125–2025 B.C. Louvre. *Archives Photographiques*

betray a considerable refinement in the shaping of the nose, the modeling of the mouth, and the stylized delineation of the eyebrows. Large eyes tend to obscure other variations in the treatment of the features. There are too few examples from which to obtain a broader basis for appreciation. The sculptor was limited by culture, not by lack of ability. For a truer understanding of Mesopotamian art, the reliefs must also be studied.

Ill. 24 Seal impression: lion, winged horse, and foal, Middle Assyrian, 1350–1000 B.C. *Copyright British Museum*

Lion, winged horse, and foal (Ill. 24)

Assyrians of some social standing had personal seal cylinders perforated and engraved on the exterior with pictorial designs, in some cases combined with the name of the owner. Seal cylinders were made of marble or some semiprecious stone. This cylinder was rolled onto written documents in the form of soft clay tablets; the writing itself was in Sumerian small wedge-shaped, or cuneiform, characters. Thousands of tablets of all periods represent our chief source of information on religious, political, social, literary, and commercial matters.

Small as they are, these pictorial seal impressions represent Mesopotamian art at its best. The subjects are often animals—lions, monsters, and figures in combat, arranged in the manner of a frieze or facing each other in armorial fashion.

A roaring lion standing on his hind legs with front paws raised showing claws extended faces a winged horse. A small foal is running toward the Pegasus as if to seek protection from the fiercely aggressive lion. Details—muscles, the lion's mane, the horse's wings—are simplified, stylized, without loss of a basic realism. The action is convincing and infused with vigor, but the total design is decorative. Within the same theme of animals and heroes in combat, there is much variety. When the cylinder is impressed on clay its design, as here shown, is revealed. Seals were used for marking bales of goods; they were art for commercial purposes. The exact meaning of the subjects is often unknown, although mythology is believed to be involved. Thus art was stimulated by the needs of placing seals on documents and goods. Individual enterprise was encouraged: the Code of Hammurabi [p. 53] was also a commercial code, which regulated trading; fixed prices and wages and; provided for contracts, rates of interest, promissory notes, letters of credit and incidentally commercial art, applying a modern term to seal designs. Their variety indicates that many artists must have cut seals, and the artist was allowed a considerable measure of freedom. The state regulated the life of the citizen, but it did not stifle art.

Ill. 25 Lion Hunt, Assyrian relief from the palace of Ashurnasirpal (884–860 B.C.), Nimrud. British Museum. *After Forrer,* Reallexicon, *W. Spemann (1908)*

Lion Hunt, palace of Ashurnasirpal (Ill. 25)

Assyrian art on a larger scale is largely relief carving as represented in carved wall panels [pp. 54–55]. The Mesopotamian relief style achieved its greatest development in the carved alabaster panels that decorated the lower portion of courts and halls. The portals to these courts

were flanked by human-headed winged lions, mighty
guardian spirits that combine man's intelligence (in the
human heads) with the strength of animals (the backs of
bulls and the paws of lions) [pp. 55–57]. In two rows
forming friezes, separated by a band of inscriptions, these
panels (c. 3 feet high) describe the activities of the king
[Fig. 15] in battle scenes and lion hunts. The vitality of
the scene is impressive in the wounded lion's helplessly lift-
ing a paw to convey the agony of the dying beast, his open
mouth showing formidable teeth. The realism of the
prostrate lion is the result of firsthand observation. Both
hands of the king, one gripping the bow, the other pulling
the string, are correctly drawn, as well as the extended arms
of the driver, beside the king. The rendering of the horses is
abbreviated; the three horses are given two legs each. A
confusing complication of legs, had they all been included, is
avoided. The simplified version helps design and focuses attention on the lion. The Greeks, four centuries later, did
not avoid this problem, as may be seen in the horses of the
Parthenon frieze (Ill. 47). The Assyrian artists were not lacking in skill but were concerned primarily with the fact that
the king had killed a lion in a successful hunt. The line
drawing exaggerates the ornamental effect, and the massed
detail creates a contrast against the white background which
is absent in the originals. But the ornamental effect of the
raised portion against the flat background is more effective
and is less scattered in the originals than in the line drawing. These reliefs are, with their wealth of detail, also
historical documents; they report events that actually took
place [Fig. 15].

War Against the Elamites, section (Ill. 26)

The utmost of elaboration in relief carving is represented
in a later series of historical reliefs that describe the defeat
of the Elamites by Ashurbanipal. There is a confusing
mingling of attacking Assyrians and Elamites mostly fleeing
across a river or lying prostrate pierced by arrows. Variety
is achieved by lively postures. Correct proportions are used,
as far as needed, to tell the story, and arm and leg muscles
are stressed, but correct drawing of the figure, landscape, and
spatial depth is not attempted.

Curved lines on top of the fortress and over the portal are
meant to represent fire. Assyrians with picks and crow-
bars and the falling bricks and timbers suggest destruction
of the walls. In the middle register, Assyrians descend loaded

Ill. 26 The sack of the city of Hamann, War Against the Elamites, from Kuyunjik (ancient Nineveh), Assyrian relief, period of Ashurbanipal (668–625 B.C.). *Copyright British Museum*

with loot, weapons, and caldrons. At the bottom, two groups of seated figures are eating and drinking. Each man bends to his task in a slightly different way, and those walking

43

downhill have strides of their own. If the style of the seal impressions may be compared to lofty poetry, the historical alabaster reliefs are matter-of-fact prose.

Ashurbanipal and queen (Ill. 27)

The style achieves a sense of massive pageantry where figures are set against a background of lush vegetation and heavy-set furniture. The king reclines, the queen is seated; both are heavily robed and hold goblets, and the king also a flower. There are tables behind the royal couch (with bow, quiver, and sword) and in front of the queen. A harpist advances on the left; on the tree in front of him hangs an upturned severed head (Teumman, King of Susa). Servants bear food and whisk away the flies, birds perch in the trees, and grapevines overhang the royal couple. Among Assyrian reliefs this subject is unusual, peaceable, and idyllic. The single disturbing detail, the severed head, that shocks modern sensibilities, is irrelevant artistically. If this is interpreted as a symbol of royal victory, such victory must have pleased the gods, as all state actions, including wars, were undertaken with the consent and approval of the gods.

Ill. 27 Ashurbanipal (668–626 B.C.) and queen in the garden, Assyrian relief from Kuyunjik. H. 21 in. *Copyright British Museum*

The Ishtar Gate of Babylon, restored (Ill. 28)

Mesopotamian art accomplished another triumph in the invention of colored glazed tiles used for architectural decoration. They are believed to have been an invention of

Ill. 28 The Ishtar Gate of Babylon, restoration by Robert Koldewey. Berlin Museum. *Dr. F. Stoedtner, Düsseldorf*

the new Babylonian state under Nebuchadnezzar II (604–562 B.C.). The surface was modeled in low relief, cast, and then painted individually and glazed, unlike earlier Assyrian tiles, which were painted only.

The style is well represented by this restoration of the Ishtar gate of ancient Babylon. Yellow bulls and white, long-necked dragons against a blue background decorated the walls flanking the arched gateway. Art history has hardly anything comparable to offer except as the tradition was continued in glazed-brick reliefs of ancient Persia in the fourth century B.C. frieze of Archers from Susa (Louvre). As most countries had stone for monumental building, there was no need for glazed bricks.

Ill. 29 Prehistoric vase from Susa. From The Art and Architecture of Ancient Persia, *Penguin Books, Inc., Baltimore (1958)*

Prehistoric vase from Susa (Ill. 29)

Persian art on a major scale did not appear until the empire, but folk art produced superior painted pottery during the fifth millennium. Animal forms are highly stylized in this vase. What appears to be a delicate border of an essentially linear character is accomplished by the extended necks of birds. The bold curves of the main body are near abstractions of the mountain goat, and the upper border is based on a motif in which the bodies of hounds are still recognizable. Such elegance that turns animal shapes into a pattern that depends on purely artistic effects presupposes a long period of development. The talent for decoration for which Persia became famous in later periods is based on an indigenous tradition.

Plan of Persepolis (Ill. 30)

When Persia became an empire under Darius I (522–486 B.C.), its art produced monumental work in architecture and sculpture used for decoration. The famous bronzes from Luristan [p. 58] are part of the folk-art background. Under Persian rule Babylonia contributed to a new Persian court art. With the resources of virtually the whole Near East at his disposal, Darius created an art that used the talents of subjects drawn from many countries. Unlike the Phoenicians, who borrowed from many styles without producing an original art of their own, Persia fused these many contributions into one that took on a national character of its

46

own. Enough has been excavated at Persepolis to give us a vivid impression of the magnificence and originality of this royal palace that served Darius and his successor, Xerxes. Building operations went on for over fifty years (518–c. 460 B.C.). A new style was here established based on the use of tall columns, unknown to Mesopotamia. Raised on a huge terrace, the Audience Hall and the Hundred Column Hall are separate buildings loosely connected. This is different from the Mesopotamian palace, which was essentially a single expanse of rectangular rooms and open courts. Persepolis created the square plan and the large rectangular stone window and door frames, which thereafter became a basic element of all Western building. The Audience Hall, 250 feet square, was a lofty interior believed to have accommodated 10,000 people. As in Mesopotamia, huge guardian bulls were built into the entrance towers. Wooden columns on stone bases were plastered and painted and given many closely spaced flutes [p. 58, Ill. 36].

Ill. 30 Plan of Persepolis. *Dr. Erich F. Schmidt and Penguin Books, Inc., Baltimore* (1958)

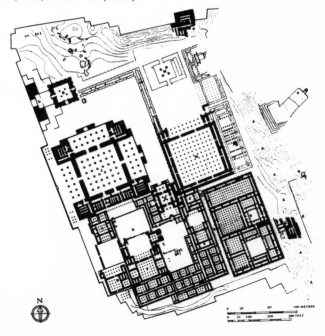

Face of bull-man, Persepolis (Ill. 31)

This motif follows closely the guardian human-headed winged bulls of Mesopotamia. Whatever differences exist seem to be toward a flat linear treatment with less emphasis on bulk and vigor. The fantastic capital of which this is a part included volutes and motifs derived from Egypt.

The refinement in the carving of this capital is typical of Persian sculpture. The motif of the bull-man was taken over from the guardian figures of Mesopotamia, repeated here in the aquiline nose, the stylized eyebrows, and the heavy beard. The snail-shell curls suggest the archaic Greek; an Ionian sculptor from the Greek cities of the coast of Asia Minor could have carried this style to Persepolis. What was sculpturesque in the original Mesopotamian model became linear and ornamental in the Persian example.

With the defeat of Persia by Alexander the Great, the ancient Near East disappeared as an empire. Persia's artistic traditions remained vital and gave the incoming Greek forms an Oriental character. Hereafter the history of Western art, still centered in the eastern Mediterranean, concerns itself with European art. European art of the historic period was reaching its early maturity in Greece as a Persian court style was emerging. Of the ancient pre-Greek styles, only that of Mesopotamia passed on to Western Europe some of its artistic heritage. Even of these contributions we have become aware largely through the researches of art historians. Europe was largely ignorant of ancient Egyptian art before the excavations of the nineteenth century. Egypt was a fabled land to the Greeks, which they knew from what Herodotus had written. But there was another culture [pp. 59–62] that produced a significant art peculiarly fascinating to our own age. This Minoan art was centered on the island of Crete.

Before Crete was excavated, the existence of a Cretan civilization about as old as Egypt and Mesopotamia was unknown [p. 59]. When Sir Arthur Evans began to dig at Knossos, an ancient site mentioned by Homer, he hoped to find a system of writing. He found much more, several stonebuilt palaces and an entire civilization. He called it Minoan after King Minos, who in the Greek legends received as a tribute each year seven youths and seven maidens. These were sacrifices to the Minotaur, a monster half bull, half man, who lived in a labyrinth beneath the king's palace and was slain by the Greek hero Theseus. The complexity of the vast palace with its many rooms and corridors, as un-

Ill. 31 Face of bull-man, part of a capital from Persepolis.
Oriental Institute, University of Chicago

earthed, gave some basis for the idea of the labyrinth. There
were bathrooms and an efficient drainage system to take care
of the island's heavy rainfall. In one part of the palace was a
theatrical area with steps intended for 400 spectators. The
palace was probably not only the residence of the king, who
may have been the high priest, but also the adminstrative
center, a religious shrine, and a place for craftsmen. The
many rooms suggest a variety of uses for living and work-

49

shop purposes. The palace at Knossos has a throne room and a shrine to the snake goddess. A double-edged ax reproduced on stone blocks is believed to have been a religious symbol. The throne, known as the throne of Minos, was of gypsum with a scalloped back in imitation of wood; it is still in place. The throne room, or council chamber, has an alabaster tank used as a fish pond or bath. All evidence points to a high state of civilized life, without emphasis on tombs, temples, or military establishments.

It is believed that Crete depended on her navy to protect her shipping, as Crete seems to have lived by seaborne commerce. Her history is unknown and her writing has but recently been deciphered by Michael Ventris, but so far her writing has not added greatly to our knowledge. Though Cretan objects discovered in excavations date back to the Stone Age (fourth millennium B.C.), the civilization was of the Bronze Age, probably developed by early settlers (c. 3200 B.C.) who had arrived from Egypt. During the so-called Middle Minoan period (c. 1800–1550 B.C.), Crete flourished. Egypt was then weakened by invasions (hyksos) and did not recover until c. 1580 B.C. (XVIII Dynasty), and Mesopotamia was also in turmoil (between Hammurabi, 1792 B.C. and the end of Babylonian civilization, c. 1350 B.C.). This Middle Minoan period brought Crete to full maturity.

Snake Goddess, Crete (Ill. 32)

Crete had no large sculpture, but small statues of terracotta or of gold and ivory (statuettes) have been found. They are female figures holding snakes, and may represent mother goddesses. This one, a well-known example, wears what may be called a crown, and her hair falls in back in curls. Holes in front may indicate that originally loose curls of gold were attached. In her hands she holds snakes of gold. The bell-shaped skirt is pleated and bound in gold, and the tight bodice has a golden girdle. Wide skirts, narrow waists, and tight-fitting bodices suggest the nineteenth century and the use of metal stays. In side view this statuette reveals its rim stand as she leans back with arms outstretched. The Cretan figures, as in the painting of the Cupbearer [Fig. 17], tall, slender, and thin-waisted, have a proud bearing unlike the stiffly devout statues of Gudea and are more akin to the Egyptians of the tomb paintings. The character of a people reveals itself in its art, and Cretan art suggests a life of ease, of comfort and peace. The crafts,

Ill. 32 Snake Goddess, gold and ivory, Crete, c. 1500 B.C. H. 6 1/2 in. *Museum of Fine Arts, Boston*

ceramics [Ill. 37], and metalwork [Fig. 15] add much to our appreciation of Cretan art.

Decoration from a burial jar (Ill. 33)

Decorations on pottery show a development from a geometric linear style in the Early Minoan period (c. 3000–2200 B.C.) to a naturalistic style in the Middle Minoan III period (c. 1800–1600 B.C.). In this border, swimming dolphins are freely executed, as they might have been drawn by any competent artist in any period. Styles in art appear and skills develop as dictated by the opportunities and the needs of the culture; there have always been talented artists wherever conditions favorable to art existed.

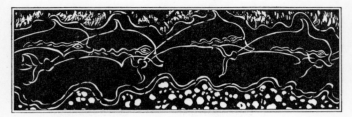

Ill. 33 Naturalistic decoration from a burial jar from Pachyammos, Middle Minoan III (c. 1800–1600 B.C.). *Metropolitan Museum of Art,* Handbook of the Classical Collection

There is much in Cretan art we do not understand, as the precise meaning of the scenes with a charging bull [Fig. 18] and figures turning somersaults. Is this a skilled circus performance or have we here prisoners trained for a dangerous sport, toreadors, comparable to the later Roman gladiators?

Plan of the palace at Tiryns (Ill. 34)

After the fall of Crete, Aegean civilization in Greece succeeded to the power of the kings of Crete (Late Minoan III, 1310–1100 B.C.). This last period of Minoan art reflects a period of warfare and migrations that extended to the Greek islands. Troy was a part of this culture, which eventually succumbed to the Dorian invasion from the north. This is the period of the Homeric poems, which were recorded later (probably in the ninth century B.C.) The centers were the hill fortresses of Tiryns and Mycenae in southern Greece (Peloponnesus), after which the period has been named Mycenaean. These fortresses, built of huge boulders for defense, were ascribed by later Greeks to a race of giants, Cyclopes, from which stems the term Cyclopean masonry, illustrated in the Lion Gate [Ill. 38] of Mycenae. The main gateways to the fortress palace of Tiryns were rectangular structures with columns set within the open ends (propylaea) as used again in more elaborate fashion on the Athenian Acropolis. A rectangular hall (megaron), the center of sociability, had a hearth and was entered through a porch with columns or portico. This use of the rectangular plan with columns is found again in the Greek temple. The palace at Tiryns developed out of single structures placed together. Each retained its individuality. Courts in between connect with narrow passageways but do not allow for easy communication. In a warlike society such an arrangement facilitated defense. (Knossos had an open plan in which the several parts grew together but were not planned for defense.) The walls, up to fifty feet thick, had interior passageways roofed over by corbel arches in which the stones laid horizontally projected out more in each layer until the two sides met to bridge over the aisle. This principle, used on a circular plan (Tholos), was used to form the so-called beehive tombs, as in the one at Mycenae [discovered by Schliemann, p. 61]

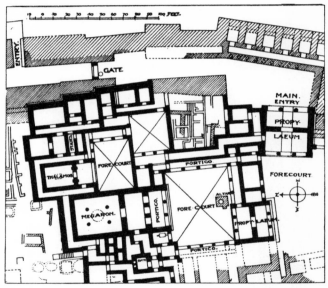

Ill. 34 Plan of the palace at Tiryns. *After Schliemann. From* The Architecture of Greece and Rome, *by Anderson and Spiers, Batsford, London* (1907)

Entrance to the treasury of Atreus (Ill. 35)

The bare masonry still stands. The columns and the architectural decoration are restored, after fragments now in museums. A feature is the half-column slightly diminishing from the top down (upper diameter, 22 1/2 in.; lower, 20 1/2 in.). Chevrons and spiral ornaments, slightly con-

cave, cover the surface of the porous limestone. Originally
they were probably stuccoed, painted, or perhaps gilded.

Ill. 35 Entrance to the treasury of Atreus (known as tomb of
Agamemnon) at Mycenae. Restored by R. Phené Spiers. *From*
The Architecture of Greece and Rome, *by Anderson and Spiers,
Batsford, London (1907)*

IV

Greek Art

THE LATE art of the ancient Orient came in contact with Greek civilization as a result of the conquests of Alexander the Great. After Greece had become a Roman province (146 B.C.) the influence of Greek art continued in the Greco-Roman period until about the beginning of the Christian era.

During the brief period of only two centuries, when Greek art was at its maturity, the city-state of Athens made an enduring demonstration of the significance of art in human culture. During the second half of the fifth century [p. 69, Pericles] and the ensuing fourth century [pp. 72–73, Great Period] architecture, sculpture, and painting, supported by state funds, became a matter of public interest. Temples and statues were for all to see. Art was not, as in the Near Eastern empires, created for the palace, to glorify a despotic ruler [p. 51, Sargon, or p. 54, Ashurnasirpal] or to be concealed in tombs made possible only through vast expenditures of labor as in Egyptian temples [p. 37, Karnak]. Greek art dealt with the gods, who were conceived in the image of man. Egyptian tomb paintings tell us much about daily life, Greek art practically nothing; no major works of Greek painting have survived. Greek religion, as represented in literature by Homer, furnished art with major and minor gods who were like men and women in appearance, though more perfect and more powerful. The animal world was no longer merged with divinity except where the gods were associated with the animals sacred to them. Mountain streams were personified as centaurs, wild creatures half man, half horse; and satyrs, lesser gods of woods and fields, had short horns and feet like goats'.

Sculpture was expressed in the human figure in repose during the period of Phidias, without violent action or strong emotional expression. Greek sculpture reflects an ideal of human dignity, self-assured, calm, and without infirmity. Greek sculpture had many imitators in later periods. But art is more than skill and imitation; hence Greek art as an expression of a culture has never been duplicated. The particular combination of circumstances that produced Greek art never occurred again. Among these circumstances [p. 97] was the existence of leisure and discrimination on the part of a small group of males who enjoyed citizenship in Athens. They alone made the decisions that put artists and craftsmen to work. Domestic chores and much, but not all, manual labor were performed by slaves. Among those who worked on the Parthenon, many were probably freemen (Plutarch, Pericles, as quoted by Grant, 1913), the craftsmen particularly. Moreover, Athens, as the chief trading center of Greece, lived by export and import. Trade was in the hands of the metics, who, though not citizens, were freemen and constituted a large and prosperous part of the population. Free Athenian citizens owned the land and cultivated it during the earlier period before the Peloponnesian War. That was the period of Phidias and the classic masterpieces of Greek art, the Parthenon and the large statues of gold and ivory of the second half of the fifth century. In literature Sophocles embodies the qualities also expressed by Phidias—proportion, restraint, reverence, purity, and harmony. What is enduring and reposeful in art and literature is the essence of the mood of the classic spirit.

With the fourth century, after the Peloponnesian War, which ended Athens' position as a powerful state, a new motif entered literature and art: suffering and compassion in the tragedies of Euripides and an emphasis on feeling in sculpture. Scopas introduced pain and passion, Praxiteles a gentle mood that concerns only the individual. In both cases literature precedes the visual arts; sculptors and painters follow the path set by poets and dramatists. Realism followed in the late period when sculpture broadened its scope to include portraiture as in the victorious boxer (Ill. 59), as well as types from everyday life (Ill. 60). Greek sculpture developed from the self-limitation of the archaic style to the self-expression of the Hellenistic. It began in the small city-state and ended in the Roman empire. Art flourished where political power was concentrated; surplus wealth and leisure provided conditions that made the major arts possible. When such conditions do not exist, there is at best only folk art. At one stage in history, in fifth-century Athens, conditions combined to produce an art we look back to with nostalgia. As significant as the quality of the art itself was the cultural background that favored so broad a development of human potentialities.

From the study of a few selected examples, chiefly sculpture, arranged approximately in chronological order, we may get an impression of the artistic significance of each work, the stylistic development, and the place each work occupied in its original setting.

Hera of Samos, marble (Ill. 36)

The inscription on the statue says "Cheramyes [a man] dedicated me to Hera," who may well be represented, as the statue was found near the temple of the goddess Hera. Even without the head and with only a trace left of her bent arm, the statue has an elegance of shape and a delicacy in the garment, expressed by closely spaced grooves. The cylindrical, columnlike figure tapers down, the feet protrude at the base. The sculptor aimed to get the utmost effect from the heavier drapery of the upper garment, contrasting against the thin lines on one side and the broad, smooth surface on the other. He was absorbed in the play of pattern applied to form and never reached the point of being concerned with a struggle to express a living figure. It is a mistake to look upon the archaic artist as one who contented himself with only a partial solution, because a complete rendering of the figure would have been too difficult for him. He began with a cylindrical block; his aim was to get the most rewarding carving from the block, not to turn it into a figure inspired by a living model.

The figure was originally painted, so details like textile patterns were expressed through color. We know that wood was also used for sculpture, but no wooden statues have survived. This particular statue is often said to show the influence of wood sculpture in its tree-trunklike shape. But we need not accept this theory as an explanation of sculpture. Though tree worship is at times linked to wood carving, whether or not this is the case here is problematical.

Maiden, marble (Ill. 37)

In this figure from Athens, carved perhaps a few decades after the Hera of Samos, the sculptor has sacrificed slender elegance in favor of robust proportions. The thin ripple of

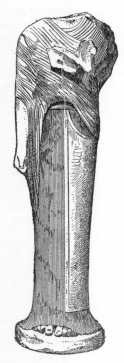

Ill. 36 Hera of Samos, marble, c. 550 B.C. H. c. 6 ft. Louvre. *After Collignon (1866)*

Ill. 37 Maiden, marble, c. 540–550 B.C. Acropolis Museum. *Copyright Spyros Meletzis*

many parallel folds of the Hera of Samos has become real drapery. Fewer and broader folds define several surfaces, one recessed behind the other. The garment no longer cuts off on a horizontal line above the feet, but parts of the drapery are of different lengths. The modeling of the out-stretched arm sets off the upper arm from the lower, and the hair falls down in front in long, neatly separated curls. Drapery falls in vertical lines instead of clinging to a cylindrical shape. The love of ornamental pattern is still strong, but a sense of a living figure is beginning to emerge. Such figures of well-bred Athenian ladies making offerings to Athena were set up in the sacred temple areas as individual dedications to the goddess.

Ill. 38 Maiden, marble, c. 540. Acropolis Museum, Athens.
Copyright Spyros Meletzis

Maiden, marble, c. 540 B.C. *(Ill. 38)*

The sculptor here aimed at perfection of details of hair
style and a pleasing expression; the smile is almost natural.
The sculptor had in mind a concept of feminine charm, not
an expression of individual character. Surface elaboration
rather than structure, pattern more than form, fascinated
the archaic sculptor, particularly of the Ionian style. The
wide-open stare of the primitive eye is here narrowed and
the lower eyelid is differentiated from the upper. A bronze
rod set into the back of the head held a wooden disk lifted
above the head. This was a necessary protection against the
birds, for the painted figure dedicated to Athena must not be

defiled. Such female figures are believed to have been developed first in the centers of Asia Minor, in Ionia. In Athens the Ionian style fused with a second trend, the Dorian, which emphasized anatomy. Vestiges of color remain in the borders of the textiles, on earrings, and on eyes and mouth; it was used for accent, not to cover the surface fully.

Statues like these were probably offerings made to the goddess and represent a survival of sacrifices in primitive ritual, or worshipers symbolically dedicating themselves to Athena. They were themselves neither priestesses nor goddesses.

Statues from sanctuary of Apollo (Ill. 39)

An archaic seated type is known from seven male and three female statues that lined the sacred way from the harbor to the temple. One, bearing an inscription, represents a local ruler, Chares, who dedicated his statue to the god. The inscription giving his name and rank adds, "this statue is the property of Apollo." To ingratiate oneself with a god by dedicating a statue to him was an ancient custom; Gudea, the Sumerian king of Lagash [p. 52] had done so long before the Greeks.

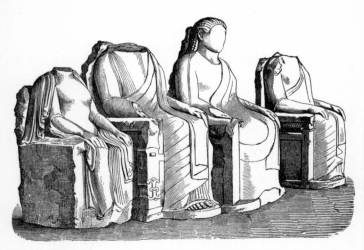

Ill. 39 Statues from the sanctuary of Apollo at Branchidae, near Miletus, marble, Archaic period, c. 550 B.C. British Museum. *After Lübke (1871)*

Ill. 40 Female head, limestone (poros), Archaic period, c. 550 B.C., from Sikyon. *Museum of Fine Arts, Boston*

Proportions are massive; figure and chair seem to be of one piece. There is little to suggest the body beneath the heavy drapery. The cubical block is rounded off to define only the main contours, and the folds lying flat are carved on the surface. The interest in drapery, to the neglect of anatomy, characterized archaic sculpture of the Greek Ionian settlements along the coast of Asia Minor. This stylistic trend was carried to Athens, probably through a patron of art and literature.

Ionian artists invited to Athens by Pisistratus (560–527 B.C.),

Female head (Ill. 40)

This head once belonged to a statue about half life-size. It is of a soft, coarse-grained stone, poros, that carved easily; hair and lips were painted red, and earrings in the form of concave disks were originally painted blue. The carving of the softly rounded cheeks shows a delicacy rarely found in limestone. In an attempt at expression, the lips

61

curve up to produce a smile, which does not yet involve the corners of the mouth. The slanting, almond-shaped eyes still protrude unduly, and the upper and lower lids are not yet differentiated; the eyes are too large, though the ears are at the proper level. The hair, dressed in ringlets above the forehead with long locks front and back, no doubt is in the fashion of the day. With no models to follow, the Greek sculptor had to solve each difficulty unaided. An art student today learns to carve or model a head or figure in the course of his art-school training. To acquire the skill of representing the figure freely took Greek sculpture two centuries. As we have all stages of the historical development before us, we can see the trend toward realism.

To the extent that all art is experimental, the archaic artist experimented, but he was satisfied, with reservations perhaps, with his own achievements. He could not know that in due time the works of a Phidias or a Praxiteles would make his work look old-fashioned to his descendants.

Standing male figure (Ill. 41)

Many local centers contributed to the archaic style [625–480 B.C., p. 65]. The list would include the Peloponnesus, of which the Apollo of Tenea, in marble, is an example [p. 66, Ill. 40]. Bronze was also used, but few bronze statues have survived. There are two basic types of freestanding figures, the draped female of the maidens of the Acropolis and the nude male of the "Apollo" type, here represented in a later, more advanced stage of development, with arms extended; one hand holds a small stag; the other originally held a bow. The pose is free, and the modeling hard, making the muscles stand out. Through observation of athletes at practice, the sculptor learned his anatomy. Statues of the victors in athletic contests were set up at Olympia; portrait statues were dedicated to those athletes who had won three times, a generalized type serving for others. Statues by the leading masters were imitated or copied by others to supply the demands.

Grave relief of a man and dog (Ill. 42)

Grave reliefs represented scenes of daily living. Veneration of the dead was a part of Greek civilization, though the emphasis was modest compared with the Egyptian's concern for an eternal resting place. The beehive tombs [pp. 61–62] of the Mycenaean kings were monuments of considerable

Ill. 41 Standing male figure, bronze. British Museum. *After Lübke (1870)*

Ill. 42 Grave relief, marble, about life-size, from Orchomenos: a man playing with his dog. National Museum, Athens. *After Lübke (1871)*

splendor. But the Greeks of the archaic period had among their ancestors northern tribes including Dorians. These new Greeks never rivaled the luxury of the gold and jewelry found in Mycenaean tomb furnishings. Their carved grave reliefs reflect the taste and participation in art of a well-to-do middle class. The monuments recovered are from this group rather than from those of the great men like Pericles, which have not survived.

Unlike the Egyptians, who aimed at portraiture in tomb sculpture, the Greeks ignored both name and appearance but suggested in their carved figures a person's station in society. The man leaning on a staff holding out a grasshopper to his dog seems to indicate a man living in the country. An incident from life, playful, casual, passes on to posterity the idea of life itself; sentiment is here memorialized.

The relaxed posture attempted by the carver exceeded his skill. The eye in front view in a profile head is combined with a smile, a fleshy neck, and a muscular arm and well-rendered though slightly twisted hand. The left foot is forced into an awkward frontal position. No dog with his legs in the position here represented could possibly get his head into a normal side-view position. The artist was unconscious of any shortcomings of his work, for he signed it at the bottom: "Alexnor of Naxos made me. Just look at me."

Figures from pediment, Aegina, restored (Ill. 43)

In this restoration some figures, originally included to fill the space, have been left out. The heads, some restored, show the curved mouth, intended to give expression. The sculptor was more experienced with the male than with the female figure. If the immobility of the central goddess is not due to a restraint proper in the representation of deities [p. 67], it may have resulted from the sculptor's hesitancy to court difficulties. The sculptor's name is not known, but sculptors from Aegina were experienced in bronze, a material that facilitates action and a diversity of contours.

Ill. 43 Figures from west pediment, south side, of temple of Aphaia, island of Aegina, c. 500–480 B.C. Munich Glyptothek. *Restored by Bertel Thorwaldsen. After Lübke (1870)*

Ill. 44 West pediment of temple of Zeus at Olympia (Peloponnesus), marble, Transitional period (480–450 B.C.). *Restoration after Treu, Jahrbuch (1888)*

Before casting, the form is modeled in clay, which gives the sculptor more freedom to use a variety of postures. This earlier training in bronze may explain the invention of motifs of action, bent knees, extended arms, and precise detail. Such emphasis on line rather than mass is more readily achieved in clay than in marble and may have prepared the sculptor to attempt a comparable freedom when he had to use marble, as in the pediments at Aegina.

The Dorian school of sculpture with its emphasis on the nude, athletic male type here reaches a stage of development that is free without having cast off all restraints. Though immobile in effect, the postures are free; what is missing is a sense of life, though we must keep in mind that in restoration the original surface of the marble may have been removed in an effort to clean the surface free of dirt.

West pediment of temple of Zeus (Ill. 44)

The most important ancient site for "Transitional" sculpture and architecture is Olympia, on the Peloponnesus, where representatives of the Greek states assembled every four years for their national festivals and contests. In this temple, as large as the Parthenon [Fig. 36], built of limestone, stood the famous gold and ivory statue of Zeus by Phidias [p. 69.]

The west pediment shows a battle between Greeks (Lapiths) and centaurs, mythological creatures part human (head, shoulders, and torso), part horse (body and legs). Apollo, in the center, supervises the battle. As at Aegina, the figures are adapted to the space with balanced groups on either side of the center. But in contrast to the Aegina sculptures, the groups combine into a unified composition. The struggle is fierce, and the contestants come to real grips; there is none of the artificiality of the Aegina marbles.

The centaurs try to seize the women; the Lapiths try to protect them. Color was used to clarify the composition, and the finish is less perfect than at Aegina. Clothed, partially draped, and nude figures make for variety. Ends of drapery wrapped around parts of the figures emphasize the curvature of an arm or a leg. The originals themselves have not been restored to deceive the eye as was done in the Aegina figures [p. 67.]

Centaur holding a young woman (Ill. 45)

The occasion for this battle between Lapiths and centaurs was the wedding feast of Pirithous, rudely interrupted by the centaurs, who attacked the bride. Pirithous stands to the left of Apollo, about to slay the centaur. One of the most engaging groups is this one of the bride resisting her attacker. Bending back, she tries to free herself; but her features betray no strain, and her composure contrasts with the brutality of the centaur. The sculptor thereby suggests superior Greek restraint even under trying conditions. The head is close to our conception of classic beauty. The hair was probably painted; forehead and nose are nearly in line; the cheeks are drawn in. In the fall of the broadly carved drapery this sculptor has been completely successful. Drapery expresses form without entirely abandoning the delight in pattern for its own sake. The style fits the period just prior to the grandeur of the Parthenon sculptures and the clarity of the painted murals of Polygnotus. The pediment was probably designed by a Peloponnesian artist who had been influenced by the Ionian school.

Zeus, bronze (Ill. 46)

This bronze statue of Zeus about to hurl thunderbolts is of about the same period as the Olympia pediment. Except for his beard, Zeus, the father of the gods, is hardly differentiated from the youthful Apollo, god of the Muses; all Greek gods are eternally youthful. The fact that this bronze statue was modeled first in clay accounts for the freestanding locks on the forehead and the sharp ridges above the eyes, set in to add color. The figure is slim compared with the compact and sturdy warriors from Aegina. The extended long arms show veins, the torso is lean, showing the ribs, and the thighs are slender. Calm but determined, the god poses for the final thrust, effortless except for his forward stride.

Ill. 45 Centaur holding a young woman, from west pediment of temple of Zeus at Olympia, marble. *Copyright Professor Walter Hege, Karlsruhe Staatliche Kunsthalle*

Young riders, marble relief (Ill. 47)

The well-known frieze of the Parthenon was placed high on the exterior of the cella wall, where it was hardly visible, as the columns obstructed a free view [Plan, Ill. 59]. To compensate for this difficulty, the carving of the upper portion projects out farther from the wall. Among the finest

Ill. 46 Zeus, bronze. *National Museum, Athens*

portions are the seated gods over the eastern door [Ill. 42]. They witness the central ceremony, which represents the acceptance by the priests of Athena of the new gown, the peplos, which each year the women of Athens wove for her. Here are represented youthful riders in the festive procession. The small horses are vigorous and spirited, the riders are relaxed, and their cloaks flutter in the breeze. There is no duplication of postures; in places the horsemen are two abreast so that the legs cut across the surface in a bewildering variety of positions.

Ill. 47 Young riders, marble relief, from Parthenon frieze. *After Lübke*

68

Coin from Elis with Zeus (Ill. 48)

The greatest work of Phidias was his seated statue of Zeus made for the temple of Zeus at Olympia [p. 69]. What we know of the actual appearance of this work is derived from Roman copies that are believed to reflect the type. Even in this small coin replica there is majesty combined with mildness, which characterized the statue at Olympia. The forehead is low and shows a wreath, which was in

Ill. 48 Coin from Elis with Zeus. *After Lübke (1876) and Overbeck*

bronze on the original statue. Compared with other heads of Zeus, which perpetuate the type initiated by Phidias, this coin and a head in Boston have set a standard for comparison. After Phidias had carved the statue of Zeus, the god's image as described by Homer was fixed. Power was his attribute as told in the Iliad (ll. 528–80, v. 6, A.T. Murray): "The son of Cronos spake, and bowed his dark brow in assent, as the ambrosial locks waved from the king's immortal head; and he made great Olympus quake."

Head of Zeus, marble (Ill. 49)

This colossal head has absorbed later influences from Lysippus in an expression of power; force is added to benevolence. The forehead, intended to convey wisdom and will power, seems to be yielding to an internal pressure of thought. The brows are arched and the hair is piled high, a style unnatural in men but proper to Zeus, the ruler of

Ill. 49 Head of Zeus from Otricoli, marble, Hellenistic or Roman period. Vatican. *After Lübke (1876)*

Mount Olympus. His beard is symmetrically divided, as becomes his dignity, not disheveled as the beards of river and sea gods, which were in contact with water.

Hera Ludovisi, marble head (Ill. 50)

This colossal head of Hera, wife of Zeus, is recognized today as representing not a goddess, but a Roman lady of the imperial family, idealized after the manner of Greek sculpture. Greek artists, the Neo-Attic school of Athens, worked for Romans in the styles of the great masters. It is not surprising that this majestic head was mistaken for a copy of a famous Hera by Polycleitus. The combination of mature dignity with youthful charm found enthusiastic approval from Winckelmann, founder of classical archaeology; Goethe; and Schiller. Their words of appreciation are valid today, as they were when written. The fact that this head cannot be specifically related to a Hera made by Polycleitus does not detract from its beauty. The Hera Ludovisi and another comparable head in the Naples Museum have contributed greatly to a concept of classical art that prevailed until later excavations gave us more works that helped to broaden our knowledge of Greek sculpture.

Ill. 50 Hera Ludovisi, marble head. Museo delle Terme, Rome. *After Lübke (1876)*

Amazon, marble (Ill. 51)

Polycleitus, a contemporary of Phidias, worked in bronze. He was known for a statue of an Amazon, of which this statue is a Roman copy. Like his famous statues of athletes [p. 71], this Amazon, one of a group, has the square-shaped head and a heavy jaw. The Amazon, though weary of battle, shows no sign of emotion. The soft, clinging folds of her chiton and the easy, graceful pose show the sculptor was an excellent craftsman. The pillar is a restoration suggested by the position of her left arm. She is probably represented as resting.

Ill. 51 Amazon, marble. Berlin. *After Overbeck*

Ill. 52 Victory fastening her sandal, marble relief from the balustrade of the temple of Nike, Acropolis, Athens. Acropolis Museum, Athens. *Copyright Spyros Meletzis*

Victory fastening her sandal (Ill. 52)

This figure of Victory (Nike) is one relief of several that formed a balustrade around the small temple that stands on the southwest corner of the Acropolis in Athens. In its style of carving it is associated with the three Fates of the east pediment [p. 70, Fig. 26]. Pausing in flight, Nike stoops to fasten her sandal; she rests her foot on an elevation in the ground. The drapery is given a transparency that real cloth garments probably did not possess. It is used to reveal form; the folds and creases contrast with the smoothly clinging portions.

72

Head of a Youth, marble (Ill. 53)

This head belonged to a statue of a victorious athlete who wears the fillet of victory above his forehead. This is not a portrait; the features are idealized, as in an Apollo or a Hera. Within subtle variations, eyes, nose, mouth, and the shape of the head are standardized. The gradation of the light reveals the modeling and the beauty of the smoothly finished marble. A comparison with the poros head (Ill. 40) reveals how sculpture changed in the course of a century. The rapid advance of Greek art was one of the miracles of history.

Ill. 53 Head of a Youth, marble, Roman copy, fifth century. *Metropolitan Museum of Art*

Ill. 54 Roman copy of the Athena Parthenos by Phidias, Varvakeion statuette, marble. H. 3 ft. 4 in. National Museum, Athens. *Alinari*

Phidias: *Varvakeion statuette, copy (Ill. 54)*

Phidias represented the gods in idealized human form, relaxed in posture, and calm in expression. Those qualities that are enduring—serenity, dignity, and repose—found expression in the work of Phidias [p. 69]. In this he may have been benefited by the painter Polygnotus, as painting, more flexible than sculpture, anticipated the great sculptors who followed. A Roman copy of the great Athena Parthenos

of Phidias, which stood in the cella of the Parthenon, re-
produces the elaborate helmet with a sphinx between two
Pegasi, all three surmounted by crests. The cheekguards of
the helmet are turned up. In her right hand Athena holds a
statue of Nike, thereby symbolizing Athena presenting victory to the Athenians. The column here used as a support
may have been required in the original as a support for
the six-foot Nike statue. A wealth of ornamentation was
made possible by the size of the original Athena figure,
which was about forty feet tall. Though the copy is believed
to reproduce the original in its essential parts, it lacks the
rich contrast of the ivory flesh against gold drapery.

The weight rests on the right leg, concealed by the vertical
drapery folds. The left leg, set back, allows the thigh and
knee to show through the drapery of the long peplos. With
her left arm she supports a spear, and the shield rests on
the ground. The full, round face is probably true to the
original. The restful pose was meant to impress, and the
almost symmetrical design conformed to the severity of the
Doric temple.

Scopas: *head from the temple of Athena (Ill. 55)*

Freestanding colossal statues, like the Athena Parthenos
and the Zeus at Olympia, are exceptional in any period.
This lofty concept of sculpture, resulting in statues undertaken by the state, did not last long. The Athena Parthenos
was finished in 438 B.C. After the Peloponnesian War, when
Athens ceded political power to Sparta (404 B.C.), a new
spirit of individualism and realism in philosophy and literature affected art. The great sculptors of the fourth century,
Scopas [p. 72] and Praxiteles, turned to the lesser gods
and heroes, representing them in their more human aspects.

In the plays of Sophocles, the great dramatist of the fifth
century, emotions are given universal significance. He
created types that were in conflict with the general laws of
society. Phidias also generalized; his gods are idealized,
dignified, and serene; he raised human beings to the level
of divinity. Euripides, the dramatist of the fourth century,
abandoned generalized types and created individuals in conflict with themselves or with other men. The individual
and human emotions replace types of persons who are in
conflict with society.

In art this emphasis on the individual is represented by
Scopas and Praxiteles. In a head—one of two found—that

once belonged to a group representing the Calydonian Boar Hunt, the short mouth with parted lips and the deep-set eye half as wide as it is long reflect the strenuous action the body was subjected to. Until these originals were discovered (1879), the basic stylistic differences between Scopas and Praxiteles were not realized.

Ill. 55 Head from the temple of Athena at Tegea (Peloponnesus) by Scopas, marble. National Museum, Athens. *After Lübke*

Praxiteles: *satyr, copy (Ill. 56)*

With Praxiteles we enter the realm of Roman copies. Except for his Hermes [p. 73] no originals of Praxiteles are known.

Satyrs were the wild companions of Pan, pastoral gods of hills and woods with goat legs and goatlike faces. This satyr is human but betrays a kinship to the animals in his elongated ears. The tree trunk and a leopard skin slung over his shoulder suggest his closeness to nature. Given to piping in the woods and dancing with the nymphs, a satyr is averse to work. Unused to physical exertion, a satyr is soft and lacks the muscular development of the athlete. Relaxed and well pleased with himself, he devotes his days to the pursuit of pleasure; this is the character expressed here by Praxiteles.

Praxiteles: *Apollo Suroktonos, copy (Ill. 57)*

In this statue the great god Apollo, relaxed, is leaning against a tree trunk. He is lost in reverie, for the shy and timid lizard has dared to climb the tree trunk. The incorrectly restored right hand once held an arrow aimed at the lizard, and in this drawing the round head is faulty; even in this marble copy the cheeks are more slender. As in the satyr (Ill. 56) one leg bears the weight of the body as the other rests. Hips and shoulders incline in opposite directions, and arms and elbows contrast; thereby movement is introduced. The motif of the standing posture that began with the immobile Apollo statues has achieved complete freedom in the course of two centuries.

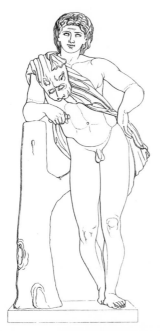
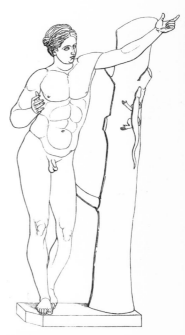

Ill. 56 Satyr, marble copy after Praxiteles. Capitoline Museum, Rome. *After Overbeck*

Ill. 57 Apollo Suroktonos, marble, Roman copy after an original bronze by Praxiteles. Louvre. *After Overbeck*

Ill. 58 Hegeso, fourth-century grave relief. *National Museum, Athens*

Hegeso, fourth-century grave relief (Ill. 58)

As in the archaic period, fourth-century grave reliefs show scenes from daily life. Here a seated lady removes a necklace from a box of jewelry offered her by a servant. The

78

style is in the Phidian tradition; the carver either had
been trained in this style or had worked for a craftsman
who had assisted on the Parthenon sculpture. Through the
sensitive carving of the drapery, attention is drawn away
from faulty anatomy. The freedom suggested in the action
of the hands is combined with insufficient skill to master
the anatomy of the wrists. Conservative carvers of tomb
reliefs carried the style to which they were accustomed into
the fourth century.

Silanion: *portrait of boxer Satyros (Ill. 59)*

This original fourth-century (c. 330 B.C.) bronze head is
a portrait of a man along in years. The boxer Satyros belonged
to an ancient and distinguished family. He had been champion for sixteen years, having won twice at the games at

Ill. 59 Portrait of boxer Satyros, by Silanion, bronze, fourth
century. Olympia Museum. *Copyright Professor Walter Hege,
Karlsruhe Staatliche Kunsthalle*

Delphi and twice at Olympia. The head belonged to a statue that stood in the open at Olympia in the sacred grove for statues of victors (Rodenwaldt, 1936).

This bronze fourth-century head might be compared with the late-fifth-century marble head (Ill. 53). Both represent victors in athletic contests. The marble head is typical, the bronze a portrait. In the marble head the curls of hair are treated as a mass, round and smooth, left that way after the sculptor finished chipping away the flakes of marble. In the bronze head, the curls are pulled up in freely twisted ends and show numerous grooves and ridges. The soft clay from which the sculptor made his model made it easy for him to include as much detail as he pleased. The bronze cast, made from the molds of the clay model, retained every imprint left on the clay.

Old Market Woman, marble (Ill. 60)

The wrinkles of face and neck and the parts left bare were meant to represent old age. The drapery, carved in the conventional style of classical sculpture, might have belonged to a statue of a Hera, though advanced in years. Her sturdy legs seem to belie any necessity for bending forward as she walks. This is realism adapted to traditional Greek sculpture, which depended more on memory and general observation than on a study of a particular model. The drapery clearly shows that artistic conventions were not easily abandoned; the addition of a few new traits as symbols of old age did not produce a new vision. This is still late classical art; the retention of classicism in the drapery is as noteworthy as the appearance of realism in parts of the figure.

Greek vases have today assumed an importance that they did not enjoy in ancient times. Vases are a form of pottery that has been manufactured in many countries since the Neolithic period. Most of those made for household use have not survived. What has been best preserved are vases for decorative purposes or those used in connection with the ritual of the dead. Thousands of painted vases have been found well preserved in cemeteries in Greece and Italy. Greek vases were exported widely and were imitated in all Greek countries on the Mediterranean. Some fine vases made in Athens or Corinth have been recovered from the necropolis of Vulci. Out of the study of these finds, a school of classical research has grown up that in the course of

Ill. 60 Old Market Woman, marble, Hellenistic period, second century B.C. *Metropolitan Museum of Art*

over two centuries has developed generations of specialists.

From the names of the vase shapes, we know their practical uses, even though many of the vases we have today were articles of luxury. The names apply to a basic type; individual vases vary in proportion and size [Ill. 58]. The two-handled amphora was used for holding water, wine, or oil. Richly painted amphoras were wedding presents; large amphoras in the geometric style were for sepulchral purposes (Ill. 61). The kraters (Ill. 64), usually large, were for mixing water with wine [also Fig. 33.] The oinochoe, or wine jug, corresponds to our pitcher. The kylix was a drinking cup, the lecythos an oil flask [Fig. 35], the skyphos a beaker [Fig. 34].

The student derives some satisfaction from recognizing how a vase should be classified according to its place in the stylistic development. The pre-Greek Minoan or Mycenaean vases [Ill. 37] are rare, but larger museums have reproductions. Vases of historic Greece fall into four major styles: geometric (900–700 B.C.), often called eighth-century style; Orientalizing, also called early-black-figured (700–550 B.C.) or seventh-century style; black-figured, also called later-Attic black-figured (550–480 B.C.) or sixth-century style, corresponding to archaic sculpture; red-figured (525–300 B.C.), divided into severe style (525–460 B.C.), fine or free style (460–400 B.C.), and late style (400–300 B.C.). Concurrent with the red-figured style is another white-ground technique, fifth-century Attic.

Greek vases were turned on the potter's wheel; neck and handles were attached afterward. The outlines of the decoration were traced with a stylus on the clay after the first firing to mark the main outlines. The red background is the natural color of the clay. On the black-figured vases the figures are filled in as black silhouettes; for details a dry point is used on the black figures to bare the red background. On red-figured vases the figures were drawn with a fine brush and the background filled in around the figures; details were drawn in with a fine brush.

Geometric-style vase (Ill. 61)

In this first truly Greek geometric vase the shape itself partakes of an organic quality that in the later Doric style of architecture comes to its full maturity. This organic sense relates to the structure of the human figure, where each member is shaped to carry out its function. Though still tentative and uncertain, the base is emphasized as a separate part to stand on, like a foot. The neck meets the body with a determined break; like a real neck, it comes to a halt before the shoulders slope off. Such a clear differentiation between base, body, and neck echoes the marked contrasts in the structure of the human figure. A Chinese Kang-hsi vase of the same type softens the transition in an easy, languid flow of line, soft and graceful without this exacting vigor. The Egyptian figures of the tomb paintings were like mannikins [Ill.

Ill. 61 Geometric-style vase, amphora, Dipylon ware. *National Museum, Athens*

21]; even in their most graceful shapes [Ill. 30] they seemed stolid, ever ready to return to simple horizontal, vertical, and oblique lines. Greek art has a basic character that reveals itself in the various arts, however they may differ in general appearance.

Order and restraint characterize all Greek art. In sculpture the human figure was virtually the only motif; in architecture it was the Doric order that was perfected. In this vase, stripes and meander border, with minor breaks, are repeated with modifications from top to bottom. A geometric pattern covers most of the surface, but a picture panel shows mourners flanking the bier with kneeling and seated figures beneath. The Neolithic (Ill. 5) and Bronze Age figures are here given an unprecedented refinement. A triangular torso connects to shapely thighs; the mourners raise their arms to their heads like the mourners [2] on the Egyptian XVIII Dynasty painting of Ramose's tomb (Ill. 19).

Exekias: *Ajax and Achilles playing draughts (Ill. 62)*

The geometric style in vase painting was followed in the seventh century by a fashion for Oriental motifs [Ill. 51]; pictorial elements combined with ornamental. This trend continued to produce masterpieces of vase painting in the black-figure styles in vases by such artists as Exekias, who was both potter and vase painter. The foot of the vase has now become a wide flat base that emphasizes firm support. The handles are also more functional; they are placed beside the neck, and are related to the profile. In this position they follow the outline yet do not interfere with it. Borders are used as accents to enrich the total effect. The narrow and still timid figure border of the geometric style (Ill. 61) and the profuse elaboration of borders in the François vase [Fig. 33] attained a balance in the black-figured style: a forceful concentration on a large figure panel is combined with utmost refinement. Decoration strives for elegance and delicacy in its sophisticated crispness of line, which is cut through the black. The artist imbues his figures with a sense of tense concentration. Feet almost fade away, but the toes are all accounted for. Hands are anatomically incorrect but they are not slighted and are by no means clumsy. This calculated preciousness did not last; the full-view eye and the indifference to anatomical correctness gave way to an ever-increasing measure of visual truth.

Ill. 62 Black-figured-style vase, amphora painted by Exekias. Ajax and Achilles playing draughts, 550–480 B.C. Vatican Museum, Rome. *Alinari*

Apollo between Leto and Artemis (Ill. 63)

The black- and red-figured styles overlapped and some painters worked in both styles, like Epictetus [Ill. 53], the early master of the red-figured style. Of the same period are the masters of the red-figured style Euphronius [Ill. 54], Douris [Fig. 32], Brygos and Hieron. These painters belong to the earlier fifth century, before the completion of the Parthenon.

In the "severe" style the figures are in one plane without indication of depth of space; they have profile heads and may be in side or front view. Action seems free; there are occasional effects of foreshortening, and the narrow eye tends toward a true profile. In this procession, as if it were a fashion parade, the same dress is displayed by the two goddesses, the end figures, in different poses. Artemis (right) also wears a stole, perhaps a leopard skin; she shows off bracelets as she drapes her cloak over one arm and holds up her trailing dress with the other. Apollo plays a lyre. Artemis, goddess of the hunt, is also guardian of the animals. The hind, approaching Leto, was especially sacred to Artemis. The beauty of the design is in its wealth of linear rhythms and variety of textures in truly intoxicating profusion.

As on earlier vases, an upper palmette and a lower meander border frame the panel.

In the fifth-century red-figured style the painter no longer had anything to do with the making of the vase.

Ill. 63 Apollo between Leto and Artemis, from a red-figured amphora, severe style (525–460 B.C.). *After British Museum catalog (1908)*

Ill. 64 Red-figured krater of Euphronius, contest between Apollo and the giant Tityus. *After Collignon (1886)*

Contest between Apollo and Tityus (Ill. 64)

The krater, a bell turned upside down, is widest at the top as if to suggest outgoing conviviality. An oil flask [Ill. 58, lekythos] has a narrow neck with a cuplike top for pouring out oil when needed by the athlete. On this krater the painted anthemion borders are quiet and restrained in their jewellike delicacy. In their repose they contrast with the moving rhythm of the figures. Outstretched arms repeat the horizontal borders; drapery lines on Artemis repeat the flaring sides, which are stabilized by the left legs of Apollo and Artemis. A commotion is caused by the giant caught in the middle, his leg dragging as he clutches Artemis. Figures in motion are combined in a single well-integrated design expressive of the same exuberant grandeur that is suggested in the vase itself.

Ill. 65 Judgment of Paris, preparation of the goddesses, fine or free style (460–400 B.C.). *After Percy Gardner, Macmillan (1908)*

Judgment of Paris (Ill. 65)

Complete freedom in drawing was reached during the second half of the fifth century. All suggestion of the lingering archaic traits of the severe style has vanished without the introduction of spatial depth. The straight-line draperies are here replaced by clinging drapery that defines the form of the figure and is reminiscent of the Phidian style of the Parthenon sculpture. With a gain in naturalness for each figure, there is also a loss of simplicity in the total effect that distinguished the severe style.

The goddesses prepare for the shepherd king, Paris, who is to decide who is the most beautiful. Hera, holding a mirror, adjusts her veil; Athena, having set her armor aside, bathes her arms at a spring; Eros assists Aphrodite to put on her jewels. Aphrodite, who had bribed Paris with the promise of the most beautiful woman in the world, Helen of Troy, for his wife, was given the prize in the judgment that followed.

Model of the Acropolis, Athens (Ill. 66)

Of the numerous buildings here shown in a recent model the ruins of only four buildings remain today. They are [Plan, Ill. 59]: the small temple of Nike (1), shown in this model on the extreme right above the monumental entrance; the Propylaea (3); the Parthenon (9); the main temple and

Ill. 66 Model of the Acropolis, Athens, first century A.D. *After G. P. Stevens. I. T. Hill,* The Ancient City of Athens, *Methuen (1953)*

the smaller Erechtheum (16), a temple of Poseidon and the finest example of the Ionic order. The placing of the buildings follows no overall symmetrical arrangement as was later used in Roman architecture. A Greek temple was an isolated structure to honor a god, and was placed on sacred ground.

The Parthenon from the northwest (Ill. 67)

Although the Parthenon has been in ruins since it suffered its most damaging attack [1667, p. 91], the columns of the north and south sides have gradually been restored with the use of new materials when necessary [Plan, Ill. 59]. The work of cutting marble for restoration is going on today. What was originally a paved terrace is today an uneven collection of rocky boulders and newly cut slabs awaiting their turns to be fitted into place. Old and new parts are combined with no attempt to deceive the eye but to preserve the integrity of the original. On the interior, now open to the sky, the essential divisions of the cella, the spot where the statue of Athena stood, and the separate treasury behind can be recognized.

South Caryatid Porch of the Erechtheum (Ill. 68)

This small porch projects from the south wall of the main cella [Ill. 59] of the Erechtheum. This temple had to be placed on narrow, sloping ground because it was designed for

Ill. 67 The Parthenon from the northwest, Athens. *Greek Embassy, Washington, D.C.*

two different cults, those of Athena Polias and of Erechtheus, an ancient king. In addition, the same structure had to enclose two sacred spots. One, the north porch [Fig. 37; Ill. 63, 59] marked the spot where Poseidon's trident hit the ground to produce the sacred salt spring. The other, the south porch, covered the tomb of Cecrops, mythological founder of Athens. Pericles selected this site for a temple, later called the Erechtheum, because it had such time-honored religious significance. Thereby Pericles hoped to ingratiate himself with the conservative Athenians whose faith his companions had shocked. After the completion of the Parthenon a religious appeal, civic pride, and love of art all combined to justify the further beautification of the Acropolis. The Erechtheum was built 435–407 B.C. The architect is not known. The architrave of this so-called Porch of the Maidens rests on the heads of six female figures used in place of columns.

Caryatid from the Erechtheum (Ill. 69)

The echinus [Ill. 60 M] interposed between architrave and head suggests the baskets carried by Athenian women in the Panathenaic festival as shown in the Parthenon frieze. Arms, no longer intact, were probably extended and held in restful posture. In each figure the thigh on the inner side shows through the drapery as the knee is bent. The drapery descends, flutelike, concealing the leg bearing the weight. Due to the sturdy build of the figures the weight appears to be carried without effort. Braided locks draped over the shoulders relate to the earlier "maidens" [Fig. 21], votive figures broken up by the Persians. Here we have the mature Attic development of the Ionian beginnings. This porch is one of the most attractive creations of Greek architecture.

Ill. 68 South Caryatid Porch of the Erechtheum. *Greek Embassy, Washington, D.C.*

Ill. 69 Caryatid from porch of the Erechtheum, Athens. *After Overbeck*

Mausoleum of Halicarnassus, restored (Ill. 70)

Greek architecture reached its finest development in the buildings on the Acropolis during the fifth century. But there were other important examples of Greek architecture outside Greece itself, in southern Italy and Sicily. At least one, in Ionia (Asia Minor), had a wide celebrity, as it was included among the seven wonders of antiquity: the Mausoleum at Halicarnassus (after 353 B.C.). It is known from architectural and sculptural remains and from restoration (on paper) based on a description by Pliny. Numerous restorations have been made; the British Museum catalog (1908) illustrates six. It was the tomb of Mausolus, King of Caria, erected by his wife,

Artemisia. Pliny's suggestion of a lofty basement surmounted
by Ionic columns accounts for numerous monumental buildings in the United States during the early decades of this
century. They are always put to some modern use, but never
as tombs.

Ill. 70 Mausoleum of Halicarnassus, restoration by A. D. F.
Hamlin. *Longmans, Green & Co., Inc., New York (1909)*

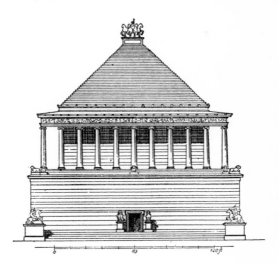

V

Etruscan and Roman Art

UNLIKE NORTHERN Europe, Italy [800 B.C.—Empire period], had a civilized and literate population. The several Italic tribes, each controlling its own city-state, were eventually conquered by the city-state of Rome. With the beginning of the Empire the Romans had a literature inspired by contact with the Greeks. Roman art, though indebted to Greek art, made itself felt at the time of Augustus. With the expansion of the Roman Empire, Greek Hellenistic art became the foundation for Western art. When it has been modified by Roman taste, we call this basically Greek art Roman, acknowledging that the Romans made artistic contributions of their own. Had the Etruscans conquered Rome, there would have been no art called "Roman"; instead its name would have been "Etruscan." Until conquered by the Romans, the Etruscans dominated a large part of Italy. But Sicily and southern Italy with many Greek settlements became known as Magna Graecia, with Tarentum as the largest Greek city. The impressive ruins of Greek temples (Doric style) at Paestum (southern Italy) and at Selinus and Girgenti (Sicily) represent Greek architecture in Italy. The discovery of quantities of Greek vases in Etruscan tombs, to which we owe so much of our knowledge of Greek vase painting, points to an active commercial interchange between Italy and Greece. In return for ceramics the Etruscans furnished Greece with household utensils made of bronze.

The Etruscans had a native art of their own. Remains of their civilization survived in town walls, ruined temples, tomb paintings [Fig. 39, Ill. 65], statues, terra-cottas and bronzes.

When the Romans needed a statue they commissioned an Etruscan artist (Vulca's sixth-century terra-cotta statue of Jove [Fig. 40]). After the Roman capture of the Etruscan city of Volsinii (265 B.C.), two thousand bronze statues were carried off to Rome. On native Roman art, actually created by artists of Rome, art history has little information; no works remain from this early period. This suggests the Romans had no art of their own but appreciated Etruscan and Greek art. What later is known as Roman art was probably executed either by Greeks or by Italian artists of Etruscan origin. The Etruscans emerge as the gifted artists of Italy. Etruscans created architecture, tomb painting, and small bronze and terra-cotta sculpture intended for tombs. Terra-cotta sculpture was applied as decoration to the lids of sarcophagi and to the temple. There was portrait sculpture and jewelry, and a few individual works of merit have survived. What the Etruscans lacked was a consciousness of the artist as a creative individual esteemed by the public. The Etruscans also failed to develop a significant literature. Without the stimulus of literature there could be no goals to aspire to. Since the Etruscans produced no writers and since their language was dying out, nothing in writing was passed on to posterity that compares with what Greek and Latin texts accomplished for classical culture (Pallottino).

Bronze bucket (Ill. 71)

Bronzes found in Tuscany are often indistinguishable from Greek, as is the case here. Those found in tombs were probably for funeral and not for domestic use. The palmetto border is raised (repoussé) relief; the other borders of shells and scrolls are typically Greek and so is the mythology. The plaque beneath the handle shows a Harpy-like winged figure holding up two children. As goddesses of storm and death, Harpies carried away their booty "on the wings of the wind." Above the foot in a relief, Heracles wrestles with the Nemean lion, a familiar Greek subject. If the Harpy relief has any meaning, it might relate to some story involving the death of two children, perhaps of the fourth century B.C.

Etruscan sarcophagus (Ill. 72)

In this group of two figures, man and wife reclining on a couch, the spirit is Etruscan rather than Greek. Women were accorded a social position equal with men; hence the woman

Ill. 71 Bronze bucket, decorated in relief, Etruscan and Greek. British Museum. *British Museum* Guide (*1908*)

is placed in front, the man tenderly resting his arm on her shoulders. She is wearing shoes; he is barefoot. The costume and a sober, matter-of-fact spirit mark the sarcophagus as Etruscan. The painted borders of the couch are as purely Greek as those found on Greek vases.

Ill. 72 Etruscan sarcophagus, known as the Lydian tomb, terracotta from Cervetri. Louvre. *After Seemann* (1879)

Maison Carrée (Ill. 73)

Roman temples combine Etruscan and Greek elements. Like the Etruscans, the Romans raised their temples on podiums approached by flights of steps; in front was a deep porch. The cella was often given the full width between exterior columns. Greek temples had interior colonnades to reduce the span. Trusses instead of simple beams were used by the Romans, as this enabled them to roof over wider spaces than those attempted by the Greeks. This is an instance of the greater emphasis the Romans placed on solving practical problems through improved structural techniques. Roman temples required interior spaciousness, as they were virtually museums for exhibiting bronze and marble statues taken from Greece. Whereas the Etruscans used wood, brick, and terra-cotta, the Romans used marble for columns and entablatures; and for slabs on the exterior of the walls, which were

Ill. 73 Maison Carrée, Roman temple, Nîmes, southern France.
Archives Photographiques

of concrete faced with brick, hard tufa or travertine. The
Romans preferred the Corinthian order, which they elaborated, especially the capitals [Fig. 43]. The frieze bases
and moldings were carved with continuous leaf and foliage
scrollwork based on the acanthus and other plant forms.

The Maison Carrée, so called because of the rectangular
plan, is the best preserved of Roman temples.[3] It has been
variously dated (periods of Augustus, and of Antoninus Pius,
138–161 A.D.). Its fine proportions and excellent workmanship are generally acknowledged; its refinement may be due
to a contribution from early Greek settlers. Technically the
temple is classified as hexastyle (six columns in front), pro-
style (porch on one end), and pseudoperipteral (freestanding
columns on both ends, but engaged on the sides).

Plan of the Pantheon (Ill. 74)

The circular plan (rotunda) shows a templelike entrance
(portico) placed in front, using material left over from an
earlier temple that had ten columns in front. Only eight were

used for the present building. The rectangular plan of the entrance portico does not gracefully fit a circular plan when the two are joined. To disguise the juncture a lot of useless masonry had to be made into walls and niches. The thick walls of the rotunda on the ground floor permitted niches for statues. The niches were later converted to Christian altars. The dome on a circular plan to obtain a spacious interior was a great engineering accomplishment; but it was only a first step, which was improved upon by the Byzantine builders with the construction of a dome over a square plan [Ill. 84].

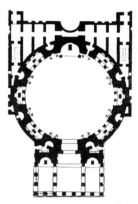

Ill. 74 Plan of the Pantheon, a Roman temple on a circular plan enclosed by a semispherical dome. *After Luckenbach*

Pantheon, interior, restored (Ill. 75)

The vast spaciousness of the Pantheon[4] [p. 103, Ill. 69, Fig. 42] has aroused universal admiration. The height (140 ft.) about equals the diameter of the circular base (142 ft.). If the semisphere of the dome were completed, the sphere would about touch the floor. For nearly fifteen centuries the Pantheon was the world's largest interior uninterrupted by supports. Its only illumination comes from above; the center of the dome is an opening 30 ft. in diameter through which sunlight and also rain enter freely. The slightly concave floor takes care of the drainage. Actually rain causes only minor inconvenience due to the area of the interior. The effect of the light streaming in from above is impressive: "by far the noblest conception of lighting a building to be found

Ill. 75 Pantheon interior, restoration. *After Bühlmann and Dell*

in Europe" (Fergusson). This reconstruction shows five ranges of coffers once plated with gold and thirty-two vertical ribs. Originally each coffer had its bronze rosette. The arches opening over the seven niches correspond to the arch of the barrel vault forming the entrance. In one of the several restorations the building has undergone, these arches disappeared.

A new design for the attic of rectangular panels was created [Ill. 69] in 1747, and the present stucco replaced the original marble paneling. The pediments on columns, flanking the central niche, inspired architects of the Renaissance. As the section shows [Ill. 69], the exterior walls are higher than the base of the dome. This was to counteract the thrust of the dome, an unnecessary precaution since the dome was one homogeneous mass.

Colosseum, air view (Ill. 76)

An air view of the Colosseum ("the largest [5] of all Roman ruins") reveals the several basement levels. They contained, in addition to wild-animal dens, mechanical equipment serving for elevating tools and for providing water to turn the arena into a lake. The performances staged to celebrate the opening of the amphitheater lasted 100 days, and 5,000 wild animals were killed. The arena is said to measure 287 by 180 feet (Anderson and Spiers).

On the right is the substructure showing the inclined planes that supported the seats in three main tiers. The front rows were for the emperor, the senators, and the vestal virgins [Ill. 71]. A colonnade with wooden benches for women was on the uppermost level. Above, on the roof, there was room for the lesser spectators and for the sailors who managed the canvas (velarium) to provide shade. The structural walls were of concrete (tufa) faced with brick. The outer wall was of travertine blocks, which provided an ornamental shell. The plan and the construction are Roman; the design of the exterior is based on the Greek heritage of columns and entablatures, combined with the Roman arch [Roman arch order, p. 108]. To the left the Arch of Constantine is visible above the Arch of Titus; above the Colosseum, the temple of Venus and Roma. Originally the arena had a floor covered with sand.

The Romans conquered Greece in 146 B.C. In A.D. 313 the Roman emperor Constantine legalized Christianity. Roman art may be said to belong to these five centuries, but the great Roman monuments fall into the Christian era, before Christianity had been officially adopted. By correlating major works of art with the rules of emperors we have:

1. (27 B.C.–A.D. 68) Early emperors: Augustus and the Julian emperors, Tiberius to Nero—Statue of Augustus, Altar of Peace
2. (A.D. 69–96) Flavian emperors, Vespasian, Titus, and Domitian—Colosseum, Arch of Titus

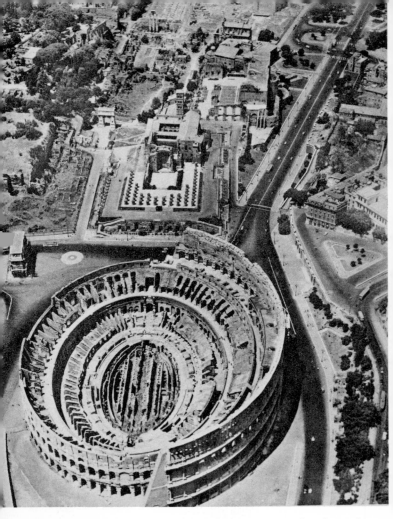

Ill. 76 Colosseum (Flavian Amphitheater), Rome, view from air.
Pan American World Airways, New York

3. (A.D. 98–180) Trajan and Hadrian, Antoninus Pius, and
   Marcus Aurelius—Trajan Forum and Columns of Tra-
   jan, Maison Carrée, Pantheon
4. (A.D. 211–377) Late Empire: Caracalla, Diocletian, and
   Constantine—baths, Basilica of Constantine, Arch of
   Constantine reliefs.

Colosseum, exterior, restored (Ill. 77)

Each of the 80 arches on the ground floor formed an entrance to one section of the arena. Four were for the emperor, for the entry of processions, and for bringing in animals and stage sets. As each entrance led to a section that was separated by walls from adjoining sections, the crowds at each entrance were kept small. For controlled cir-

Ill. 77 Colosseum, exterior, restoration. *After Lübke (1908)*

culation the Romans set a standard hardly excelled by our modern stadia.

The arches of the second and third stories were filled with statues. On the corbels of the uppermost story between the pilasters rested the poles that supported the canvas to shade the arena. The wall of the third story is set two feet back from the wall below. The fourth story is recessed less. Because flat pilasters are used in place of engaged columns, the section does not appear top-heavy.

Arch of Titus (Ill. 78)

Arches were built as separate structures in honor of victorious emperors or as entrances to towns, forums, or approaches to bridges. Rome at one time had thirty-eight (Simpson); others were in the provinces.[6] They symbolize triumphant returns after successful campaigns. All have an arched entrance, a part of a substructure that was surmounted by an attic with a base for a bronze chariot. Some triumphal arches had a single arch, others three. The Arch of Titus [p. 108], of Pentelic marble, gets its effect by contrast of the unadorned side against the sculptured center. Figures of winged victories carved in low relief fill the spandrels of the arch. The main sculptural reliefs, placed within the arch on either side [Fig. 46], are outstanding examples of Roman high-relief sculpture. An important part of the design is the high attic above the arch, with its central panel framing the dedication, cut in the marble in Roman capitals:

SENATVS

POPVLVSQVE ROMANVS

DIVO TITO DIVI VESPASIANI F

VESPASIANO AVGVSTO

Here, as in other stone-cut inscriptions, capital letters are used. For distinction this alphabet has set a standard of perfection that is valid today. Letters are carefully proportioned; there are both wide and narrow ones, as those of the base of the Column of Trajan. The wide letters are round (O or D) or square (M); narrow letters are P, B, E, R, S, and others. For readability and beauty, used for monumental inscriptions, Roman capitals have held first place since their full development nearly 2,000 years ago. They consist of thin and thick strokes and of straight lines and curves; they were probably developed from the use of an instrument that was used rapidly like a brush or pen. A master writer prepared the

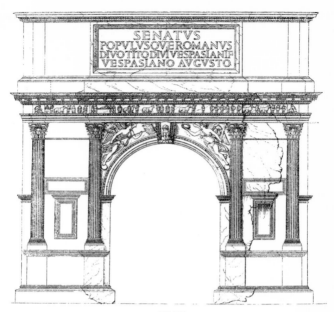

Ill. 78 Arch of Titus. *After Durm (1885)*

copy for the stonemason. Traces left within these letters suggest that they were originally filled in with bronze.

Statue of Augustus, marble (Ill. 79)

Roman sculpture, taking over where Greek sculpture left off, modified the Greek (Hellenistic)-Etruscan heritage through a varying emphasis of realistic or idealistic elements. The mingling of these two trends constitutes a Roman contribution.

In this statue of Augustus the posture is Greek, in the tradition of Polycleitus [Fig. 28]. The weight rests on one leg, the other is set back. This motif for the standing figure became part of the Western tradition in art and persists in subsequent styles particularly during the Renaissance period. Bare legs and feet suggest divinity, as in the statue of a Greek god. The spear that he is believed to have held originally (restored as a scepter) and the armor denote a general of the army. With dignity and repose befitting an emperor, he lifts one arm, a gesture that suffices to command attention.

105

Ill. 79 Marble statue of Augustus, after 20 B.C. Vatican, Rome. *After Leitfaden (1882)*

The head, attached separately to the statue, is treated as a portrait, as we know from other portrait busts of Augustus. This too is in the Roman realistic tradition based on the wax masks traditionally kept in Roman families. The workmanship is superior; texture is expressed to bring out the difference of materials in metal breastplate and leather straps, and there is a contrast between the thinness of the linen tunic, which was painted red, and the heavy folds of the mantle, originally painted purple. The eyes too were painted, but the pupils are not indicated in the carving.

Roman emperors were still divine, though compared to a Ramesses or a Gudea the relationship to divinity was less personal. Specific references to divinities are included in the ornamentation of his armor. Augustus felt obligated to Apollo and Diana, his favorite gods, to whom he credited his victory at Actium (over Antony and Cleopatra of Egypt, 31 B.C.), which made Augustus master of the empire. These two gods are included (lower left), Apollo as the sun god driving his chariot, led by Aurora, goddess of the dawn (see the painting by Guido Reni, Ill. 210). With the gods thus relegated to a minor place, religion has become part of the background; in art religion no longer occupied a place of major importance.

Altar of Peace, section, relief (Ill. 80)

This altar (about 35 ft. square) was dedicated to the goddess of the Peace of Augustus on the field of Mars. Peace had been established through a successful war; each year priests here brought sacrificial offerings. The altar included among others the beautiful Tellus relief [Fig. 45, p. 109]. Of this Roman goddess, Ceres, or Mother Earth, Horace wrote: "May earth, fertile in fruits and flocks, present Ceres with her garland of ears of corn; may the healthful showers and gales of Jove nurse the springing plants." As such she is close to the Christian Caritas (Charity). As on the breastplate of the statue of Augustus, Ceres with the horn of plenty is represented as a symbol of the blessings of peace. Art, reflecting the culture of a period, represented Augustus as a lover of peace and the empire as a civilizing force.

The walls of the altar were decorated with reliefs showing the procession advancing toward the entrance. This relief includes many historical figures. The interpretations for in-

Ill. 80 Relief from the Altar of Peace, procession of priests and senators, south frieze, right half. Uffizi, Florence. *Alinari*

dividual figures are conjectural, and some heads have been restored. The south frieze, with wives and children, shows more variation.

These reliefs have been compared with the Parthenon frieze. If composition is made a standard for comparison, these reliefs lack the variety introduced by the open spaces on the Parthenon frieze; figures may seem crowded and the total effect monotonous. Yet the children bring in variation, and the frieze aims to suggest a crowd. Some figures, as seen in the heads, stand behind those in front; there is depth and space not attempted in the Parthenon frieze. Figures are in front, three-quarter and side views; they look in different directions, form groups, and seem to be conversing. The second figure on the left in the background places her finger on her lips as if to caution silence, and others lift their hands. Though inferior to the Parthenon frieze in clarity of composition, it represents a new style, at the beginning of Roman sculpture.

Ill. 81 Portrait Bust of a Roman, terra-cotta. *Museum of Fine Arts, Boston*

Portrait Bust of a Roman (Ill. 81)

The living quality of this bust of a forceful, intelligent, elderly gentleman suggests that this was made from a life mold. The anatomically correct structure of the head and the softness of the flesh with many tiny wrinkles seem to prove this. Contrasted with these characteristics is the sketchy indication of the eyelids. In the corners of the eyes the artist added strokes of his own, which stand out against the delicacy of the rest of the modeling. In the sensitive mouth the transfer of the living flesh to the soft plaster is particularly noticeable [p. 110]. The bust is probably of the late Republican or Early Empire period.

Column of Trajan relief (Ill. 82)

The sculptural bands of the Column of Trajan illustrate for European art a concept of narrative, or story-telling, art. The events of the two Dacian campaigns (Trajan) are illustrated by consecutive scenes (called "continuous style"). These reliefs, though not the first example, have been preserved. A historic interest attaches to the subject matter of the everyday incidents of the campaign, the army advancing in boats on the Danube, fording the river, fortifying a camp, and other scenes; the emperor Trajan appears frequently. Artistically important in their own right, the reliefs set examples for art to emulate after the content had become Christian, as in Raphael's frescoes and in scrolls and cycles of painting telling of events as they happened.[7]

Ill. 82 Column of Trajan relief, Rome. *After Lübke (1871)*

Column of Antoninus Pius, base (Ill. 83)

Emperor Antoninus Pius and his consort appear as half-length figures behind the outstretched wings of a male figure. This "genius" holds the globe, symbol of power, encircled by the serpent, symbol of eternity. The deified couple is being borne to heaven (apotheosis). The eagles symbolize consecration, and two seated figures personify the place where the apotheosis takes place. The goddess Roma is on the right, reposeful and with a shield bearing the emblem of the wolf suckling the twins Romulus and Remus, children of the war god Mars. The other figure, holding the obelisk of Augustus, is the Campus Martius, personifying the place of the funeral.

Elegance in the classical tradition of Greek sculpture indicates an eclectic taste with little vitality of its own. The disposition of the drapery on Roma recalls that of the three Fates of the Parthenon pediment. This relief illustrates the conservative trend of Roman art. Only the base of the column exists today. Figures ascending to heaven and the use of globe and eagles as religious emblems reappear in Christian art under a new symbolic interpretation.

Arch of Constantine, section, relief (Ill. 84)

In this late example of Roman relief carving, the figures appear isolated, though their arms still suggest that an event is being represented, a *congiarium,* a distribution of gifts. The seated figure of Constantine (in the original his head is chiseled out, leaving a void) is dispensing favors, surrounded by officials. Here medieval Christian art is foreshadowed: the seated emperor was later replaced by an enthroned Christ. An earlier point of view emphasized that this late Roman art is decadent and lacking in skill. In comparison with the Altar of Peace or the reliefs of Trajan's Column, these reliefs have regressed to an archaic stage. But according to Riegl, the champion of late Roman art, "what appears to be coarse and inartistic is positive artistic intention clearly to differentiate figures and parts of figures from one another, while calling forth at the same time the optic impression of a rhythmical alternation of light and shade" (Eugenie Strong, *Roman Sculpture,* 1907, p. 315).

Ill. 83 Base of Column of Antoninus Pius, marble. Vatican, Rome.
After Lübke (1876)

Ill. 84 Central portion of a relief from the north facade of the
Arch of Constantine (erected 315 A.D.)

Ill. 85 Altar of Peace, lower frieze, Museo delle Terme, Rome.
Alinari

Altar of Peace, lower frieze (Ill. 85)

Acanthus-leaf decoration enriched with scrolls, rosettes, buds, flowers, and birds was further developed during the Hellenistic and Empire periods [Ill. 64]. Meanders (Ill. 61, 63); dentils, eggs and darts [Ill. 62a]; and anthemions, or palmettes [Ill. 62b], had been part of the Greek tradition. All these motifs were perpetuated and elaborated by the Romans and revived by the Renaissance.

Here broadly based acanthus foliage sends off on either side of a central axis one major and one supporting scroll encased in clinging acanthus leaves. From each scroll another curves up or dips down to carry on the movement. The central stem ends in a magnificent flower, others terminate in leafage or flowers, and one at the top supports a swan with delicate outspread wings. The convolutions decrease in size and fill the voids gracefully and without crowding. Each bend, descending or pressing forward like a bursting rocket, expands to fit a space, and compact clusters adhere to the confining limits of a spiral forming its center. An endless variety, lively and spontaneous, is developed with skill and restraint. This is an end result of the Greek tradition, a self-conscious performance that uses familiar motifs. We admire the elegance, good taste, and fine craftsmanship; originality is only secondary [see also Ill. 64].

A step beyond this ornamental surface carving against a uniform flat background was taken by the carvers of the following "Flavian" period (Arch of Titus). This "illusionistic" style is well illustrated in two carved pillars, one entwined with roses in bloom, the other with quince and lemon foliage (from the tomb of the Haterii, now in the Lateran Museum, Rome). Here some leaves and flowers and fruit are almost detached from the background. Others melt into the stone to create a sense of distance termed "illusionism" by Wickhoff. The reliefs from the Arch of Titus are in that style [Fig. 46].

Roman acanthus scroll, relief (Ill. 86)

A rich and truly sumptuous manner of Roman decoration is illustrated in the closely packed convolution of this acanthus scroll. What is light and elegant in the carving of the Augustan Altar of Peace here takes on an extravagant luxuriance, combined with precision and crispness in detail.

Ill. 86 Roman acanthus scroll, relief. *After Moore (1903)*

Hercules finds his son, mural painting (Ill. 87)

The infant son of Hercules, Telephos, guarded by an eagle, was brought up by the nymphs. The seated Arcadia is relaxed and reposeful. Telephos was destined to become the ancestor of the royal family that ruled Pergamum [p. 74] under the kings of the Attalid Dynasty, the sponsors of the famous Hellenistic school of Pergamum sculpture [Fig. 30]. In myths the human and animal worlds are closely related, not only in classical mythology, but the world over. Thus a hind plays mother, nursing the infant son of a demigod. The lion too rests peacefully in this heroic setting where all nature is kin. Ancient painting has the human figure as its main topic; landscape was secondary. In this painting there is a sense of weight; heavy forms in figures and landscape are massed in a concentrated, closely packed composition. In the design, diagonals are stressed in repeating parallels. The raised arm of Arcadia is placed on

Ill. 87 Mural painting from Herculaneum, first century A.D.: Hercules finds his son Telephos in the Arcadian Mountains. National Museum, Naples. *Alinari*

the central vertical axis. This is the style of Pergamum sculpture, as in the massive figures of the famous altar [Fig. 30]. The young satyr enjoying himself is true to his natural bent of seeking the pleasure of the moment. This is a mature style, developed as to drawing, modeling, foreshortening, and composition. Cast shadows are used with restraint so as not to obscure the contours of the figures. Color in ancient painting is restricted; black and white, yellow and red dominate, but other hues are contained in the general tonality. There is spatial depth, but no deep space. Though art did not stand still during the Middle Ages, Western painting did not advance beyond this stage in the representation of space and depth until the Renaissance, some thirteen centuries later.

The painter of the original, of which this is believed to be a copy, was probably a Greek from Pergamum. If this is true, it illustrates the importance the Romans attached to Greek art. A culture that is not sure of itself is satisfied with copies of acknowledged masterpieces from artistically more advanced countries.[8]

Mural decoration from Pompeii (Ill. 88]

The names of a few Roman painters have been handed down but they are known as mural painters; no works have been preserved. But numerous painted wall decorations (National Museum, Naples) from the destroyed city of Pompeii (A.D. 79) give an impression of early imperial painting.

This painting is a wall decoration in which the whole wall is divided into sections separated by colonettes, friezes, panels, and floral garlands. Smaller enframed panels of mythological subjects represent Perseus liberating Andromeda, or Theseus as conqueror of the Minotaur. Fruit and flower still-life pictures are also used, and occasionally landscapes where outdoor settings are part of the myth, as in the landscape of Odysseus (Vatican, Rome). Pompeii at the time of its destruction had painting of several styles, mostly of the so-called "fourth" style, with painted architectural elaboration. The style was rich, playful, and fan-

Ill. 88 Mural decoration from Pompeii. *After D'Aurelio (Richter) and Simpson (1929)*

tastic. Though the attenuated architectural members may suggest metal, probably no actual imitation was intended. The ruins of Nero's "Golden House" furnished examples that still existed at the time of the Renaissance, when they inspired Raphael.

Portland Vase, glass (Ill. 89)

The design is cut in opaque white glass over a blue-glass ground in the manner of a cameo. The difficulty of carving brittle glass subject to fracture during the cutting makes such carved glass rare. The subject is doubtful, but may be Thetis reclining on a couch consenting to be the bride of Peleus, as Poseidon is seated on the right.

With the invention of the blowpipe during the Roman period, glass was blown; the handles were attached separately. The blue vase acquired a coating by being dipped in the molten white glass. By applying the design to the white coating after cooling, the white background was cut and carved away, leaving the figures standing in relief.[9]

Ill. 89 Glass vase, known as Portland Vase, Early Empire period. *British Museum*

VI

Early Christian
and Byzantine Art:
A.D. 100 — 1453

ROME WAS transformed from a pagan into a Christian city
in the course of the first three centuries of what became
known as the Christian era.[10] The final "conversion" of the
emperor Constantine (306–337) was but an official recognition of a development toward Christianity that had long been
in preparation. The new religion gave hope and reassurance
to the masses of the people for whom conditions of living
had become intolerable. What eventually led to the fall of
Rome was not so much the barbarian invasions as the internal social decay. Poverty increased along with corruption,
and civil government itself lost control to the army. The
praetorian guard elected emperors as their puppets (third
century). Constantine had transferred the capital from Rome
to Constantinople; thereafter (395) the empire was divided
into west and east. When finally the western part lost its
title to an emperor (476), the final "fall of Rome" had been
accomplished.

Earlier barbarian invasions into Italy of the third and
fourth century had been resisted or thwarted. Those of the
fifth century finally succeeded, under the East Goths (Ostrogoths) and the Longobards (Lombards). These two Teutonic
invasions left their mark on art [p. 130]. An elaboration of
the imperial court was another deteriorating influence introduced by the emperors from Constantine to the final collapse. The earlier emperors, from Augustus on, had ruled
with the aid of the senate, *senatus populusque Romanus*
(the senate and the Roman people). Constantine introduced
a monarchial system with officials and servants that depended on a virtually hereditary caste system and ruinous taxa-

tion to support the state. This disintegrating social pattern affected art, but only gradually and unequally and not in any catastrophic manner.

As late as Diocletian (284–305) the magnificent baths [p. 105] that bear his name, the Basilica of Maxentius and Emperor Constantine, and the Arch of Constantine were created. This arch is well proportioned but some of the carved reliefs betray a declining skill (Ill. 84). With the introduction of Christianity all construction of temples and carving of statues based on pagan mythology ceased. But carvers of ivory did not lose their skill, and mosaic decorations were turned to Christian subjects.

Rome, the center of the secular empire, became the ecclesiastical capital of Christianity. As a new religion, Christianity became a reality before there was a Christian art. That required centuries to complete and finally matured in the Gothic cathedral. Had it been historically possible for a new religion to exert its civilizing influence solely as a spiritual force, a Christian art might never have developed.

Christianity's success as a popular religion was due in part to the fact that it incorporated many local customs, which added to its own worldwide appeal, addressed to all people. Basic terms from the classical and pagan world acquired a Christian meaning. The word for church, *ecclesia,* was the name of an ancient Greek assembly; *basilica,* the early Christian church, denoted a hall; *episcopus,* bishop, was first the title of a Roman municipal officer in Asia Minor.

In early Christian communities the few adherents could meet in a room around a table like a family, without formal leadership. The first Christian church, the early Christian basilica, came into existence after the Christian congregations had outgrown the meeting places provided by private homes. With the growth of the clergy and the development of a ritual, it became necessary to give expression to the importance of the new religion in the church building—the basilica [p. 119]. Unlike a pagan temple, the basilica was not to be admired from the outside. Exteriors were of plain brick, without architectural or sculptural elaboration. The purpose of the Christian church was to accommodate a congregation that came to hear the gospel and participate in sacred rituals; hence the interior was made attractive. The altar was placed over the tomb of a martyr, at times developed on a lower level as a crypt; a marble canopy like a protecting roof was placed over the altar [p. 121, Ill. 80]. A semicircular niche, the apse, terminated the basilica with a bench for the clergy. The apse, like the plan itself, had formed part of the Roman basilica used as a law court.

Basilica of Old St. Peter's, section, restored (Ill. 90)

The old basilica of St. Peter's was demolished during the Renaissance to make room for the Church of St. Peter. A rectangular forecourt for those not yet baptized was placed in front of the basilica. This section through nave and side aisle is more or less typical. Some basilicas had only three aisles (nave and one aisle on either side). In early basilicas following those of Constantine, the facade rather than the apse faced east. The reverse became the established custom and was usually followed for all Christian churches during the Middle Ages. Constantine had erected this basilica over the tomb of St. Peter, near the place where St. Peter was crucified. The basilica was built partly on the walls of the Roman circus of Nero, apparently in a hurry, as classical fragments were used liberally. The same is true of other basilicas still standing. Though a patchwork in details, the general design was one of simplicity. In size, meaning the ground covered, Old St. Peter's was exceeded only by the Gothic cathedrals of Milan and Seville. Its nave was nearly

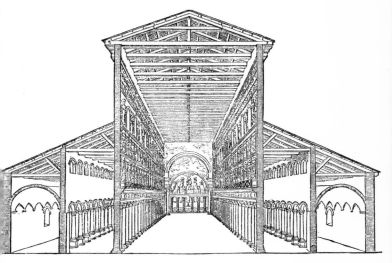

Ill. 90 Basilica of Old St. Peter's, section, restoration, Rome. *After Fergusson (1883)*

as wide as the basilica of Maxentius and the halls of the great Roman baths. Of the many basilicas Constantine erected, one in Bethlehem (Palestine) is still standing. Others in various cities in Palestine exist only in isolated ruins.

Ill. 91 Basilica of St. Paul's (S. Paolo fuori le mura), interior, Rome. *After Lübke (1876)*

Basilica of St. Paul's, interior (Ill. 91)

The basilica of St. Paul's appears to have been conceived as an attempt to improve upon Old St. Peter's. The bema (later called transept) was broadened. After its restoration (1823), following a fire, the originally open ceiling was replaced by one closed by coffers. Otherwise the general impression, if not the modern decoration, probably reflects the character of the original [p. 121, Ill. 81]. Roman basilicas were not used as churches as they continued to serve as law courts. Until later periods, prejudice against Roman temples stood in the way of converting these pagan structures. A Roman building used for storing grain was restored as a church, S. Maria in Cosmedin. The basilican plan concentrated the attention on the altar at one end. A different intent was achieved in the central-type plan, in which the altar was placed in the center of a circular, polygonal, or cruciform plan. Illumination came from above through windows at a higher level, at times under a cupola, or dome. This type achieved the greatest development in the eastern part of the empire, in Jerusalem, in the Church of the Holy Sepulcher by Constantine, and in Anatolia.

Statue of the Good Shepherd (Ill. 92)

After the classical age freestanding figure sculpture plays no major role until the Renaissance. During the Early Christian period sculpture continued in reliefs in marble sarcophagi [p. 118] or in small ivories. Of the few examples of

Ill. 92 Statue of the Good Shepherd, marble, half life-size, Lateran Museum, Rome. *Alinari*

figure sculpture, the Good Shepherd [p. 119] continues in the classical tradition. Of several versions this, the earliest one, is of the middle of the third century, and the best. The figure is still freely posed, with arms detached and the head turned to one side, the eyes gazing into the distance. The idealized classical head is now intended to suggest the youthful Christ. Gradually this style recedes into a more primitive, ornamental treatment. The Good Shepherd posture becomes frontal, drapery flat and proportions clumsy. Monumental sculpture had run its course, and no new motifs appeared to retain or further develop the classical heritage. With no incentive to develop an art that stood for a pagan way of life, life-size sculpture lost its vitality and gradually disappeared.

Church of Hagia Sophia, interior (Ill. 93)

The plan for Hagia Sophia [Ill. 84] was prepared by two earlier central-type domed structures, the church of Saints Sergius and Bacchus (Constantinople) and the Church of Saint Irene. Elements of both plans were ingeniously combined in the plan of Hagia Sophia; niches are from Saints Sergius and Bacchus; the central type, a single dome on a square plan, is Saint Irene. Innovations in architecture or in any of the arts do not appear suddenly as inventions of a single individual. They are the end results of a slow growth that advances step by step. In retrospect each new work reveals itself as a link in a chain. To have forged a new link constitutes a major step forward, which only the more daring and inspired artists have taken. The normal procedure was to adhere to tradition and build, carve, or paint as others had done before.

This interior view should be related to the plan [Ill. 84] for a better comprehension of the structure. The great eastern apse adjoins the central square plan with the three smaller niches opening out from the great apse, semicircular in plan. The thrust of the dome, the problem of supporting its weight, caused concern to the architects of all domed buildings. If the dome, like a semicircular shell, had simply rested on a cylinder, the cylinder would have held up the shell-like lid. There would have been no problem but also no sense of a spacious interior, but only a towerlike, cramped space. To open up the interior and get a sense of space was the aim of all architects since the Pantheon. This the architect was able to do by using large half domes east and west and arched galleries north and south. Thus space opened up

Ill. 93 Church of Hagia Sophia (532–538), Istanbul, interior. *After a painting by John Singer Sargent. The Speed Art Museum, Louisville* *

in all directions. The dome now rests on a square plan, no longer on a circle, and the square plan itself has been extended for greater spaciousness. The lofty dome impressed

* This painting, though without details, gives the effect of spaciousness.

contemporaries by its lightness, as in fact the dome was constructed of lightweight tiles. The present structure was inaugurated (562) four years after the dome had collapsed, only 20 years after its completion. At this second opening, Paul the Silentiary recited his famous poem [p. 128].

Little Metropolis Church (Ill. 94)

The first Golden Age of the sixth century under Emperor Justinian (527–565) is separated from the new "Golden Age" by a period that discouraged representation of the Divine in art, the period of iconoclasm (image breaking, 717–843). Churches of this period favored the Greek cross plan with a dome over the crossing and barrel vaults over the arms. In the later churches of this period the corners of the cross are filled in, making the plan square; the cross as here appears at the upper level. Churches are smaller and related to such examples as Saint Irene. The dome in this church, only eight feet in diameter, is raised on a high drum and becomes an external feature. Through brick, stone, and carving, the exterior received texture and color.

Athens today still has numerous Byzantine churches and

Ill. 94 Little Metropolis Church (St. Eleutherion), mid-twelfth century, Athens.

Ill. 95 Angel, mosaic. Church at Daphni, end of eleventh century.

Salonika has Byzantine churches from all centuries. Athens also has a wealth of Byzantine stone carvings, panel paintings, textiles, silver, utensils, and related objects. Though she lacks a Byzantine Parthenon or a National Museum with its classical antiquities, the Byzantine churches are virtually treasuries of art. The Benaki and the Byzantine museums are rich in Byzantine art in all materials and techniques.

Angel, mosaic (Ill. 95)

This church on the outskirts of Athens has distinguished mosaics. How much of the classical spirit lives on in the ease and naturalness with which the figure moves! Drapery falls into natural folds, as in any late-classical marble. Form

127

is not flattened to a rigid surface pattern; the drawing is free, anatomically correct, and with little if any primitive hardness. Though styles change, the fine craftsmanship and the meticulous taste of Byzantine art reflect a Greek spirit.

Ill. 96 Chair of Maximian, carved-ivory plaques, after 548, Ravenna. *Alinari*

Chair of Maximian, ivory (Ill. 96)

Furniture before the Gothic period has been preserved only in exceptional cases. What is known of ancient furniture, outside of occasional instances of stone seats or thrones, comes from Egyptian tombs and other incidental pieces or is known from paintings [Fig. 9] on walls or from vase paintings [Fig. 32], from Roman sculpture [Ill. 73], or from Roman bronze pieces like a bed from Boscoreale (Berlin Museum). As a throne, this chair demonstrates the architectural character of much early furniture, especially when the importance and dignity of office had to be expressed. Permanence and stability were more important than comfort, which could be provided by cushions.

In this case it is less the chair as such that is important than it is the attached carved ivory plaques. The carving is no longer classic but Eastern in derivation. A basically pagan symbolism is given a Christian meaning. The grapevine stands for Christ, the peacocks for immortality; other animals suggest a Christian reference. St. John the Baptist and the four evangelists are placed in niches. The action of each figure is expressed through gestures. The emphasis is on detaching arms and legs from underneath the drapery; and the vigorous carvings have been related to a Syrian-Egyptian influence, even if carved in Constantinople. The central monogram stands for an abbreviation of *Maximianus episcopus*.

Ivory triptych (Ill. 97)

The apotheosis of Christ is represented on the interior of this triptych; in the upper center panel Christ enthroned is between St. John the Baptist and the Virgin (*Dëesis*). In the lower center panel the five Apostles are, from left to right, James, John the Evangelist, Peter, Paul, and Andrew. Eight warrior saints are depicted on the side panels. All figures are inscribed. The exterior, reverse side, is also carved. Originally such ivories were colored in a subdued way; in other examples the color has been retained. The evenly spaced figures betray the Oriental preference for an emphasis on pattern. A sense for form and the minor differences of action that characterize each figure suggest an underlying Greek tradition of naturalism. Though a single formula is carried through all figures, the heads and handling of drapery show subtle variations. All are graceful, delicate, and exquisite in craftsmanship.

The majestic Christ is seated on a cushioned throne, contrasting in his expansive splendor with the shrinking Virgin and St. John the Baptist. Their simplified drapery concentrates attention on their hands, raised in adoration. The smaller saints of the side panels, crowded into respectful subordination, make the Christ panel seem magnificent. Here is late Byzantine art in its most distinguished manner.

Ill. 97 Ivory triptych (Harbeville), tenth century. Height of central panel, 9 1/2 in. Louvre. *Archives Photographiques*

VII

Early Medieval
and Romanesque Art:
100 B.C. – A.D. 1150

CLASSICAL ART was gradually absorbed by medieval art. Early
Christian and Byzantine art represent largely the reaction
of Italy and countries to the east to classical art modified by
new contributions. The classical contribution lasted longer
in Italy and southern France than in the countries to the
north. The period here covered, more than the first millennium of the Christian era, includes Italy, but particularly
the newly emerging western and northern countries. During
the migration period, we touch upon Italy where the invad-
ing Teutonic tribes, Ostrogoths and Lombards, left some
works behind in northern Italy as in sixth-century Ravenna
[p. 141]. The Irish manuscripts and the Carolingian Renaissance are of the seventh and ninth centuries. More important was the Italian Romanesque style [pp. 145–49] that
developed after the year 1000. The major Romanesque development in all countries took place toward the end of this
period. Architecture, in the form of the Romanesque church,
is the leading artistic expression. Sculpture is largely architectural decoration, but the arts of metal, ivory carving, and
manuscript illumination maintain a high level of distinction.

As the new styles develop, the classical contribution,
Roman or Italian, is felt in Carolingian manuscripts. It is
only in the Irish manuscripts that an entirely new style makes
itself felt. A Greek element that still played a part in Byzantine art, executed as it was on Greek soil, has disappeared.
During this first millennium we witness the emergence of
new forms on the one hand, as well as the continued use,
at least in fragments, of the very stones that had been
carved by the ancients.

So great was the supply of ancient carved stones left over from Roman ruins that they continued to be worked into contemporary structures. Classical fragments inspired also contemporary imitations. The Roman round arch, the idea of the Corinthian capital, and the draped classical figure in sculpture became a part of the Western heritage. These are but a few examples of a much larger number of classical forms that merged with Romanesque. In the Gothic style the classical element almost disappears, but even here it is occasionally recognizable. With the Renaissance the whole classical repertoire started on a new lease on life, and classical reminiscences have not entirely disappeared even in the twentieth century.

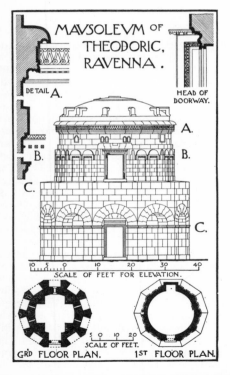

Ill. 98 Mausoleum of Theodoric: Ostrogothic Kingdom in Italy (493–555), Ravenna, Migration period. *After Simpson (1929)*

Mausoleum of Theodoric (Ill. 98)

The circular Roman temple or the Roman mausoleum was imitated in the circular or polygonal plans of baptisteries attached to cathedrals and occasionally in Christian churches. This small polygonal (ten-sided, circular in the second story) building of cut stone, the tomb of the Ostrogothic king Theodoric, in Ravenna [p. 141], combines vigor and originality in the frieze (Detail A) with refinement in the egg-and-dart molding. Theodoric's tomb has been claimed both for Teutonic as well as for Byzantine Greek architecture; the frieze is more northern than classic in style. Whether we have here a reminiscence of a prehistoric dolman [p. 22] or a Roman mausoleum can hardly be settled. Hadrian's huge tomb, the so-called Castle of S. Angelo in Rome, was begun in A.D. 135 and later made into a fortress. It had a total height of about 300 feet; originally it was faced with marble and adorned with statues. Compared with Hadrian's monumental mausoleum, this 30-foot tomb reflects the architectural decline that had settled over Italy during the intervening four centuries. Theodoric's government no longer had the labor and trained craftsmen necessary for large stone buildings. After Constantine had moved the capital to Constantinople, large stone buildings were no longer erected even in Rome, and Ravenna was but a small provincial town.

Church of San Michele (Ill. 99)

Romanesque building activity followed in the decades after 1000. Although that year may have been thought of as bringing the end of the world, according to the Apocalypse, there was no panic as the end of the first Christian millennium approached.

All Romanesque styles have the round arch in common, but all countries that developed Romanesque styles—Italy, France, Germany, and England—had local variations. Three factors contributed to the formation of local variations: [1] classic elements from Roman, Byzantine, and native ruins; [2] unskilled labor; and [3] local materials, usually excluding marble. They made for a new type of architecture totally unlike the ornate character of classical architecture. Where the native influence dominates, the resulting style has a new vigor, though often uncouth and lacking in the perfection of craftsmanship that distinguished classic architecture. Refinement and precision of carving, especially in marble, may

Ill. 99 Church of San Michele, Lucca, begun c. 1210, Tuscan Romanesque. *After Lübke (1905)*

indicate a Byzantine influence. Italy produced three major Romanesque styles: Sicilian in southern Italy [p. 149], Tuscan in central Italy [p. 148], and Lombard in northern Italy [p. 145]. Of these the Tuscan Romanesque is the most emphatic Italian expression, just as the Tuscan language became the literary Italian language. The best-known examples were produced in the Tuscan cities of Pisa, Lucca, Florence, and others [p. 148]. The Romanesque church naves have flat timber roofs, and the side aisles have groin vaults [p. 102, Ill. 67] in a basilica type of plan adapted from the Early Christian style. Unlike the Early Christian basilica, the Tuscan exteriors are ornamental.

Lucca, a financial center, had twenty to thirty churches. The Church of San Michele was influenced by the cathedral of Pisa [p. 148], the best-known example of the style. Arches and columns form a blind arcade for decoration on the ground level, and as superimposed open arcades on the facade. Roman arches had a stately grandeur, but here they are used in mass formations. Being on a smaller scale, they take on a playful elegance, enhanced by the use of dark-green and white marble. The facade, designed for its own sake as a frontispiece, is totally unrelated to the building; the square bell tower, or campanile, is in the Lombard Romanesque style. Architecture here recedes to a provincial expression. This made for variety in the absence of the kind of authority that had given Roman architecture its unified expression. The Tuscan Romanesque is essentially pictorial, developing no new principles of structure. This was the aim of the Lombard Romanesque style, which was functional, and developed vaulting to become the foundation for the Gothic. Before that stage was reached the Italian Lombard and particularly the German Romanesque developed an impressive style, which was more than a transition to the Gothic.

Ill. 100 Worms Cathedral, west end, twelfth century. *After Lübke (1905)*

Worms Cathedral, west end (Ill. 100)

The basic elements, ornamental and structural, of the German Romanesque were already present in the Lombard Romanesque of Italy. Germany further developed the Lombard and produced unified exteriors in the large Rhenish cathedrals of Speyer [Ill. 90], Worms [Ill. 91], and Mainz. All have in common a plan that is essentially the three-aisle basilica now vaulted, hence fireproof. The crossing of nave and bema, now called transept, is made externally important through a low octagonal tower, or cupola. Most German Romanesque churches have two apses, the usual eastern choir apse and an additional one at the west end. The west choir resulted in less conspicuous side entrances [Ill. 91]. Two towers east and west, with stairs leading to the galleries over the aisles, give to the total mass a sense of uplift. The west choir produces a forceful termination of great vigor. Choirs, cupolas, towers, and a steep roof pile up to produce a closely knit, unified effect, more fortress than church. Lombard pilaster strips, corbel courses, and recessed arcaded galleries under the eaves are eminently fitting decorations for so vigorous a structure.

Earls Barton Tower, west end (Ill. 101)

Existing stone churches in England are largely from the period after the Norman invasions. The typical Irish and English church of the Pre-Conquest period had a square eastern tower rather than the apse common on the continent. They were decorated with string courses and pilaster strips,

as in the more elaborate churches of Italy. Projecting strips and round arches form a framework for rough rubble stone walls. Such churches are small and plain and do not compare with the fully developed Romanesque style as represented by Durham Cathedral.

Ill. 101 Earls Barton Tower, west end, early eleventh century, Early Romanesque in England. *After Simpson (1929)*

Ill. 102 Durham Cathedral, nave looking east, c. 1096–1133.
Judges Ltd., Hastings

Durham Cathedral, nave looking east (Ill. 102)

The great cathedrals that were created in England after the conquest were inspired by those in Normandy [pp. 152–53] and Lombardy. This nave with ribbed vaults represents the English Romanesque in its later, twelfth-century development. The main piers rise without interruption from floor to vaults. On the nave arcade two arches are used between these main vaulting shafts. In between, cylindrical columns alternate with continuous shafts; hence this system is called the alternate system [Ill. 95]. It was first used in Lombardy in the well-known church of San Ambrogio [Ill. 88], where piers alternate, only every other pier rising to the full height of the vault. Durham, like any Romanesque nave, has a basic massiveness, which is here pronounced. Other characteristics of the style are the cubical capitals and the use of chevrons (zig-zag lines) in moldings and on the cylindrical columns. The fact that the nave was completely enclosed in the stone vault gave it protection against fire.

Arches that cross the nave at the main piers are called transverse arches. The triforium is the middle section of the nave arcade at the level of the gallery over the side aisles. Above the triforium is the clerestory, through which the nave receives light. The compact massiveness is characteristic of the Romanesque style. During the half century following the conquest (1066), more than thirty cathedrals and monastic churches, exclusive of parish churches, were erected in England, Scotland, and Wales. Durham represents the English Romanesque in its finest and most homogeneous manner.

Ill. 103 Ivory chess figures from island of Lewis (west of Scotland), h. 4 in., twelfth century. *British Museum*

Ivory chess figures (Ill. 103)

A sense of style in a work of art may indicate a measure of artistic quality, as being "without style" denotes its lack. One characteristic of a style is the fact that it finds expression in different materials and in works of art that on the surface seem to be quite unrelated. Such is the case of a Romanesque church and these carved-ivory chess figures [11] [p. 163]. Though these chess figures are small, like toys, they show the same compact severity found in the exterior of Worms or in the nave of Durham. Contours are firm and adhere to the same direction as in the line of the backs of horse and rider that continues without break.

Ill. 104 Last Judgment, tympanum of Church of St. Lazare, Autun, Burgundian School, twelfth century. *Giraudon*

Last Judgment, tympanum of Church of St. Lazare (Ill. 104)

Romanesque sculpture in France found its most intense expression in the representations of what awaited mankind at the Last Judgment. On that day angels—one in each corner —blow trumpets, and the dead, in the lower frieze, rise to be judged by Christ. Souls in the shape of little children are to be weighed by St. Michael in the psychostasis—the weighing of souls. The good and evil of each soul is written in an open book held by a figure above. This is like the weighing of the heart against the feather of truth by Anubis before Osiris, as depicted on an Egyptian funerary papyrus (Ill. 20). On the right of Christ, placed in the almond-shaped mandorla, symbolizing light, are those who are saved. St. Peter with a large key stands at the gate of heaven as angels assist the souls into the heaven overhead. On the right the condemned are taken by the devil. A demon casts the sinners into the funnellike entrance to hell, and another below reaches for other victims. In the resurrection scene below, the saved raise their heads, the wicked cringe in agony. Huge hands close viselike on the head of a sinner, and serpents gnaw at the breasts of unchastity. Intemperance, in the corner, scrapes an empty dish; an angel in the center drives the damned. Agony and suffering speak from the distorted features of the sinners, who seem to be well aware of the terrible retribution awaiting them. The utmost of repulsive ugliness, more bestial than human, is expressed in the grotesque heads of the demons. Sin distorts and causes grief and suffering, virtue calms and relaxes. Man's experience in life here finds expression in art. Underlying all is a sense of guilt that made life on earth a preparation for heaven or hell.

The thin, linear character may owe something to pendrawn manuscript illustrations. The elongated figures of apostles and angels are more ethereal than agitated. Their lack of substance gives them an unearthly, immaterial quality, suggesting the reassurance of divine grace. With loving care the angels hold up the souls as the demon opposite pulls them down. A child's soul reaches back, seeking comfort from the angel (left side) as others cling to the drapery of the angel with the scales (right side).

With a gesture of the hands pointing right and left, Christ the Judge points to the inevitable that is taking place. In the figure of Christ the meticulous precision of the pleated drapery suggests that he, in monumental grandeur, remains aloof. Like the figure of Apollo in the pediment of the temple at Olympia, Christ stands above the strife but metes out justice even-handed. There is here a blending of grace and terror that sums up medieval thought. The Greeks affirmed the meaning of life in the beauty of the human form improved and expanded; the medieval Christian sought escape and deliverance from the bonds of the flesh, which were but the temptations of the devil.

Facade of Church of St. Trophîme, detail (Ill. 105)

We find an entirely different style of Romanesque sculpture in the south of France in Provence. This region had long been a flourishing province of the Roman Empire, where Roman art had left numerous monuments, like the Maison Carrée (Ill. 73) and the Pont du Gard, still standing today. It is understandable that this classical tradition, indigenous to the country, should have affected medieval art. Even so this portal is medieval; it could never be mistaken for a Roman building. It is only when we study the details that we become aware of the fact that two of the three capitals here shown are Corinthian and that the base reflects a Roman design. The portal, like a Roman entablature, has architrave, frieze, and cornice. The artistic language is as different from Roman as French is from Latin. Our illustration

Ill. 105 Facade of Church of St. Trophîme, detail, Arles, twelfth century. *Archives Photographiques*

represents in the frieze the Last Judgment. The part here illustrated shows a demon on the right corner leading the condemned bound by a chain. The recessed statues suggest Roman toga-clad figures, as well as the stolid figures of the Lombard sculptor Antelami [Fig. 83, p. 164], both in the same type of pleated drapery. Another resemblance of style relates the carving of St. Trophîme to the sculpture of Chartres. The date of St. Trophîme, whether before the middle of the twelfth century or later, has been much debated by art historians. Its eclectic character rather than its originality seems clear; according to another view, the style of Lombardy, southern France, and Spain was international (Porter) due to the traffic that connected Lombardy with Spain along the road taken by the pilgrims to Santiago de Compostela [p. 164].

Romanesque lectern (Ill. 106)

With the Romanesque style, the larger forms of sculpture began to assume importance, but the large freestanding figure to be seen from all sides had not yet been developed. This mid-twelfth century lectern from Freudenstadt (Swabia, southern Germany) suggests a step in that direction. The figures of the four evangelists are detached from the shoulder up and treated as a group in high relief below the elbows. Only the head and neck convey a sense of fully rounded form. On the figure itself drapery lines are incised; they are like cylindrical tubes below the knees. Geometric shapes are emphatic and anatomical form is generalized. The inspiration is derived from linear designs, as in ivories, and adapted to the figure. Romanesque carving, originally painted over a layer of gesso, is largely derived from other works of art and shows no firsthand observation of the living figure. The heads are essentially alike, of a type found in other examples of twelfth-century art. The evangelists are identified by their symbols: John by the eagle (left), Matthew by the angel (facing), Luke by the ox (right). Our illustration represents the lectern in its original condition, after restoration (the wings of the formerly restored Matthew, symbolized by an angel, have been removed). Dignity and severity are expressed as well as a sense of submissiveness; the evangelists willingly submit to carrying the burden of spreading the Gospel.

Ill. 106 Romanesque lectern with four evangelists, wood, painted, mid-twelfth century, Freudenstadt, Germany. *Hans Retzlaff, German Tourist Information Office, New York*

Ill. 107 Ornamental page with letters Chi-Rho, Book of Kells. *Trinity College, Dublin University*

Ornamental page, Book of Kells (Ill. 107)

The ornamental style of Irish book illumination was used in metalwork before it was adapted to the more flexible pen-drawn ornament of the scriptoria of the monasteries. A wealth of motifs, enhanced by brilliant color, makes such pages as this from the Book of the Irish monastery of Kells [pp. 142–44] one of the great miracles of art. Even a reproduction, without color and reduced in size, gives a hint of the magnificence, invention, and craftsmanship of the original. Self-effacing monks dedicated themselves to their work with complete disregard of the time expended. An examination of the page with a magnifying glass becomes a journey of discovery. The careful observer will find human heads, parts of figures, hints of open-mouthed animals, and interlocking scrolls that merge with others, fade out, lose themselves, or turn into hands or claws. There are no real floral shapes; animals are disguised; only human heads are easily recognized.

Portrait of the Evangelist Mark (Ill. 108)

Easel pictures or panel paintings did not appear until the late Gothic period. Medieval mural paintings have been preserved, but not in quantity [p. 155], whereas medieval miniatures from all periods exist in many illuminated books, but are usually accessible only to scholars or when placed on exhibition by museums or the Morgan Library in New York. On such occasions the student is afforded a glimpse into a world of rare beauty.

This is one of four full-page miniature paintings, representing St. Mark seated reading from a book placed on a lectern before him. The sky is blue, St. Mark's gown dull green, the earth light brown. He rests his chin on his folded hands, supported by an upright scroll. This illumination belongs to the period 845–882, following Charlemagne, who died in 814. France as a nation separate from Germany dates from 843, the Treaty of Verdun; hence this may be taken as an early example of French art.

Here we still have a degree of realism, a seated figure in space, wrapped in a Roman toga. The footstool shows lines, meant to be converging, as if existing in space. A wall creates a sense of seclusion; the drapery shows modeling without any sense of form; and the figure is on the front edge of the picture. Space exists in outlines, but not convincingly in depth. This neglect of visual truth turns gradually to its complete negation during the Romanesque period [Fig. 79].

Ill. 108 Portrait of the Evangelist Mark. Illuminated manuscript, Carolingian School of Rheims, ninth century. *Morgan Library*

VIII

Gothic Art:
1150—1400

THE TWO and a half centuries of the Gothic style are dominated by architecture. This is the age of the great cathedrals of northern Europe. A new style has emerged that is original and has an emotional appeal quite different from the reasoned perfection of the Greek temple. These northern countries arrived at a new style roughly a millennium after the peak of classical art (from A.D. 200–1200), whereas Greece accomplished her triumph in the course of a few centuries. Greece is a small country with a warm climate; her culture followed earlier civilizations that bordered on the Mediterranean. Moreover, Greece was in contact with a Hellenic culture through her maritime commerce.

France, Britain, and Germany constituted a much larger area, inhabited by primitive tribes, without a unified, central government. Villages had to grow into towns and cities, with diversified economies and social structures that were above a mere subsistence level. After a long migration period (A.D. 370–800) stable governments were established. During the following Romanesque period progress was more rapid. It is this final culmination (1150–1400), the Gothic period, that in rapid progress is comparable to the advances made by Greece. During the earlier centuries, civilizing contributions came from Italy, and Christianity itself furnished a unifying element. The astonishing originality of the Gothic cathedral is due in part to this long evolution, during which the Roman vaulting system was transformed into the Gothic. The development of Greek sculpture was a simpler and

147

more rapid process than the transformation of the Roman groin vault into the high naves of Amiens Cathedral.

Gothic sculpture remained subordinated to architecture and became independent only gradually. Its real development hardly belongs to the Gothic period, but came during the Renaissance. There was little painting, except mural decoration; its place was taken by stained glass. Panel painting came only at the end of the Gothic period, during the fourteenth century, with such painters as Duccio. Illuminated manuscripts and the arts of metalwork and goldsmithing reached a high degree of perfection. Gothic art, like Egyptian and Greek, has a unity of expression. The Gothic style was based on line and surface decoration and development of form; an interest in volume and space is hardly present and did not develop until the Renaissance and Baroque periods. The human figure and the individual personality of the artist remained undeveloped; there are no Gothic portraits.

A division of history by centuries is convenient but also suggests separations that do not fit the facts. We include Giotto (b. 1266) in the Gothic period, though he set painting on a modern, ungothic trend toward mass and volume. Before the late Gothic had come to an end, a new Renaissance style had made its appearance. This however did not mature until the fifteenth century, chiefly in Italy. In the northern countries the Gothic continued, at times merging with the Baroque.

Cathedral of Chartres, south facade (Ill. 109)

Rising above the rooftops the cathedral forms the important accent in the silhouette of the town. Two western towers terminate the nave crossed by the transept, with impressive side portals. The choir continues the nave roof beyond the transept [Plan, Ill. 99], and radiating chapels terminate the apse on the east. The original plan of Chartres called for eight towers; only the western towers were completed, but the three on the south side were carried to the height of the eaves. Gothic spires were usually executed for the western towers only. The steep, pitched roof, which diverts rain and snow, protects the vaults. In place of the continuous heavy walls of the Romanesque, the Gothic used buttresses to strengthen the high nave walls. Buttresses are small sections of walls turned at right angles to the nave to function like props. Buttresses form a support for the flying buttresses that connect with the nave walls at the

Ill. 109 Cathedral of Chartres, south facade. *French Government Tourist Office*

places where interior piers and vaulting ribs meet. According to theory, the thrust is counteracted by the flying buttress, which transmits the thrust across the roof of the side aisle to the massive buttress. This traditional explanation of thrust and counterthrust has been modified to the extent that an aesthetic preference for lightness—an emphasis on the linear as well as a structural advantage during building operations—suffices to explain the Gothic rib vault. One reason to cast doubt on the theoretical explanation, that thrust and counterthrust kept the vaults in equilibrium, was the effect of war damage to vaults. Even where vaults had been damaged they did not always collapse as theory would have led one to expect. Instead the structure maintained a measure of coherence. By starting a vault in which the stone ribs were erected first, these narrow ribs required little centering (meaning wooden supports to hold up the ribs till the mortar had set). Thereafter the ribs fused into a self-supporting structure. Solid groin vaults required continuous wood centering to support the whole stone surface, which meant a great deal of wood was required for temporary use during construction. Compare a groin vault [Ill. 67] with a rib vault, as in Amiens [Fig. 92] or Sainte Chapelle (Ill. 110), to see the difference.

Ill. 110 Interior of Sainte Chapelle (upper church), Paris, dedicated 1248. *French Government Tourist Office*

Interior of Sainte Chapelle (Ill. 110)

The Gothic structural system gains the full effect of lightness and spaciousness for the interior. In this small nave the piers are extremely thin, almost metallic in appearance. Walls have disappeared; the space between the thin piers is filled in with windows.

Cathedral of Siena, west facade (Ill. 111)

Italian Gothic is the least Gothic of the several variations developed in the European countries. Italian Gothic lacked the structural unity developed out of the vaulting system from the inside out. It had no system of buttresses, no large windows, and except for the cathedral of Milan, no choir or radiating chapels. The Cistercian monks of France introduced the Burgundian Gothic system to Italy, but it produced no

Ill. 111 Cathedral of Siena, west facade. *After Lübke*

truly Gothic monuments. Italian builders applied Gothic details to a basically classic structure. Roofs were flattened; naves were made broad rather than high and without the triforium; windows remained small, wall surfaces large; and tie rods were used in place of buttresses. The cathedral of Florence, Santa Maria del Fiore, is an example [p. 185, Fig. 104]. Siena and Orvieto cathedrals show the Italian Gothic in its most extravagant expression.

The facade of Siena Cathedral rises high above the low-pitched roof; for comparison note the exterior of Chartres. "Buttresses" are but thin pilaster strips that do not act as buttresses, and the side elevation shows more walls than windows; for comparison note the interior of Sainte Chapelle. Red, black, and white marble and mosaics (nineteenth century) intermingle color with carving that is architectural rather than figure sculpture. As in the Romanesque cathedral of Pisa, the elaborately diversified facade is a false front (frontispiece), for decoration only. The total effect is one of profusion; no surface is left untouched. Before such magnificence, criticism is silenced, though the purist may point out that structure is not expressed.

Crockets line the steep gables over the portals. Elaborated corner turrets mask empty spaces above the roofs of the side aisles; innumerable turrets end in finials; niches are filled with statues, and have cusped, pointed arches surmounted by steep gables; the corner turrets have waterspouts and gargoyles. Virtually every French Gothic ornamental device here in Siena is used in marble. It took years to transport the marble to the building site [p. 169]. The present nave was planned as a transept for a larger cathedral, which, because of the plague of 1348, was never completed. The one completed transept was begun about 1245; the designer is believed to have been a sculptor, Giovanni Pisano.

Ca d'Oro Palace, detail (Ill. 112)

Italian Gothic of the fifteenth century assumed a peculiarly Venetian expression in palatial architecture in such buildings as the Ducal Palace [p. 187] and the palace, once gilded, that was called the Ca d'Oro (house of gold). Except for its use of pointed arches, it owes as much to classic and Byzantine inspiration, but none of these sources is as emphatic as the manner in which these details are fused into an original expression. In a totally novel fashion, cusped, pointed arches, huge quatrefoils, columns, and delicate balustrades create a screen for an open loggia. Texture is

Ill. 112 Ca d'Oro Palace, Venice, detail. *Alinari*

created by the contrast of smooth panels of marble, architectural relief carving, and the tracery of the balconies. The palace was designed by Giovanni Buono (1430) for the Patrician Marino Contarini.

Amiens Cathedral, west facade (Ill. 113)

Gothic sculpture, as applied to church architecture, was building-stone sculpture, carved out of the stone that was used throughout the church building. The sculptor was a skilled mechanic who carved a statue to fit the space and the stone. Originally color and gilt gave these figures a spectacular brilliance quite different from the graystone we see today. Sculpture does not yet individualize the carver to any extent. The sculpture of Amiens (1225–1236) is later than the west portals of Chartres. The figures are robust and fully rounded, the weight is evenly distributed, and the drapery is seemingly of heavier material [p. 190]. Arms and hands move freely; the figures are idealized; they seem gentle as is appropriate to express heavenly bliss. The serene figure of Christ, "Le Beau Dieu" of the central portal, adjoins on the left [Ill. 109].

Ill. 113 Amiens Cathedral, west facade, south portal of the Virgin, Figures of the Annunciation, the Visitation, and the Presentation. *Clarence Ward*

Pisano: *pulpit, Church of S. Andrea (Ill. 114)*

In Italy Gothic sculpture was applied especially to marble pulpits that combined sculpture in relief with figures in the round attached at the corners of an octagonal balustrade [p. 198]. Such a pulpit is not only a monument of sculpture but of architecture as well. The pulpit rests on the backs of lions and is served by an iron staircase. In the Crucifixion relief the space is packed with figures, moving, gesticulating, and wrapped in voluminous drapery. Heads turn and twist to express pity as well as grief. Autun has a severe grandeur with no depth of space; here there is foreground and distance but no pictorial perspective. The Burgundian sculptor may have developed his style from pen-drawn illumination; the sculptors of the Pisan school drew inspiration from Roman reliefs and statues. Styles spread when individual artists, seeking better working conditions, left one region for another. Nicola Pisano, also known as Nicola d'Apulia, left southern Italy (c. 1260) for Pisa, where

154

he carved his famous pulpit [Ill. 112]. Eventually the Pisan style was carried to Florence, where Andrea Pisano became famous for the first bronze doors of the Baptistery of Florence.

Ill. 114 Pulpit by Giovanni Pisano (executed 1298–1301), Church of S. Andrea, Pistoia. *Alinari*

Ill. 115 The Creation, detail of relief, ·Orvieto Cathedral, west facade, designed (c. 1275–1330) by Lorenzo Maitani. *Alinari*

Maitani: *The Creation, detail of a relief (Ill. 115)*

The entrance portals of Orvieto Cathedral are flanked by broad marble piers, each covered with reliefs that constitute the most important Gothic sculpture of the Sienese school. Among the subjects treated are the stories of the Creation and the Last Judgment. The scenes are arranged in superimposed bands, but a slight suggestion of distance anticipates the later achievements in perspective by Ghiberti. The nude figures are well modeled as they recline gracefully. Sienese art becomes synonymous with grace and delicacy, in painting as well as in sculpture.

Duccio: *Angel Announcing the Resurrection (Ill. 116)*

The event here represented is slight: the three Marys draw back at the sight of the angel seated on the lid of the open tomb. The compact group of figures, the angel as the center, with lines converging on the angel's head and the lines of lid and tomb creating a base, are combined with consummate skill. Note the play of line and the soft, graceful curves in the drapery of the women; the sharp, crinkly edges in the cliffs; and the expansive folds draped across the edge of the tomb. The picture demonstrates linear composition; it owes much to line and form; color adds least to the effect.

Gothic painting in Italy developed local schools, of which the school of Siena during the fourteenth century produced masterpieces and supplied the rest of Europe with models. Duccio di Buoninsegna [p. 202] was the founder of the Sienese school, and with Simone Martini, its greatest master. He painted the great altarpiece for the Cathedral of Siena, for which he was paid by the day with expenses added. His contract required that he should paint the altarpiece with his own hands, which meant he could not hire assistants, which was common. On the day the altarpiece was finished it was carried in "solemn procession" from his shop to the cathedral. It was a day of celebration and prayer, as an expression of religious devotion. This panel, painted on wood in the usual tempera manner [p. 205], is about 20 inches high and is one of a series depicting the life of Christ and that of the Virgin.

Ill. 116 Angel Announcing the Resurrection to the Women, by Duccio. Panel from back of altarpiece, 1309–1311 [p. 202, Fig. 128], Cathedral Museum, Siena. *Alinari*

Madonna and Child with Donor (Ill. 117)

Medieval wall painting outside of Italy has not survived in many examples [p. 155], but painting on wooden panels, the altarpiece, represents a transition from mural painting to easel painting. Duccio's altarpiece [Fig. 128] and this panel belong to that group. Over six feet high, it suggests a wall divided to form a throne, a pedestal, and arches, with columns and much architectural detail, a worthy seat of honor for Mary, Queen of Heaven. Like a ruling monarch she holds the orb surmounted by a cross, symbol of power, and a scepter; the halo signifies her sanctity. Color [12] enlivens the effect, a soft pale rose for architectural parts, light blue for the angels, gilt for all halos. Two angels above hold a tapestry back of the throne, another leans out from underneath a Gothic vault. Depth is suggested by converging lines, but the modeling of the drapery stands by itself. There are no cast shadows, no uniform illumination. Light from above is hinted at by the lighter tint of the horizontal surfaces. This is still painted in the "mode of line and flat tone" verging on the "mode of relief" [p. 209]. There is relief, but it is used arbitrarily to suit the painter and not as observed in nature.

Note that amidst this celestial splendor the Christ Child clasps one finger of his mother's hand, and he no longer sits upright. The drapery of her mantle breaks into irregular folds, her head is inclined. These seemingly minor variations from strictly formal postures are due to the Sienese influence, the first signs of a trend toward naturalism that a half century earlier Giotto had introduced into Florentine painting [p. 204]. The small figure kneeling in adoration in the lower corner is the first Bishop of Prague, who commissioned the painting. He studied in Italy and visited Avignon, then the seat of the Papacy. This painting represents the Bohemian version [p. 201] of the international style, which Duccio began in Avignon and which spread throughout Europe. With Duccio and the expansion of his influence, painting now concentrated on this type of panel painting, though miniature painting for the illustration of books and fresco painting and mural decoration for walls also continued. Giotto is the best known fresco painter of this period.

Ill. 117 Bohemian school, about 1350: Madonna and Child with Donor, Berlin Museum. *Photograph, National Gallery of Art*

Ill. 118 Giotto: Presentation of the Virgin, fresco (c. 1306)', Arena Chapel, Padua. *Alinari*

Giotto: *Presentation of the Virgin (Ill. 118)*

Giotto's contemporaries were impressed with his ability to represent his stories true to nature [pp. 204–05]. To a modern eye Giotto's trueness to nature seems unconvincing. This is so because we have been conditioned by the impact of all that an enriched tradition of over six centuries has added to our artistic heritage. On the other hand, we have also become accustomed to simplification in painting so that Giotto's severely monumental style should present no obstacles [p. 204]. His forms lack detail and texture. Flesh, drapery, and stone are painted as if made of a single substance. Figures are modeled to bring out roundness, but there are no shadows, nor is there atmosphere or a unifying illumination. This "mode of relief" does away with the flat surface without creating any great depth of space; action takes place in the foreground.

According to the legend of the childhood of the Virgin, a supposedly miraculous event took place when the little girl, unaided, mounted the stairs of the temple. Here all

160

eyes converge on the child as she pauses between her mother and the high priest. A small structure, almost toylike, stands for the temple, and the figures are types without individuality. Giotto's claim to fame is the skill with which he composes his figures and relates them to the architectural framework. Giotto as yet has no command of anatomy, but he tells his story with absolute clarity. Giotto's figures stand on real ground; though space is shallow the ground is continuous, more so than in Duccio or in the Bohemian school altarpiece. Giotto's style marks an early stage of realism in Western painting. This is one section, about half life-size, of a cycle of wall decorations.

IX

Renaissance Art:
1400–1600

THE TERM Renaissance art means what it implies, a rebirth of classical art, particularly for Italy [pp. 214–15]. It was a conscious return to the culture of classical antiquity. This included Roman ruins as well as the literature, philosophy, and mythology of antiquity, Greek and Roman. This classic heritage appeared as a rediscovery of which the Middle Ages had only an incomplete and at times distorted impression. Greek and Latin manuscripts were studied, and matters pertaining to classical archaeology became fashionable among the well-educated. Traditional Christian subjects were continued as before. Architecture and to a lesser extent sculpture were affected, and painting in the selection of classic subjects, often through the medium of Roman mosaics and wall decorations. Although little of classical painting had survived, it had some effect on the development of painting. But technically and stylistically painting still owed least to any remains of classical art, and painting made the greatest advances during the Renaissance. Architecture reintroduced the Roman orders and all carved details that could be studied in existing ruins; sculpture remained more independent. Though classical antiquity was upheld as an ideal worthy of emulation, there was, along with imitation, also originality. Even in architecture the Italians did not re-create Roman temples, baths, or triumphal arches. The cultural background had changed too thoroughly to make any close adherence to ancient buildings feasible. The nineteenth century came closer to reproducing whole classical buildings than was ever the case during the Renaissance.

In place of the centralized Roman empire there was a

disunited Italy ruled by different kinds of governments [p. 214], all more or less independent of one another. This encouraged variety and made for the growth of local centers of art and for the development of individual styles. The Renaissance was a liberating influence that contributed greatly to a new sense of the importance of the artist as a creative personality. Italy again became the leading country in art. She produced many of the great artists who carried the Renaissance style to the northern countries.

The technical development of engraving expanded the arts without benefit of any classical contribution. Next to painting, the invention of printing was the most important contribution of the Renaissance period. Stained glass, illuminated manuscripts, the arts that used the precious metals, and tapestries continued, but with less emphasis. By the beginning of the nineteenth century they had become unimportant. Furniture flourished during the Renaissance but produced its most elaborate development during the Baroque periods. In many ways the Renaissance was for art the most fruitful period of any since the days of ancient Greece.

Beginning with Netherlandish painting, we proceed to Italy and the other countries and take up the major arts in turn.

Hubert and Jan van Eyck: *Ghent Altarpiece (Ill. 119)*

This altarpiece [p. 208] when closed is as wide as the lower landscape panel of the *Adoration of the Lamb*. When the folding side shutters are open, as here illustrated, all twelve panels are revealed, except the fronts of the shutters, which are also painted. A religious ceremony is enacted, based on a theological script, the story of salvation. Through Adam and Eve sin came to the world. Salvation begins with the Annunciation to the Virgin, represented on the exterior of the shutters. The Christian believer was concerned for his soul's salvation from eternal damnation. The donor and his wife kneel in prayer and look up in devout submission to St. John the Baptist and St. John the Evangelist. The promised salvation is indicated by the bleeding lamb, symbol for Christ's redeeming of mankind. Around this meaningful event the remaining panels add stature to the celestial drama.

Voluminous draperies with jeweled borders give a massive breadth to the Virgin and St. John the Baptist, each holding a book, and to God the Father, raising His hand in blessing. This is a rare instance of Christian art's giving a concrete personification of the Almighty. The text from the Apocalypse (vii: 10), "Salvation to our God, which sitteth upon the throne," refers to the Lord as a person, and the artist followed the text. Phidias gave greater spirituality to divinity, and Michelangelo greater power.

The realism of the Van Eycks was ill-suited to express divinity; rather the whole altarpiece reflects the piety of the donors and the dedication of the artists. Painting in fifteenth-century Flanders focused on the near view, which stressed details and textures. The straining after expression is strikingly successful in the rendering of the anatomy of Adam, the features of the singing angels, and the heavy brocaded garments throughout. The calm features of God are idealized in comparison, and ornamental details are concentrated, giving to the cloth garment a sense of distinction, simplicity, and restraint.

The Van Eycks' contribution is felt most in the upper figure panel; the lower landscape scenes are still in the manner of enlarged miniatures. Figures and landscape do not fuse, and the figures receive the greater attention compared with the foreground. On the other hand, the distance close to the horizon has remarkable unity and atmosphere. For a full identification of each of the lower panels the reader should turn to the text of the Apocalypse.

Jan van Eyck: *Madonna of Canon van der Paele (Ill. 120)*

This altarpiece painted by Jan, was his most important work aside from whatever he may have contributed to Hubert's Ghent altar. The qualities of the Ghent altar are here repeated in an even more elaborate setting. The amount of detail concentrated in one panel is extraordinary. The four massive figures are St. Domitian (left) in a monumental robe; the Virgin and Child in a broadly spread cloak, with sharp angular folds; the Canon van der Paele, kneeling; and his patron saint, St. George, in armor, who tips his helmet and points out the donor. The action takes place in a church, in which the architecture seems compressed. In this ceremonial presentation the donor is recommended to the Queen of Heaven in the presence of two saints who act as intermediaries. The whole panel in breadth and depth is tightly packed with marble columns, capitals, arches, leaded glass windows, and a tiled and carpeted floor. Two groups, one of Cain and Abel and the other of Samson and the Lion, are carved on the arms of the throne. What each person holds in his hand, from Domitian's wheel with can-

Ill. 119 Hubert and Jan Van Eyck; Ghent Altarpiece, or Adoration of the Lamb, Church of St. Bavon, Ghent. *Copyright A.C.L. Brussels*

dles to the donor's eyeglasses and book, has a miniature-like quality. The figures engage in action, but the whole surface is also a continuously expanding miniature. Light and shade bring out form, but hardly obscure detail. Illumination is evenly distributed; cast shadows are present but not emphasized. A comparison of the heads is illuminating. St. Domitian is self-assured, the younger St. George is less so. The donor is a marvel of precise, full-bodied expression; every wrinkle is painstakingly indicated. His devout and even grim expression dominates detail; the character of the man is not submerged by the minute variations of surface treatment. In the Christ Child one senses the painter's desire to express an unchildlike seriousness, which makes the infant look unhappy. Flemish Madonnas, aiming to combine sweet seriousness with stately dignity, never equaled the success of a Raphael. Italian art had the advantage of a tradition of classic beauty that gave Italian Madonnas a universal appeal that is effective today. Essentially this is painting in the "mode of relief." Light and depth of space play a minor part; perspective is linear but is not emphasized; atmospheric effects are absent; drawing is by outline, not yet by brush stroke. The effect of relief is developed, but there is as yet no total visual effect.

Ill. 120 Jan van Eyck: Madonna of Canon van der Paele, 1434–1436. Bruges Museum. *Copyright A.C.L. Brussels*

Ill. 121 Jan van Eyck: Man with the Pink. Berlin Museum. *Photograph, National Gallery of Art*

Jan van Eyck: *Man with the Pink (Ill. 121)*

Character is well expressed in this portrait of a squire of the Order of St. Anthony. The contrast of textures—fur hat against tightly drawn skin, the slightly parted lips, and raised hands—gives this portrait a living quality. It is one of the most convincing character interpretations of all time.

Masaccio: *The Tribute Money (Ill. 122)*

Shortly before the Van Eycks had completed their oil painting on oak panels in Flanders, Masaccio in Florence had advanced painting through frescoes on walls. In *The Tribute Money* Masaccio's style appears in its developed form. What Giotto accomplished for the fourteenth century *(trecento)* Masaccio did for the fifteenth *(quattrocento)*. He gave painting a new direction, a trend that dominated the period of the Early Renaissance. The painting follows closely the actual story (Matthew xvii:24). The scenes of

167

Peter crouching to receive the coin from the mouth of a fish and then handing it as a tribute to the tax collector are represented on the sides (not illustrated). The main group shows the central figure of Christ controlling the angry disciples; Christ counseling obedience to the law quietly passes his right hand over Peter's left, raised in protest. The new style, advancing toward realism beyond Giotto, unifies figures and landscape. Figures are blurred in outline; they recede into space, and there is atmosphere and distance. The fresco technique reduces contrasts of color, and contrasts of value are lessened toward the distance. The tax collector, whose entry gives rise to the event, stands with his back toward the spectator. On his right, according to tradition, Masaccio introduced himself.

Masaccio, of the Florentine school, is the representative of the monumental trend in Early Renaissance painting in Italy. He died young (1428), a genius recognized by his fellow artists for his worth. To appreciate the enrichment Masaccio contributed to painting, compare these individualized heads with the empty patterns used by Giotto. His tightly drawn, sacklike gowns are here developed into loose garments hanging in broad folds.

Ill. 122 Masaccio (b. 1401): The Tribute Money, fresco, Brancacci Chapel, Carmelite Church, Florence. *Alinari*

Ill. 123 Paolo Uccello (b. 1397): The Rout of San Romano, panel (before 1457). *National Gallery, London*

Uccello: *The Rout of San Romano (Ill. 123)*

Uccello, a contemporary of Masaccio, emphasized perspective, as in the lances cutting across the picture or laid out on the ground pointing into the distance. Pieces of armor are spaced in between to aid the eye to estimate depth. Such feats of foreshortening include the fallen knight stretched out on the ground. The Battle of San Romano was fought in 1432 between the Florentines (on the left), led by Niccolò da Tolentino on a white horse, and the Milanese. This panel was one of four painted for the Medici palace. A taste for battle pictures, like the battle scenes in classic mosaics (Alexander battle) or sarcophagi, rather than a desire for a historical record of a particular battle, may have inspired these paintings. The battle is a staged affair with wooden horses assuming rigid postures like horses on a carrousel, and the rendering of space is not convincing. Uccello uses color in the manner of stained glass, with which he had formerly worked. He had also worked as a goldsmith and in mosaic. His painting style reflects these craft origins.

Piero della Francesca: *The Queen of Sheba in Adoration (Ill. 124)*

A group of painters between Florence and Umbria, bordering Tuscany on the south, Piero della Francesca, Signorelli, and Melozzo da Forli, follow the monumental and scientific trend of Masaccio [p. 218].

169

Ill. 124 Piero della Francesca (b. 1416): The Queen of Sheba in Adoration of the Holy Cross (c. 1465), Church of San Francesco, Arezzo. *Alinari*

Piero developed further the monumental style of Masaccio. Calm, dignity, and a sharp contrast of light and shade distinguish the group of the kneeling queen surrounded by her court ladies; a groom on the left holds a horse. The sweep of the trailing gowns and the defined profiles of the ladies emphasize line, which is linked to form and related to space. These stately figures are part of a real landscape, figures and space begin to merge, and the trees are related to the figures in a visually correct way. Piero's color is luminous, his figures sculpturesque. This series of frescoes depicting scenes from the Legend on the Holy Cross is his most important work. Piero, the son of a shoemaker, wrote a book on perspective, which he dedicated to Federigo, Duke of Urbino.

Signorelli: *Fall of the Damned (Ill. 125)*

Signorelli represents the monumental trend in the second half of the *quattrocento*. A pupil of Piero della Francesca, he is one of the Umbrian-Tuscan group of painters who were influenced by Verrocchio and Pollaiuolo [pp. 218, 232, 240]. Anatomical foreshortening here finds its most mature expression, a few years before Michelangelo's frescoes of the Sistine Chapel. The text for the events of the Last Day could have come to the painter from Dante's *Divine Comedy,* from the Book of Revelation, or from mystery plays and woodcuts. The fanatical sermons of Savonarola were in the same mood. Uccello's foreshortening was timid and experimental. His beginnings are here developed by Signorelli into accomplished demonstrations of skill to portray violent movement and convincing, if not always correct, anatomy.

The downward plunge has come to an end. Three archangels in armor with swords look on from above; there is evidence of sympathy in their saddened faces. Horned and winged demons push, tug, and trample those condemned to hell. One poor woman is taking a ride on the back of a demon; another demon glances at the uppermost archangel, about to pull his sword. These standing and falling figures skillfully fill the space above those who have been herded together into an impenetrable mass of writhing figures. The eye is entranced by the ever-novel combination of nudes kneeling, crouching, or lying prostrate on the ground. Suffering is suggested, but there is no bloodshed. Knit brows, screaming mouths, and twisted torsos convey the horror of the event, but coercion and fear are more in evidence than torture. All this is like one great stage play, such as only an artist could have contrived.

Ill. 125 Luca Signorelli (c. 1447–1523): Fall of the Damned, fresco, Orvieto Cathedral. *Alinari*

Mantegna: *Calvary (Ill. 126)*

Mantegna, of the school of Padua, is the representative painter of the second half of the *quattrocento,* in North Italy. A grand, wide-open space forms the setting for a tragedy enacted as on an open stage. In contrast to earlier painting, space is here continuous. The figures diminish in the distance to suggest that there is no break as the platform recedes. A great calm prevails. The figures are grouped beneath the tall crosses on which Christ and the two thieves are suspended. To the left of Christ is St. John, with hands clasped, who, grief-stricken, looks toward Christ. The Virgin, opposite, is supported by her mourning companions. The man on horseback gazes at the bad thief, who is on the side of shadow; the standard-bearer indifferently turns away from Christ. There is deep feeling on the side of light, indifference on the dark side, where the soldiers in armor throw dice. Mantegna's study of classical antiquity accounts for his treatment of drapery, of helmets, shields, and the Roman standard with SPQR. Mantegna is an excellent draftsman with a thorough command of anatomy, down to the details of hands and feet correctly foreshortened in many varied postures.

Ill. 126 Andrea Mantegna: Calvary. Louvre. *Alinari*

Ill. 127 Vittore Carpaccio: Dream of St. Ursula (1490–1495). Academy, Venice. *Osvaldo Böhm*

Carpaccio: *Dream of St. Ursula (Ill. 127)*

So far we have noted Renaissance painting as decoration for churches. In Venice Carpaccio (active 1478–1522) painted large canvases (h. 9 ft.) for various associations for mutual benefit, called *scuole* (schools). Though the painter is dedicated to telling of the events in the life of a saint, the action takes place in a Venetian room of a well-to-do burgher. The story to which this scene refers is a fantastic account of religious folklore. Though too long to report here, the whole story is well worth reading.[13] As St. Ursula, who is a princess, sleeps in her four-poster bed, the door opens and in a flood of moonlight an angel appears, as in a vision, wearing a slashed-sleeve Venetian gown and carrying a palm suggesting the martyrdom awaiting the saint. A crown is placed at the foot of the bed, a dog rests on the floor. Two potted plants on the windowsill, myrtle and carnation, say in flower language "I love you," as a prince is also involved. The spacious emptiness of the room in its architectural features is severe but delicate. Illumination adds depth to linear perspective. A real interior here becomes the setting for a fairy tale. Though this painting belongs to the last decade of the fifteenth century, the thinness of form is typical of the *quattrocento*. The tall figure of the angel is echoed in the spindlelike bedposts; the slender chair; and the sleeping, shadowlike princess, who is almost without substance.

Ill. 128 Giorgione: Pastoral Symphony. Louvre. *Archives Photographiques*

Giorgione: *Pastoral Symphony (Ill. 128)*

Here a fullness of form fuses figures and landscape into a closely knit design. Wherever the eye enters the canvas, lines and masses merge without losing their identity. Drapery clings in soft folds to the nude figure on the left, and is given a broader treatment in the seated mandolin player. It appears in simpler form on his companion and is given a striking accent in the crumpled cloth underlying the seated nude. Around the center of the canvas the dark profile of the seated player is contrasted with the patches of light on his neck, his right hand, and the tip of his knee. In this "Venetian pictorial mode" light is used for purposes of dramatizing effects, not to give a naturalistic impression of a scene actually observed in nature. Whatever the unknown story may be, this is an idealized interpretation of an event. Realism is constantly modified by light and made to serve the purpose of design.

Gozzoli: *Journey of the Magi (Ill. 129)*

Italian painting in the fifteenth century *(quattrocento)* developed a style that has common characteristics that are different from the sixteenth-century *(cinquecento)* style. Briefly they are (1) painting by mode of relief, (2) modeling to give roundness; an effect of light and dark, but with few cast shadows, (3) no sense of depth of space, (4) a lack of transition that would give continuity of space, (5) emphasis on line rather than mass, (6) drawing by outline rather than painting by brush stroke, (7) linear rather than aerial perspective, and (8) diffused illumination. In color (9) primary and secondary colors are preferred to grays or contrasts of values, which means contrasts of light and shade; (10) what is called realism is an emphasis on detail that is sharp and crisp; (11) what may be called idealism is a tendency to stress composition and to avoid what is mean and trivial; (12) painting is surface decoration rather than surface imitation.

With exceptions, one or more of these stylistic descriptions apply to almost any *quattrocento* painting. Even these differentiations are not sufficient to classify Italian fifteenth-century painters. Three main trends have been pointed out: the monumental, as in Masaccio; the scientific, as in Signorelli; and the pageant, narrative, sentimental approach, as in Benozzo Gozzoli, Domenico Ghirlandaio, and Sandro

Botticelli. Differences in local styles such as Venetian (Carpaccio and Giorgione), North Italian (Mantegna), Tuscan-Umbrian (Piero della Francesca), and Florentine add to the interest. Finally, the personal style of each painter adds another dimension, the most distinguished of these criteria.

The *Journey of the Magi,* by Benozzo Gozzoli (1420–1498), was painted for the private chapel of Cosimo de' Medici's palace in Florence, where it still is. A procession of the Wise Men from the East wends its way through an artificial rocky landscape like a model for a stage set. The distance shows men on foot and on horseback, seen from many angles. This procession is headed toward the altar of the chapel for which Filippo Lippi had painted the *Madonna Adoring the Child* [Fig. 144]. Two of the kings are believed to portray Lorenzo and Giuliano de' Medici. The religious pageants of the period are reflected in this fresco. The points noted above as characterizing fifteenth-century Italian painting apply here. The right half of this fresco was copied by Lockhoff, who used the materials and techniques of the original in a "scientific recreation" (Fogg Museum, Cambridge, Massachusetts).

Ghirlandaio: *Birth of the Virgin (Ill. 130)*

This is an interior of a Florentine palace, and the persons represented are friends and members of the family of Tornabuoni, who commissioned the painting. It illustrates the costumes and the built-in furniture and decoration of Florence toward the end of the *quattrocento.* Ludovica Tornabuoni is the young woman who heads the group of women standing. Here are pilasters carved in relief, a carved frieze of dancing and music-making children, and inlaid (intarsia) wood panels. There is dignity, but no feeling. This was criticized by Ruskin, a point of view that seems irrelevant today. This "worldly spirit" in art here reflected came to a sorry end through the preaching of the Dominican monk Savonarola. "The figures you paint in your churches," said Savonarola, "are the images of your gods. People can say, on meeting them in the street, 'there goes Mary; that is John.' By so doing you degrade the divine." The fanaticism of Savonarola resulted in the burning of books and works of art and eventually led to a reaction that resulted in his own death; he was burned on the pyre. Of the impious astrologers he had said that the only argument with them was *col fuoco* (death by burning on the pyre).[14]

Ill. 129 Benozzo Gozzoli: Journey of the Magi (1469), fresco,
Medici-Riccardi Palace, Florence. *Alinari*

Ill. 130 Domenico Ghirlandaio: Birth of the Virgin, fresco, choir of Church of Santa Maria Novella (after 1485), Florence. *Alinari*

Botticelli: *Madonna of the Magnificat (Ill. 131)*

Botticelli is commonly characterized as the master of line. This is shown here in the flow of line from one focal point to another. Follow the lines from the hand of the angel holding the ink to the hands holding the starry crown over the Virgin's head. The main lines conform to the circular frame. Within selected areas shapes are related through interweaving contours. With what loving care the heavy strands of hair mingle with the looped shawl. In the long, shapely hands each finger is articulated, the ivorylike flesh tones show little modeling, and all features are Botticelli's most personal invention. A sweet melancholy speaks from the Virgin's downcast eyes, barely visible beneath heavy lids. The reason for this resignation is hinted at in the message written on the left page of the book, *"Ave Maria,"* and the answer she has just written on the right side, *"Magnificat anima mea Dominum"* ("And Mary said, my soul doth magnify the Lord." Luke i:46). The hands of mother and child rest on the pomegranate, symbol of sacrificial death.

Ill. 131 Botticelli: Madonna of the Magnificat. Uffizi, Florence. *Alinari*

Savonarola preaching, woodcut (Ill. 132)

Ill. 132 Woodcut, Savonarola preaching, from Compendio di Rivelazione (Florence, 1495). *After Hind (1935)*

Illustration from De claris mulieribus (Ill. 133)

Italian woodcut illustrations are book illustrations. Soon after the invention of printing, from about 1470 on, woodcut illustrations became closely associated with book production, competing with illuminated manuscripts. At first the printed book was looked upon as "artificial script." Early books were in fact barely distinguishable from manuscripts; both were written in the Gothic Fraktur. Roman type forms, perfected in Venice by the Frenchman Nicolas Jenson, eventually came into general use. Florentine woodcuts usually have strong contrasts of black and white, enframed by a narrow ornamental border. Savonarola's sermons were printed in small format with woodcut illustrations. The designer is unknown; though not a master draftsman, he is also above the primitive level. He is at his best in the drawing of the figure, for example the agitation of the preacher and the expressions in the faces of his listeners.

The small cut, showing one of the famous women of history, has the quality one would expect from a painter of note. It also has the breadth appropriate to a woodcut. The open linear treatment of the figure is close to that of the Venetian woodcut style; the use of black for the starry sky is in the Florentine manner. Ferrara lies between Florence and Venice and here combines elements from both styles.

Ill. 133 Woodcut, illustration from De claris mulieribus (Ferrara, 1497). *After Friedländer (1921)*

Coriolanus Cepio Clariſſimo uiro Marco Antonio Mauroceno equiti apud illuſtriſſimũ du-
cem Burgundie Venetorũ oratori felicitatem.

Vom prefectus triremis ad claſ-
sem proficiſceret/quam feliciſſi-
mus imperator Venetoꝗ Petrus
Mocenicus contra Othomanum
Turcoꝗ principẽ ducebat:uehe-
menter rogaſti me/ut quicqd in hac expeditione
geſtum eſſet litteris mandarem: affirmans ea te
Apollinis oraculo uetiora habiturum que a me
ſcripta forent. Igiꝗ ut tibi more gererem que ab
imperatore Mocenico ꝓ quadrienniũ geſta ſunt
annotaui: Tanto enĩm tempore & ille imperiũ
geſſit/ & ego prefectura functus ſum. Quapꝓter
opuſculũ in quo hec ſcripta ſunt tibi mitto:quod
cũ perlegeris/ nõ minus te egregias imperatoris
uirtutes q̃ magnifica ipſius geſta admiratuꝗ cer-
tũ habeo: meritoꝗ damnabis eotũ ſententiã qui
affirmare ſolent effoetam eſſe naturam: nec pro-
ducere tales uiros quales priſcis temporibus ex-
titerũt:omniaꝗ mundo ſeneſcente degeneraſſe:
q̃ falſi ſint uel ex hoc maxime apparet. Nam ſi

a 2

Ill. 134 Page from the Gesta Petri Mocenci of Cepio, printed at
Venice by Erhard Ratdolt, 1477. *After Rhead (1903)*

Page from the Gesta Petri Mocenci of Cepio (Ill. 134)

This printer, originally from Augsburg, settled in Venice,
where he developed the woodcut for purposes of decorating
printed books. Ornamental borders of scrolls, tendrils, and
leaves in the classic Renaissance style, showing white against
a black background, are well related to the printed page. The
initial letter is made into a feature, an ornamental accent
balanced by crossed shields in the lower border. For the
proportioning of the border of unequal width, with its brilliant contrast of white against black, and black type against
white paper, this page sets a standard of perfection. Achievements of this kind have received the unqualified admiration
of connoisseurs everywhere. Whether Ratdolt or someone
else was the designer of the woodcuts is not known.

Ill. 135 Detail from page from Hypnerotomachia Poliphili
(Venice, 1499). *After Friedländer (1921)*

Page detail, Hypnerotomachia Poliphili (Ill. 135)

The supreme accomplishment of Venetian book illustration is the famous *Hypnerotomachia Poliphili,* translated
freely as "The Strife of Love in a Dream." It was published
by Aldus Manutius, perhaps the most famous Venetian
printer. It is the only illustrated book from the celebrated
Aldine Press. The designers of the 168 woodcuts are unknown, but they have never been surpassed. It was translated into French and English, and even the woodcuts were
redesigned in a late French version. Many cuts are architectural, others show outdoor settings. All are linear with no
blacks, in a style that is vigorous yet retains an ornamental
beauty.

Leonardo: *Madonna with St. Anne (Ill. 136)*

After this brief excursion into the arts of the printed book,
we return to painting, which we left with Botticelli, the last
great master of the Early Renaissance [pp. 216–21]. The
style that prevailed between roughly 1500 and 1550, the High

Renaissance, is dominated in painting by Leonardo da Vinci, Raphael, Michelangelo, and Andrea del Sarto in Florence and Rome. In Venice Titian, Tintoretto, and Veronese are the leading masters, and Guido Reni [pp. 221–30] represents the late academic school.

Each painter developed a personal style that differentiates his work from that of his contemporaries. At the same time, a few stylistic characteristics apply to all. They are: (1) details are simplified, drapery folds are broad and massive, figures are voluminous and free in posture; (2) spatial depth

Ill. 136 Leonardo da Vinci: Madonna with St. Anne. Louvre. *Archives Photographiques*

leads the eye into the distance; (3) a contrast of light and shade creates a rounded, plastic appearance; (4) there is greater facial expression.

These points are illustrated by Leonardo [p. 221], especially by the facial expression in the smiles of his women. Freud speaks of feminine traits [p. 313, (Note 10)] in Leonardo, encouraged through his having spent his early years, as an illegitimate child, according to tradition, exclusively with his mother. Leonardo affords an exceptional case where a specific characteristic has been linked psychologically to early childhood influences.[15] Leonardo here develops a traditional problem of combining three figures into an involved pyramidal composition, replete with expression and movement. The contrasted action, the mother reaching out, the Child looking back and St. Anne at the apex, enlivens the basic pyramid so that it is absolved of all rigidity. A religious element is suggested in the Christ Child's playing with a lamb, hinting at his sacrificial death; the lamb was the symbol for Christ. The unfinished mantle of the Virgin and a later broadening of the painting by a few inches on the sides detract from the effect.

Ill. 137 Leonardo da Vinci: Study for the Head of St. Anne, black chalk, c. 1508. *Royal Library, Windsor Castle, Berkshire*

Leonardo: *Study for the Head of St. Anne (Ill. 137)*

The chalk medium of this drawing is well suited to Leonardo's *sfumato,* his soft, atmospheric tone. The resemblance to the St. Anne of the painting makes it seem that this is indeed a study for the painting. Her youthfulness is surprising. Where grandmothers or older women occur in other paintings of the period, some difference is made to show that one woman is older than the other. If we were to hazard a guess, it would be that Leonardo's attachment to his mother could account for this dedication to a single ideal of feminine beauty wherever an opportunity presented itself.

Leonardo: *Five Grotesque Heads (Ill. 138)*

Leonardo was the keen observer who made drawings of whatever interested him. This included what others would have avoided, the unusual that seemed repulsive and perhaps unworthy, particularly in a period that tended to idealize. Art and science were closely related in Leonardo,

Ill. 138 Leonardo da Vinci: Five Grotesque Heads, pen and ink drawings, c. 1490. *Royal Library, Windsor Castle, Berkshire*

and his curiosity led him to seek what was uncommon. Leonardo, the master of the subtle expression, also left us studies of these ghastly old men, horrible and yet human. All this forceful characterization is expressed with great delicacy. Leonardo was left-handed and used a slanting stroke from left to right.

Raphael: *The Small Cowper Madonna (Ill. 139)*

Raphael [pp. 222–24], one of the great painters of the world, was born in 1483 in the little town of Urbino, Italy. During his short span of only 37 years, he accomplished what for other artists of perhaps equal stature required a lifetime.

Today Raphael is still a popular favorite. As the painter of Madonnas he created a type admired universally for its loveliness. "Beautiful as a Raphael" is an expression the French use in praise of beauty.

Raphael's *Small Cowper Madonna,* in the National Gallery of Art, appears meditative, self-forgetful. She has soft brown eyes and a thin veil covers her blond hair. The heads of mother and child incline in opposite directions. We can imagine the Christ Child about to nestle up to His mother when He paused. His foot came to rest on the relaxed hand of His mother. This stopping short in the midst of action brings out the pensive mood. Mother and Child are unaware of our presence and have their thoughts on His mission on earth, the central theme of the Christian dogma.

To give full play to the silent drama, costume is subdued. The thin veil curving around the Madonna's shoulders gives weight to the figure, and heavy drapery folds call attention to the simple tunic. Raphael has enlivened his group to make every gesture meaningful. Dark tones enframe light flesh tints, and a luminous sky rises above the distant hills.

We do not know for whom the panel was painted. The building in the background is probably the church of San Bernardino, near Urbino, from which town this painting is said to have come.

Raphael: *Portrait of Pope Julius II (Ill. 140)*

The fifteenth-century portrait would show the sitter in his usual self-possessed appearance [Fig. 141], but not so in Raphael's portraits. The head of Julius is bent, there is tension in the tightly closed lips, his piercing gaze suggests that he is lost in thought as his left hand clutches the arm of the chair. Through a fuller use of light and shade concentrated

Ill. 139 Raphael: The Small Cowper Madonna. *National Gallery of Art, Widener Collection, 1942*

on the head and an emphasis on expressive gesture, the individual personality is brought out. The High Renaissance advances portraiture to a level of great individuality, of which the more descriptive style of the fifteenth century was not capable. The "mode of relief" is abandoned and we are closer to the "mode of full visual effect," even though there is as yet no sense of daylight. The dark background checks any sense of depth and the armchair hardly contributes to bringing out the third dimension. The Renaissance still depends on individual modeling and an appeal to our sense of touch. Light as an element to suggest space was a creation of the Baroque.

Michelangelo: *Holy Family of the Doni, detail (Ill. 141)*

This panel painting is in a circular frame. Only the upper two thirds of the group is here illustrated. In spite of forceful modeling, this is a painted relief; light is used to model

Ill. 140 Raphael: Portrait of Pope Julius II. Uffiizi, Florence.
Alinari

details. The effect is based on drawing—line—and a complicated composition to create a closely knit design in which the heads of the group and the indented left side contrast with the unified smooth contour of the right. The Virgin is about to reach for the Child. The presence of these three persons makes it a Holy Family, but it failed to satisfy the commissioner Angelo Doni, who, according to Vasari, did not want to accept it.

Three figures interlock to produce a rich pattern of arms and hands in profile and foreshortened view. All this bending, twisting, and reaching is for artistic purposes. Forms interweave as they emerge from light or dark; action serves to create an involved composition, to demonstrate a design that was difficult and unprecedented. Perhaps Michelangelo wished to compete with Leonardo's Madonna, Child, and St. Anne. A religious element, obscured by all this commotion, may also be present. The Christ Child is given a significance of His own. His eyes are downcast with a premeditated em-

Ill. 141 Michelangelo: Holy Family of the Doni, detail. Uffizi, Florence. *Alinari*

phasis, as if looking upon mankind with deep concern. His outspread arms are self-conscious, hardly those of an infant seeking support. His well-placed right foot is unchildlike; a little muscular giant acts gravely as if aware of His superior intelligence. Only Raphael was able to give a divine element to a human infant as in his Sistine Madonna and in the *Small Cowper Madonna*.

Ill. 142 Michelangelo: Sistine ceiling, Separation of Light and Dark, Rome. *Alinari*

Michelangelo: *Sistine ceiling, section (Ill. 142)*

According to scripture (Genesis i:1–4) "In the beginning . . . the earth was without form, and void; and darkness was upon the face of the deep. And the Spirit of God moved upon the face of the waters . . . and God divided the light from the darkness."

Through a mighty thrust of His arms, God separates light from darkness. The Spirit of God is mentioned before God speaks "Let there be light." Michelangelo obscured the face of God through the upturned, foreshortened head. His theme is mysterious power, which is set in motion to accomplish the first act of creation. By retaining in the background a sense of formless void, and by emphasizing dynamic power in the Creator's mighty figure, Michelangelo made himself the perfect interpreter of the opening lines of the Old Testament. Michelangelo used fresco and had a whole ceiling at his command. He could also represent the Creator in action, and at a distance from the spectator. All this was to his advantage. On the other hand, Van Eyck in the Ghent altar (Ill. 119) had to place the Lord on a throne, inactive, but made to appear important. Realism was a handicap for an expression of divinity that Michelangelo escaped.

Michelangelo: *The Prophet Jeremiah (Ill. 143)*

Jeremiah in silent sorrow broods over the defeat of his people. His name has become almost a synonym for woe. Michelangelo's mighty figure expresses profound dejection. There is no despair; the prophet was a tower of strength, but he is seized with weariness and indifference. His left hand has dropped off his thigh aimlessly. His lowered head with eyes closed rests against his right hand in a listless way— Michelangelo reveals character in the action of hands. The inert, massive figure in its undisturbed simplicity seems weighted down by hopeless resignation. His garment, a sculptor's smock, has led to the suggestion that Michelangelo may have identified himself with the prophet; his own temperament was akin to what we know of Jeremiah's.

Michelangelo: *Study for the Libyan Sibyl (Ill. 144)*

The Sibyl of classical mythology foretold the coming of Christ and was thereby associated with the Christian faith. The five sibyls [p. 226] had no individual character, they

HIEREMIAS

Ill. 143 Michelangelo: The Prophet Jeremiah, fresco, Sistine Chapel. Vatican, Rome. *Alinari*

had only prophecy in common. Michelangelo represents them as purveyors of spiritual messages, which come to these women as they are immersed in study. Michelangelo gives the sibyls an individuality of his own invention; some are aged and of powerful build, others are youthful. As messengers of God conveying to man his fate, they are made impressive but devoid of feminine charm.

Reaching back to lift a huge tome, the Libyan Sibyl assumes a task of importance. A touch of sadness is suggested in the turned head. The figure is a study in anatomy for the draped figure of the fresco. Action of hands and feet is analyzed in detail. The spreading of the toes of her left foot is repeated in the three sketches.

Ill. 144 Michelangelo: Study in Red Chalk for the Libyan Sibyl. *Metropolitan Museum of Art*

Andrea del Sarto: *Madonna of the Harpies (Ill. 145)*

The motif of the Madonna and Child, raised above the level of the accompanying saints, appears here in another variation. In larger altarpieces she is often seated on a throne like a queen [Figs. 137, 142]. Raphael envisioned her as floating down from the clouds [Fig. 148]. Here Andrea del Sarto places her, statuelike, on a pedestal, the corners of which have carved half-human half-bird monsters, or harpies,

Ill. 145 Andrea del Sarto: Madonna of the Harpies (1517). Uffizi, Florence. *Alinari*

hence the name *Madonna of the Harpies*. Her pose is exceptionally grand. Of Florentine madonnas this is the most monumental, and in this painting Andrea appears at his best. Her outstretched arms hold a book that helps support the Child, no longer an infant, without effort. Two putti at the pedestal help to create a broad, stable base by filling in the voids and linking the two saints into a closely knit group. Two pilasters draw the composition together, a masterpiece of calculated design. Variety is achieved through using opposite motifs of posture on the two sides. St. Francis, on our left, is in profile showing no exposed arms; St. John, opposite, is in three-quarter view with both arms showing. One putto looks up, the other down. Andrea's Madonna is of the heroic type. His young wife, Lucrezia del Fede, is believed to have served him as a model. A peculiarity in Andrea del Sarto's style is his well-known emphasis on draperies; in his *Assumption*, for all their clothes, the figures look hollow. This trend is here hinted at in the end of the cloak, which, like extra cloth, the Madonna holds up on the book.[16]

Titian: *Young Woman at Her Toilette (Ill. 146)*

In Titian's style the concept of a painting as being something resembling a relief existing in a comparatively shallow space is replaced by the Venetian pictorial mode. Light, texture, and soft outlines replace sculpturesque form [p. 228].

The woman here represented may be only a generalized type rather than a known person. The man may be Alfonso d'Este of Ferrara or Federigo Gonzaga of Mantua. The whereabouts of this painting is known almost from the time it left the artist's studio.

Tintoretto: *The Miracle of St. Mark's (Ill. 147)*

Titian and Raphael represent the spirit of harmony and serenity of the Renaissance, derived from comparable trends of ancient art. Tintoretto is closer to Michelangelo, as he imbues his figures with movement that leads the eye into the picture. The painters of the late sixteenth century introduced a new style, known as Mannerism. Tintoretto was an early Mannerist painter of Venice. This painting represents the freeing of a Christian slave who was to be martyred. St. Mark, unseen by the onlookers, sweeps down from above to perform a miracle and save the slave. The broken instruments of martyrdom are held up by the would-be executioner. The presiding Roman praetor rises in astonishment from his seat

Ill. 146 Titian: Young Woman at Her Toilette. *National Gallery of Art, Kress Collection, 1939*

on the right at a higher level. The crowd, a surging mass, looks in the direction of the slave, stretched out, foreshortened, on the ground. Each person bends, twists, and turns; one is placed behind the other so that depth is emphasized in constantly varied poses. The most extravagant feat of foreshortening is shown in the downward plunge of St. Mark. With fluttering mantle his head stands out dark against light, as his body casts a shadow over the group. Light and shadow intermingle; in the manner of the "Venetian mode" there is no consistent illumination. Even Titian's involved compositions [Fig. 155] develop groups evenly distributed to emphasize breadth as much as depth. Tintoretto, inspired by Michelangelo's late style, stresses depth.

Veronese: *Marriage at Cana (Ill. 148)*

Compared to the innovations of Tintoretto, Veronese's paintings of great feasts, of which he painted four, are stately spectacles [p. 229]; this one is the most impressive. In parallel rows the richly gowned guests, seated and stand-

Ill. 147 Tintoretto: The Miracle of St. Mark's (1548). Venice Academy. *Alinari*

Ill. 148 Paolo Veronese: Marriage at Cana (1563). Louvre. *Alinari*

ing, are crowded over a marble floor. In the rear is a balustraded terrace, between magnificent colonnades, against a clear sky. The figure of Christ gives a focal point to the composition. Musicians in the foreground suggest the importance of music in Venetian life. The viola player is believed to represent the painter himself, followed by Tintoretto with cello and Titian as the bass player. Such biblical feasts were commissioned for the refectories of chapters maintained by the monks of Venetian churches. The miracle itself is but an incident, represented by one man who is filling a pitcher from a large jug.

Ill. 149 Donatello: David, bronze, h. 5 ft. 2 in. (c. 1433). National Museum (Bargello), Florence. *Alinari*

Donatello: *David, bronze (Ill. 149)*

Italian Renaissance and ancient Greek sculpture were once accepted as the only significant styles of Western art. Since then sculpture from other periods has also gained recognition; today Italian Renaissance sculpture has its rivals. Gothic sculpture in Italy formed a part of church furniture as in pulpits [Ill. 112] or was part of the church itself (Ill. 115). Late Gothic sculpture in the northern countries included wood-carved and painted altarpieces [Figs. 116, 119]. A close connection between sculpture and architecture in Italy during the Renaissance contributed to the advance of sculpture, as in Donatello's sculpture for niches for the campanile in Florence. This bronze David [p. 231] was intended to be seen from all sides as a fountain figure for the court of the Medici palace. Its S curve is in the manner of Praxiteles but the pose is less flexible and the muscles are firmer. The lean proportions are those of a lanky boy in his teens. He holds in his left hand the stone that struck Goliath. A classical wreath forms the base; his left foot is placed on Goliath's head. The features are expressionless; the nudity may be due to an intent to suggest a heroic quality. Naturalistic elements are combined with classical, as is characteristic for the Early Renaissance.

Della Robbia: *The Adoration of the Child (Ill. 150)*

Andrea, the nephew of Luca della Robbia, worked only in terra-cotta. His Madonna is close to Filippo Lippi's painted *Madonna Adoring the Child* [Fig. 144]. She wears a halo and a crown; drapery is in thin pleats; her features are sweet and delicate and she looks down. The relief includes four rather prominent winged angels. This emphasis on the religious element is due to Andrea's having worked for village churches, convents, and foundations rather than for the noble Florentine families. His commissions included tabernacles, pulpits, and whole altarpieces in glazed terra-cotta. Andrea did what sons of great artists incline to do; in this case, after his uncle, Luca, had exhausted the more fundamental possibilities of the craft, the young Andrea could only elaborate the same theme. With a large family and no fortune, his brother having inherited the family real estate, he had to work and get all the commissions he could.

Ill. 150 Andrea della Robbia: The Adoration of the Child, terra-cotta relief. *National Gallery of Art*

Da Settignano: *The Young Christ with St. John (Ill. 151)*

One of the best known of Donatello's pupils is Desiderio da Settignano. Desiderio is his name, Settignano his birthplace. He was less versatile than Donatello, but in his own specialty of youthful figures his delicacy and charm are unsurpassed.

Desiderio's relief is flat, close to drawing, hardly over a quarter of an inch deep. The head of the young Christ is given in three-quarter view against the pure profile of St. John. To keep his halo out of the way, it is shown in perspective as a narrow ellipse, whereas Christ's halo with the cross inscribed is a full circle. The light, almost sketchy rendering of the young Christ gives this head a vaporous, apparitionlike quality, which stands in effective contrast to the more positive rendition of St. John. The marble itself has a mellow, waxy quality; its warm gray color is streaked with yellow.

Ill. 151 Desiderio da Settignano: The Young Christ with St. John, relief, marble. *National Gallery of Art*

Michelangelo: *Madonna and Child (Ill. 152)*

Michelangelo left behind masterpieces in sculpture, painting, and architecture and in his sonnets. Art for Michelangelo was a vehicle for his thoughts and feelings. Though his art interprets the subject, what is stressed also reveals his own sensitive nature. This may be expressed by anguish and terror or by sweetness and resignation. Raphael had a well-balanced, amiable personality, and Leonardo was the dispassionate seeker after knowledge, whereas Michelangelo sought through art deliverance from his own unhappy self.[17]

Michelangelo, who based much of his art on the nude figure, here revels in massed drapery. His works usually include motion; here static immobility is but gently relieved by the Child, about to take a step. With head held high, the mother loosely clasps one hand of the Child. Her right hand is relaxed, faintly recalling Jeremiah's, her eyes half closed;

Ill. 152 Michelangelo: Madonna and Child (c. 1505), marble, h. c. 4 ft. *Bruges, Church of Our Lady*

her quiet features reflect resignation mingled with sorrow. She is here like a Greek Demeter [Fig. 27] mourning the loss of her daughter. The strictly frontal pose befits a group intended as a "cult" image placed to face the worshiper. Aloof dignity and an expression of melancholy seem justified if the forward step of the Child suggests symbolically his mission, hinting at the Passion. Whereas sweet meditation serves Raphael in his *Small Cowper Madonna*, Michelangelo strikes a more serious note.

Giovanni da Bologna: *Rape of the Sabine Women (Ill. 153)*

This Flemish master, who became a naturalized Italian, was the last great sculptor of the Italian Renaissance. In this, his most famous work, three types of nudes are combined: the feminine, the youthful masculine, and the old man. Each figure exists in several planes but keeps within the limits of the block indicated by the base. An upward movement continues from bottom to top through a spiral (serpentine) line; thus the line of the leg of the standing male is carried up through the arms of the woman, and comparable linear rhythms appear regardless of the position from which the group is viewed. When first set up (1583) the group was a great success; there was no precedent for it. The composition was studied in small clay models that were cast in bronze. The title by which the group became known was invented after the sculptor had solved the formal problem. Giovanni da Bologna and his school prepared sculpture for the Baroque and for Bernini. After Bernini the major development of sculpture took place in France with Houdon and returned to Italy with Canova (d. 1822).

De Vries: *Virtue and Vice, bronze (Ill. 154)*

Giovanni da Bologna's tradition was carried on by a Dutch sculptor, Adriaen de Vries (c. 1560–1627), an able rival [p. 235]. This small group in bronze poses the same problems; again the title bears no relation to the significance of the work. Less involved, the two figures are made to relate in movement. What interests us here is the variation in contours of solids, and voids left between the figures. To this must be added the marvelous surface, the glitter of the polished bronze with its highlights, darks, and soft transitions.

St. Mark, miniature (Ill. 155)

The art of the illuminated manuscript [p. 199], for which the painter furnished ornamental borders and small paintings (miniatures), approached its end with the invention of printing. Fine manuscripts, illuminated by the leading painters of the period, were still produced during the sixteenth century for kings and queens and members of the aristocracy. In this leaf the ornamental border is drawn in outline and filled in with color. The miniature, painted in opaque

Ill. 153 Giovanni da Bologna
(c. 1524–1608): Rape of the
Sabine Women, marble. **Loggia**
dei Lanzi, Florence. *Alinari*

Ill. 154 Adriaen de Vries:
Virtue and Vice, bronze, detail.
National Gallery of Art

pigments, shows perspective but little modeling. St. Mark
with his symbol, the lion, is seated in a high-back Gothic
chair at his writing stand. Compared with architecture,
sculpture, and painting, the art of the illuminated book is
usually less accessible. On a modest scale, the heritage of
the medieval scribe and illuminator lived on into the nineteenth century in calligraphy and in folk art as Fraktur
writing.[18]

Sixteenth-century calligraphic woodcut (Ill. 156)

French printed books of the fifteenth and sixteenth centuries are distinguished for their woodcut illustrations. The

early printers were German; but after 1488 a peculiarly
French style appeared. This initial, in the tradition of the
Gothic illuminator, is turned into an elaborate design of
pen-drawn flourishes. Grotesques, apelike animals, climb up
one side and descend on the other. The books of the period
are filled with initials and borders enlivened with animals,
pygmies, griffins, birds, insects, and flowers.

Ill. 155 St. Mark, miniature, anonymous, French, from a Latin
manuscript, fifteenth century. *National Gallery of Art, Rosenwald
Collection*

Ill. 156 Sixteenth-century calligraphic woodcut, initial L attributed to Pierre le Rouge, French calligrapher and printer. *After Claudin (1914). Imprimerie Nationale, Paris*

Ill. 157 Ornamental page from Boethius,[19] De Consolatione Philosophiae, published by Jean de Vingle, Paris, 1498. *After Claudin (1914). Imprimerie Nationale, Paris*

Ill. 158 Jean Fouquet: Portrait of Charles VII. Louvre. *Archives Photographiques*

Ornamental page (Ill. 157)

As France became more familiar with Italian art toward the end of the fifteenth century [p. 236], Renaissance forms produced, besides the Gothic, a second style in book illustration. This was based on the Roman letter and the floral sprays, white on black, of Italian books. This initial C takes up almost the whole page and is embellished with a picture. The open-line technique leaves some white spaces so that the light gray is set off against the black background border in the best Venetian manner.

Fouquet: *Portrait of Charles VII (Ill. 158)*

During the French Gothic period, stained glass, tapestries, and illuminated manuscripts take the place of panel painting. With the fifteenth century the Netherlandish influence became dominant in panel painting, and during the sixteenth century the Italian, through the school of Fontainebleau [p. 236]. A French national style developed during the seventeenth century, with Paris as the art capital of the world.

Jean Fouquet (c. 1416–1480) of Tours, of the "school of the Loire," painted miniatures as independent realistic landscapes rather than as parts of text and decoration. This portrait of Charles VII is one of the few portraits.

The head stands out with uncompromising honesty to suggest the personality. It still resembles an enlarged miniature with ornamental detail. The letters of the inscription are no longer Gothic and have not yet become authentic Roman.

Title page, woodcut (Ill. 159)

Early Spanish woodcuts used for illustrations in printed books have a massive splendor. Though this is a title page, the title itself does not appear, but is placed at the end of the book. The entire page is given over to decoration. A great galley is drawn in heavy black lines and thereby gains in an expression of power. A sailor climbs a boom and looks at the moon, the sun looking over from the opposite corner. Vigor and primitive technique account for the attraction of this print.

Ill. 159 Title page for Libra de Cōsolat Tractāt del Fets maritimes, woodcut, Barcelona, 1493. *After Harberler (1897)*

Ill. 160 Title page for *Lilio de Medicina,* woodcut, Seville, 1495. *After Harberler (1897)*

Title page for Lilio de Medicina (Ill. 160)

For a combination of delicacy and strength, this title page is in a class by itself. The contrast of the black title against the all-over gray of the two angels holding the vase with lilies has a spontaneous freshness. What primitive traits appear in the small hands; the protruding knee and uncertain stance of the left angel merge into the linear pattern.

El Greco: *Portrait of a Lady (Ill. 161)*

El Greco [p. 237], who settled in Spain, became one of the great painters of Spain. In this portrait, in the tradition of the Venetian oil technique, there is a new surface quality that depends on the pigment itself. The head stands out against the dark background as if floating in space. The flesh tints are modeled to give solidity; on the right the cheek is carried through a light shadow tone into a reflected light. The transparent veil has substance, and the illumination, coming from the outside, is made to streak around the contours.

Ill. 161 El Greco: Portrait of a Lady. *Philadelphia Museum of Art, Johnson Collection*

Ill. 162 El Greco: Laocoön (c. 1610). *National Gallery of Art*

El Greco: *Laocoön (Ill. 162)*

The painting tells the same story as the late Hellenistic marble group of the Vatican [p. 78, Ill. 49]. The priest of Apollo is sprawled on the ground as his hands clutch the writhing serpent. One son fends off another serpent, as the other son is stretched out behind the father. His body is drawn at a reduced scale to denote the middle distance. Three standing figures, said to be deities, on the right balance the single standing figure on the left. In a loose, seemingly disjointed group, the three figures under attack are related in shapes; solids are interspersed with voids. The figures are elongated and flesh tints glow in a unifying light; there is no sense of natural illumination. All dark areas hang together; the houses of the distant city of Toledo are touched with flickers of light against the dark rising from the foreground. In the agitated sky, white clouds are rent by darks; the turbulence below is echoed above. There is contortion in the figures and an unrealistic posing for purposes of a magnificently integrated design. With patient and leisurely study, the artistic significance of the painting gradually reveals itself. A note of pitiful pleading in the uplifted gaze of the priest adds a human touch that gives the whole scene a note of reality in a painting that is wholly unrealistic.

Ill. 163 Zurbarán (1598–1664): St. Jerome with Sta. Paula and St. Eustochium. *National Gallery of Art, Kress Collection*

Zurbarán: *St. Jerome (Ill. 163)*

Francisco de Zurbarán, of the seventeenth century and two generations after El Greco, painted monks and saints in a sober and matter-of-fact manner. He is essentially a provincial, without the emotionalism of El Greco or the refinement of Velázquez. Not having had the advantage of Italian training, his anatomy is faulty. The three heads are not drawn to the same scale; the one on the far left is unnaturally small. El Greco's Mannerism was a reaction against the classical style of the High Renaissance, with which El Greco has nothing in common. Zurbarán, out of touch with Mannerism, continued a more traditional style. His strong contrast of light and dark and a naturalistic setting relate Zurbarán's style to Caravaggio (c. 1565–1609); he has been called the "Spanish Caravaggio."

Ill. 164 Antonis Mor (c. 1519–1575): Portrait of a Gentleman.
National Gallery of Art, Mellon Collection

Mor: *Portrait of a Gentleman (Ill. 164)*

In monumental quality, Netherlandish painting does not compete with Italian, but in portraiture, Antonis Mor is equal to the best. In the High Renaissance, the nobleman became a cosmopolitan man for whom force and action were no longer the sole purpose of life. This portrait reflects the dignity of a man who feels his worth. Man, as the lord of creation, is self-assured in his mastery. He may enlarge his humanity by recognizing that pet animals are worthy of being portrayed with him. The top of his head, his elbow, and one hand tie the figure to space. Man is still unwilling to exist in free space, which could absorb him and take something from him that is essential to his sense of self-importance. The dark tonality contrasts with head and hands; and costume, gold chain, and the hilt of his sword

213

are emphatically maintained. Externals of rank are still important, but they are subordinated to the head. The features are painted broadly with only enough detail to suggest the approximate age, but without the minute study of flesh and bone that characterizes a Van Eyck. Yet there is a more individual treatment than would be found in a Titian. This type of portraiture prepares for Van Dyck from whom Mor is but half a century removed.

Brueghel the Elder: *The Temptation of St. Anthony (Ill. 165)*

St. Anthony of Alexandria was a young man of wealth who distributed his possessions among the poor and went to live in the desert. There he dedicated himself to a life of self-denial, humility, and chastity. Such virtue displeased Satan, who feared the example set would lessen his own power. To discourage the saint, he tormented him in novel ways. St. Anthony had rejected the pleasures of the table, so an evil creature protruding from a hollow tree taunts the saint by holding out an empty basket and a knife with no bread to cut. The key to the larder hangs high out of reach. Demons in human form protrude from the ground; others, as serpents and scorpions, fly through the air. St. Anthony, barely visible in a rustic shelter, is surrounded by fearful monsters; actually the temptations are half concealed. For the desert Brueghel substitutes a walled town by the sea, a castle on a hilltop, houses, and leafy trees. Nature is realistic and fantastic, as Brueghel's human beings are often grotesque. The life of St. Anthony appealed to Brueghel the moralist, for St. Anthony's troubles of conscience have been experienced by others. Brueghel's interest in the life of the people, often outside a religious content, makes him unique in his period. His harvesting scenes [Fig. 169], peasant weddings (Vienna), and peasant dances (Detroit) expand the range of Renaissance painting. In *The Temptation of St. Anthony* landscape has a human element but also exists in its own right.

Rosendorn and Elsner: *Miniature from Choral (Ill. 166)*

During the late Gothic period, miniatures painted on vellum or parchment with Gothic lettering continued in use for

Ill. 165 Brueghel the Elder (c. 1520–1569): The Temptation of St. Anthony, . . *National Gallery of Art, Kress Collection*

choral books used in church services. After the publication
of printed books, German painting of the fifteenth century
absorbed influences from the Netherlands. As miniatures
served the purpose of ornamental elaboration, the leaf
scrolls, enclosing the miniature, are particularly effective.

Ill. 166 Frederick Rosendorn (scribe) and Jacob Elsner: Miniature
from Choral, known as the Geese Book, detail, Nuremberg. National Gallery of Art. *Rush H. Kress*

Initial B, from the Latin Psalter (Ill. 167)

The ornamental initials of the manuscripts designed and
painted by an artist inspired comparable decoration in printed books. This Latin psalter is the earliest book printed from
movable type to contain important decorations that are not
text illustrations (Hind). The initial is elaborated with a
scroll and floral design and is printed in red. Unlike the text,
which is printed from Gothic type, individual initials of this

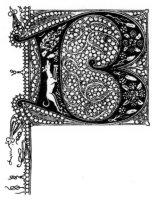

Ill. 167 Initial B, from the Latin Psalter, wood or metal, Mainz, 1457. *After Hind, v. 2 (1935)*

style were designed for this particular book. This woodcut and those to follow are fifteenth-century German of the period before Dürer.

Page from Quaestiones super Donatum (Ill. 168)

The second page of this Latin commentary on a third-century philologist shows this magnificent illustration. The initial P is filled in with a vigorous leaf border, and grotesque heads fill in the corners. In the painted miniature and in this woodcut-decorated book, the same motif of Madonna and Child appears. In the *Geese Book* the Madonna holding the Child stands on a crescent; here she is crowned by two angels. Never was type better related to illustration than in the fifteenth century. The restricted range of the woodcut, using only line and flat ornament, was eminently suited to the printed page. The contrast of black, gray, and white produces an effect of great brilliance.

St. Christopher, woodcut (Ill. 169)

Virtually all art from antiquity through the Middle Ages was commissioned by the state, kings or members of the aristocracy, the church, or wealthy burghers. The less well-to-do occasionally participated in art through ownership of religious images. These became more plentiful when paper

Ill. 168 Printed page from Quaestiones super Donatum, woodcut, Basel, c. 1490. *Joseph Baer & Co.*

came into general use in Europe by the middle of the fifteenth century. Popular prints appeared in the form of woodcuts for playing cards and religious prints; they were pictures of saints or illustrations of the life of Christ or the Virgin. They were made by artists for monasteries or churches and were produced in quantity; text and illustration were cut on the same block. This print of St. Christopher is one of the earliest dated (1423) woodcuts. It is vigorous with an ornamental design. St. Christopher, according to the legend, carried the Christ Child safely across a raging stream and became the patron saint of travelers. The Latin inscription reads, "On whatsoever day thou hast seen Christopher's face, on that day, to be sure, thou shalt not die an evil death."

Ill. 169 St. Christopher, woodcut, from Carthusian monastery of Buxheim (Bavaria), 1423. *Carl Zigrosser*

Page from Temptacio dyaboli de Vanagloria (Ill. 170)

The early-type printers did not have enough type to meet the demand without using the same type over again. Some block books have been printed after 1450, the date tentatively assigned to the invention of printing from movable type. It still paid publishers to cut the type on the same plate or on separate plates. These block books were only pamphlets, so the amount of cutting was limited. The early metal types were soft and wore out, but the wood blocks were durable. Only one side was printed, by placing the dampened paper over the block inked in brown and rubbing the back of the paper to get an impression. The text in so-called xylographic booklets was added by hand. The *ars moriendi* was of this type, which was popular and widely circulated; twenty editions are known.

This book prepared man to meet death without aid of clergy. The dying man is surrounded by devils tempting him with crowns as saints stand by to offer solace. On banderoles we read *Gloriari* (to be glorified) *Tu es firmus in fide* (Thou art firm in faith). The devils are caricatures of bestiality; the saints look on with dignity, though also with expressions of worry and compassion. The technique is primitive but vigorous and expressive. The prevalence in Europe of the plague, the Black Death, following the outbreak in 1348 explains this concern with death, which must have seemed ever present.

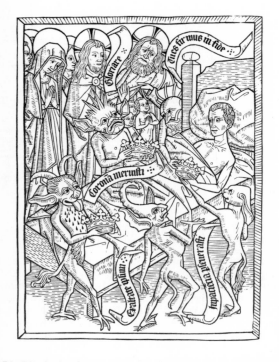

Ill. 170 Block book, ars moriendi, edition IV A, Temptacio dyaboli de vanagloria (Temptation of the Devil to Avarice), c. 1465, German. Library of Congress, Rosenwald Collection. *Photograph, National Gallery of Art*

Ill. 171 The Flight of Daedalus and the Fall of Icarus, woodcut, printed by Riederer, Freiburg im Breisgau, 1493. *Maggs Bros., London*

The Flight of Daedalus and the Fall of Icarus (Ill. 171)

According to the Greek myth, Daedalus made wings for himself and his son, Icarus, with which they escaped the labyrinth of King Minos on Crete [p. 59]. Icarus, forgetting his father's warning not to fly too close to the sun lest the wax used to hold the feathers in place should melt, plunged into the sea. The rendering of figures and geese is superior in skill to the conventional rendering of sea and land. This print is believed to be the first printed representation of human flight.

David and Bathsheba (Ill. 172)

A different style is here shown, a firm linear manner, almost geometric in its squareness. The design is divided into sections, each boxed in by itself, but all united into an attractive pattern. We are told (II Samuel, xi: 2) of David that "from the roof he saw a woman washing herself; and the woman was very beautiful to look upon." David from a Gothic balcony hails a woman taking a foot bath as her maid looks on disapprovingly. The high drama of the Old Testament is scaled down to an incident of ludicrous domesticity. What purports to be ancient Jerusalem becomes fifteenth-century Germany. Historical accuracy was an invention of the nineteenth century; it was commonly ignored in earlier representations.

Ill. 172 David and Bathsheba, woodcut, book illustration from Cologne Bible printed by Quentell, 1480

Dürer: *The Knight and the Man-at-Arms (Ill. 173)*

These last two woodcuts are contemporary with Dürer (b. 1471). Through this master draftsman the woodcut was developed to an all-time high. His work in woodcut alone can be followed year by year from 1488 to 1527 in some 340 plates, a triumph of the Renaissance in the north. The one selected here is not necessarily superior to others, but it has large areas of white and therefore retains more of its quality when reduced. It also combines figure and landscape, and there is a sense of space through a view into the distance. The pen stroke is varied but always retains its vitality. The vigor of Dürer's slashing stroke is carried into the details so that for complete satisfaction the print must be examined under a magnifying glass.

Dürer: *St. Jerome in His Study (Ill. 174)*

Compared to the pen-drawn lines used for the woodcut, the graver or burin, used on the copperplate, allows for refinement and variations [p. 242]. Dots and crosshatching are possible so that degrees of light and shade and texture appear. As a representation of an interior this print is the ultimate in Dürer's graphic work. Linear perspective and

Ill. 173 Dürer: The Knight and the Man-at-Arms, woodcut, c. 1497. *National Gallery of Art*

light flooding into the room unite to give a sense of world-removed tranquillity. The saint is absorbed in his work, the animals are quietly dozing, but light enlivens this retreat. On one occasion St. Jerome pulled a thorn from the paw of a lion, who henceforth in gratitude became the steady companion of the saint.

Ill. 174 Dürer: St. Jerome in His Study, engraving (1513–1514). *National Gallery of Art, Gallatin Collection*

Ill. 175 Dürer: Artist's Mother, charcoal, signed 1514 and inscribed. *Berlin Museum*

Dürer: *Artist's Mother (Ill. 175)*

After the death of his father, Dürer took his aged mother into his home. A few months before her death he made this drawing. Despite uncompromising realism, it is sensitive in the anxious gaze and the tightly closed lips. All his skill is given to the painstakingly accurate rendering of the eyes, letting the shawl stand in broad outlines. In this concentration on what brings out character, and a corresponding neglect of what would detract, the artist demonstrates his skill and reveals himself in his concern for his mother.

Dürer: *Mein Angnis, pen drawing (Ill. 176)*

A study of a master's drawings enlarges our concept of his capacities as an artist. If we knew only his engravings or some of his paintings of religious subjects or even his

Ill. 176 Dürer: pen drawing, inscribed *Mein Angnis. After Wölfflin, Dürer. Bruckmann (1926)*

painted portraits [Fig. 170], we would be impressed by his insistence on leaving nothing unrecorded. Dürer could also make a few penstrokes say a great deal. In this sketch of his wife (note the inscription, My Agnes) he gives pose, light, and form, but little detail.

Holbein the Younger: *Lady Barkley (Ill. 177)*

Holbein's drawings of members of the court of Henry VIII were made from life as preparations for oil portraits. They are precise statements of fact, profile and full face, often with little modeling. His sitters, persons of rank, would allow only brief sittings, during which Holbein made drawings like this one. Cool and objective, they testify to Holbein's keen eye and exquisite taste. We can visualize the individual, but the artist maintains a distant impartiality. Dürer can be warm and intimate; in these aristocratic portraits Holbein is grandly aloof. There are eighty-seven of these drawings at Windsor Castle. They are on tinted paper, reddish or bluish, with parts in colored chalk; a few are known through reproductions. Oscar Duveen tells the story of how they were first discovered, in the nineteenth century, in the drawer of a bureau.

Ill. 177 Hans Holbein the Younger: Lady Barkley, chalk drawing (1526)

Ill. 178 Holbein the Younger: Madonna of the Burgomaster Meyer (c. 1526). *Museum Darmstadt*

Holbein the Younger: *Madonna of the Burgomaster Meyer* *(Ill. 178)*

Raphael's *Sistine Madonna* [p. 223, Fig. 148] established a unity between the divine and the human. Holbein's Madonna is human and conceived in a less lofty spirit than Raphael's. The massive shell draws the Madonna into the circle of the family of the burgomaster, head of the Catholic party at the time of the Reformation. The burgomaster rests his clasped hands on his eldest son, who holds his baby brother. His first wife, no longer living, is kneeling beside his second wife and their daughter. Intense devotion speaks from the burgomaster, who rests his gaze on the blessing Christ Child. Cuddled against His mother, the small Infant with a serious expression is contrasted with the broad massiveness of the group. Except for the burgomaster, all eyes are averted; he alone conveys his plea for protection. The cloak of the monumental figure of the Madonna is draped over his back; in broad parallel folds her gown descends to the rug on which all are grouped. Holbein, against the background of the religious tension of the Reformation, shows the Madonna as protectress, drawing her mantle around the faithful.

Grünewald: *Head of a Weeping Angel (Ill. 179)*

Grünewald's style blends softness and extremes of emotion [p. 244]. This drawing shows two of these characteristics. Softness of flesh in the cheeks and tension in the wrinkled brows combine to express intense grief. There are no lines, but the shapes of the dark areas stand out. Emphasis on form is characteristic of Renaissance art, as expression through light is the invention of the Baroque.

Altdorfer: *Saint Christopher (Ill. 180)*

A specifically German element is the attention paid to the mountainous landscape [p. 244–45] of the Danube school. In Albrecht Altdorfer's woodcut this is mingled with an influence from Mantegna (Ill. 126), in the unusual foreshortened attitudes. Altdorfer derived this influence from Mantegna through the Tyrolean artist Michael Pacher. Altdorfer's crinkly drapery is German Gothic, unlike Mantegna's sober classicism, where drapery falls in orderly folds. A comparison of this crouching, bent-over saint, weighted down, as the story tells us, by the mighty load of the Christ Child, with an

Ill. 179 Grünewald: Head of a Weeping Angel, drawing. Berlin Museum.
National Gallery of Art

earlier woodcut of St. Christopher is instructive (Ill. 169). The primitive artist of 1423 has the saint crossing the stream standing up; there only halo and orb tell us that the child is

Ill. 180 Altdorfer: Saint Christopher, woodcut, 1513.
After Bock, Hanfstaengl (1922)

Ill. 181 Huber (1485–1553): View of Feldkirch, pen drawing, 1530. State Graphic Collection, Munich. *Photograph, National Gallery of Art*

the Christ. The mature Altdorfer no longer depends on emblems, but shows the exertion the Christ-bearer had to muster to accomplish his task. Crosshatching is used to bring out form, but an ornamental effect is also retained without involving the greater richness of Dürer's style (Ill. 173). With Altdorfer the Netherlandish influence on German art disappears.

Huber: *View of Feldkirch (Ill. 181)*

Wolfgang Huber, a follower of Altdorfer, here illustrates the landscape around this Alpine village, his birthplace. A brilliant light from the sun softens the distant landscape.

With detail restricted to the foreground, there is an effect of spaciousness. Form still depends on outline, and each patch of foliage retains its contour; nowhere does foliage merge with atmosphere.

Graf: *Standard-bearer of Basel (Ill. 182)*

This Swiss artist of the early sixteenth century is known for his white-line woodcuts. The artist draws on the block in pen line, which is then cut out (intaglio), leaving the background as the printing surface. Urs Graf designed initials and decorations for the printers of Basel and produced vivid illustrations from the camp life of the Swiss mercenaries (*Landsknechte*). The self-possessed, cocky posture of this standard-bearer suggests the belligerency of these professional soldiers who fought the battles for emperor or pope. Feathered hats and close-fitting doublets with large loose sleeves, slashed for decoration, gave to the costume a provocative extravagance. Urs Graf, a goldsmith by trade, also served as a mercenary. Artists have belonged to all classes. Some were distinguished personalities who led exemplary lives; others were culprits, ne'er-do-wells or worse; Urs Graf belonged to the latter group. He was warned by court order to cease his licentious life and had to promise not to jostle, pinch, or beat his lawful spouse.[20]

Ill. 182 Urs Graf (c. 1485–1529): Standard-bearer of Basel, woodcut. *After Bliss Dent-Dutton (1928)*

Ill. 183 Filippo Brunelleschi (1379–1446), architect: Church of San Lorenzo, nave, from northeast, Florence. *Alinari*

Brunelleschi: *Church of San Lorenzo, nave (Ill. 183)*

Renaissance architecture is chiefly Italian and, outside of Italy, also French. The term Renaissance as applied to architecture relates to decoration; the structural principles were basically the same in all countries; from the fifteenth to the early twentieth century architecture was largely a matter of designing facades. The longevity of Renaissance architecture is such that the style has everywhere left its imprint. With a few exceptions the Renaissance produced no buildings comparable to the Gothic cathedrals. Most churches were modest in size.

The plan of San Lorenzo is that of a three-aisle Early Christian basilica, with a flat nave roof showing a coffered ceiling and domical vaults in the side aisles. An arch order is used for the nave arcade, where the arches rest on entablature blocks, each Corinthian capital having a complete entablature. This is part of the Roman contribution. Brunelleschi's contribution is in gray stone discreetly contrasted against light walls, in the moldings that project but slightly, and in the carved portions that likewise have a flat crispness characteristic of the Early Renaissance. This flatness in architecture corresponds to a shallowness of modeling in Early Renaissance painting. The two rectancular bronze pulpits in

Ill. 184 Desiderio da Settignano: Tabernacle, white marble. *National Gallery of Art, Kress Collection*

the foreground are late works by Donatello. The facade was never completed. It was considered a separate problem, and only loosely related to the interior. This fact illustrates the inorganic character of Renaissance architecture.

Desiderio da Settignano: *Tabernacle, white marble (Ill. 184)*

Actually the Early Renaissance modified Roman forms, though originality was not the aim. Corinthianesque capitals are free adaptations of classical motifs. For the cornice only a cyma (*cymatium*) is used without a corona [Ill. 60, 72]. The architrave is reduced [Ill. 62 b] and all surfaces are richly carved without adhering to the proportions found in classical buildings. A tabernacle was used for the host, the wine and wafers used in communion.

234

Michelozzo: *Medici-Riccardi Palace (Ill. 185)*

The Italians of the Renaissance arranged life according
to a plan that was dignified and impressive. Whoever could
afford it, including intellectuals, wore clothes that were for
effect rather than comfort. Appearance counted for more
than substance; it is not what you are that counts, but what
people think you are. The palace too was designed for its

Ill. 185 Michelozzo, architect: Medici-Riccardi Palace, Florence.
Brogi

facade, visible from the street. Note that the massive cornice stops just behind the corner; what could not be seen received no attention. The high vaulted rooms were poorly lit; windows were for external effect. Open galleries around a central court provided circulation; some rooms could be entered only by passing through other rooms. This was so even in a palace and was common in less pretentious dwellings. Stairs in two runs were primitive; the grand stair-hall had not yet appeared. As to convenience and structure, the palace was medieval. Though the dark stone exterior is fortresslike, the design has many subtleties: (1) each story has its own horizontal termination, the second more elaborate than the first; the main cornice forms the crowning feature of the whole building; (2) the stories are graduated in the roughness of the masonry, rough-hewn rustication on the ground story, small rustication in the middle, and no joints in the top story; (3) the treatment of the arched openings likewise simplifies with each story.

At the street level there are iron rings for horses and torch holders above; the spiked lantern, projecting from the wall at the corner, is perhaps the most imitated lantern in architecture. The Medici coat of arms with its seven balls appears in the second story at the further corner (not visible in the illustration).

Cancelleria Palace (Ill. 186)

The palace of the papal chancellery (Palazzo della Cancelleria), later than the Florentine Medici-Riccardi palace, uses a fuller complement of classical arches [p. 246]. The round-arched windows are elaborated, each with a cornice on pilasters; the portal with a cornice on consoles recalls the doorway to the north porch of the Erechtheum [Ill. 63]. Where the structure emerges from the ground there is a projecting, pedestallike base. With the crowning cornice the whole building follows the pattern of the column, base, shaft, and cornice, or of the figure, foot, torso, head. Ever since Greek art this organic, humanizing trend has appeared and reappeared in Western art. During the Renaissance it spread to ornamental chests and precious utensils, made to stand solidly in one place (Ill. 191). This is more than a matter of practicality. Man projects himself in this way into objects of bulk because they are close to himself. Though traditionally ascribed to Bramante [p. 246], the design may be by Antonio da Sangallo the Elder.

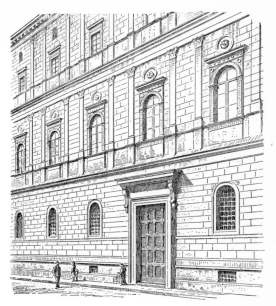

Ill. 186 Cancelleria Palace (1486–1495), Rome. *After Moore* *(1905)*

Sansovino: *Library of Saint Mark's (Ill. 187)*

Perhaps the most sumptuous Renaissance facade of a secular building is in Venice; but it is no longer used as a library. It is sculptor's architecture; its rich sculptural decorations form a unit with the architecture as if all were made of one piece. To all the common motifs used by the Romans, Sansovino has added some of his own, such as the openings in the wide frieze to form an additional story. The sturdy Doric order forms a base for the grander Ionic order above. Smooth columns contrast with sculptural enrichment, and the minor orders, also using columns, give breadth as well as elegance to the massive main entablature and balustrade. The spandrels of the arches have figures carved in relief; in the main cornice putti carry weighty swags. By all rules the facade should look top-heavy; actually the contrast of light and shade acts as a unifying element. The freestanding figures on top of the balustrade are inferior, but not the keystones.

Ill. 187 Jacopo Sansovino (1486–1570): Library of Saint Marks, Venice (1536)

Michelangelo: *stair-hall, Laurentian Library (Ill. 188)*

The Laurentian (Lorenzo de' Medici) Library adjoins the Church of San Lorenzo (Ill. 183) through this stair-hall. Here Michelangelo, free and unhampered, designed a stair-hall united to the whole architectural scheme [p. 247]. Its vigor and elegance mark the beginning of a new style called Mannerism. What is new and unprecedented is the fact that architectural forms are used unstructurally: (1) columns are recessed in niches; the wall without columns would have served the purpose of support; (2) pediments are used to frame niches—blind windows—as decoration; (3) consoles, flanking the first flight of steps, are not needed for support, nor do the consoles support anything beneath the columns; they only enhance the design; (4) where it is placed, the balustrade serves no practical purpose, but its massive breadth is consistent with the whole design. The stair-hall in fact serves its function, but in addition Michelangelo created an architectural monument that is grand

and stately. All moldings, all surfaces and forms, rectangular, curved, or round, are related. What is sharp and crisp or softly rounded or spread out in flat planes is made effective because the eye notes the quality elsewhere in the design. The flat stair treads at the ends turn out, and this extra horizontal flatness is repeated in the flat pedestal tops, to be continued in the broad bands atop balusters. The curved balusters are echoed in the curved consoles and arched pediments. Note the expanse of white wall surface and see how satisfying is the roundness of the columns. With a magnifying glass note how the console beneath the double columns is profiled (molded) and discover the same crisp elegance in closely spaced lines wherever else there are moldings. This so-called profiling introduces another motif. If architecture is frozen music, expanding surfaces may be correlated in sound to the slow vibrations of low notes, the contrasting moldings to the high notes.

Beyond the entrance to the library are visible the rows of wood-carved desks. They support the huge tomes of the famous Medici Library, each massive volume a treasure that is chained to its support.

Ill. 188 Michelangelo: stair-hall, Laurentian Library (1524–1534), Florence. *Alinari*

Renaissance carved arabesque (Ill. 189)

Architectural carving, more than sculpture, imitated Roman work (Ill. 86). Except for the slight difference of motif, the two styles are remarkably alike. Both styles aspired to the same aim; one is not strikingly superior to the other, but the Renaissance carving is more delicate.

Ill. 189 Renaissance carved arabesque, Gubbio, Ducal Palace. *After Moore (1905)*

Ill. 190 Intarsia panel, Church of Sta. Maria Novella, Florence. *After Rhead (1905)*

Church of Sta. Maria Novella, intarsia panel (Ill. 190)

The scroll pattern in a light wood is inlaid (intarsia) in the panel; design and craftsmanship are of a high order. Classical foliage is here used in a symmetrical design on the two sides of a central stem; symmetry is favored in Renaissance art, but variety and invention, subordinating minor to major motifs, are also used.

Ill. 191 Buontalenti: design for a chest. *After L'art pour tous*

Buontalenti: *design for a chest (Ill. 191)*

Furniture of the Italian Renaissance was designed in the spirit of architecture. Benches were often combined with chests, and beds, raised on platforms, were built into the wall paneling of the room (Ill. 130). Furniture had not received attention from collectors until Wilhelm von Bode, director of the former Kaiser Friedrich Museum in Berlin, called attention to Italian furniture. Our illustration, a design from the sixteenth century (sig. B. Buontalenti), shows a richly carved chest. Massive and sculpturesque, it proves that furniture designs were produced by good artists. Buontalenti, a Florentine (1536–1608) was a pupil of Bronzino and Vasari.

Ill. 192 Andrea Palladio (1518–1580): Basilica at Vicenza (begun 1549). *Alinari*

Palladio: *basilica at Vicenza (Ill. 192)*

Besides the freer tendency in architecture represented by Michelangelo, a more severe Roman-inspired style was pursued by Palladio. It was this trend that was followed in England and the American colonies. In Vicenza Palladio built a two-story arcade around an earlier town hall. Here the arches rest on freestanding coupled columns that form a second order subordinated to the major order. This became known as the Palladian motif, and was widely imitated. The end bays are wider than the others, but all bays have a comfortable breadth. On the ground floor the sturdy Doric is given a massive spread; the columns are set well apart. Note that the wide entablature above the ground floor arches, with plenty of surrounding wall, seems particularly sturdy; this makes the balustrade above seem light. Breadth and an expression of power are the result of a careful study of proportions, Palladio's own contribution. He discovered what was admirable about Roman triumphal arches and then applied his knowledge and enthusiasm to designs of his own. It was still creation; to speak disparagingly of copying as if it were mechanical fails to do justice to the Renaissance.

Ill. 193 Palladio: Villa Almerigo ("Villa Rotunda") near Vicenza. *Alinari*

Palladio: *Villa Almerigo (Ill. 193)*

Here Palladio combined the Roman temple front with the attic from triumphal arches and the central dome. Because stucco is used over brick, Palladian buildings often look dilapidated; their attraction is in the proportions. Palladio became one of the most imitated of architects.

Château of Blois, staircase (Ill. 194)

Renaissance architecture in France also elaborated the exterior. As on Italian facades (Ill. 186), orders are used to subdivide walls horizontally to emphasize the main floor against ground floor and attic. The royal emblem of Francis I, the salamander in flames, is carved in the centers of the panels. The character of the medieval fortress is overcome by large windows, carving, and sculpture. The five-sided spiral staircase, exquisite in detail, is a marvel of construction. On the other hand, the staircase is poorly related to the facade, and the difference in slope of the arches and balconies is awkward.

Art received much attention, but heating, illumination, and plumbing were primitive or did not exist. In the fifteenth century the open fireplace, with flues and chimneys, was an improvement over the fire built upon dogs of brick, stone, or logs in the center of the great hall. As before, torches or candles gave light, and water was carried into the house. What a backward technology had failed to supply was provided by servants. This lag prevailed until the Industrial Revolution started trends that produced the conveniences for living we enjoy today.

Palace at Fontainebleau, gallery (Ill. 195)

The Italian style in Primaticcio's frescoes (poorly restored in the nineteenth century under Louis Philippe) is combined with a wood-paneled dado and a coffered ceiling by

Ill. 194 Château of Blois, staircase of wing (1515–1530) of Francis I. *Archives Photographiques*

Ill. 195 Palace at Fontainebleau, gallery of Henri II (1547–1559).
Archives Photographiques

a French architect. Though fine in detail, the parts are
poorly related. The large octagons of the ceiling are crush-
ing in effect against the splendid chimney piece. The arch
at the end wall bears no relation to the flat ceiling and
may point to an early intent to use a vaulted ceiling.

Bautista and Herrera: *the Escorial (Ill. 196)*

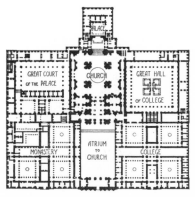

Ill. 196 Juan Bautista of Toledo and Juan Herrera: the Escorial
(1563–1584), near Madrid, plan. *After Fletcher and Fletcher
(1905)*

Ill. 197 Exterior view. *After Hartmann (1911)*

The Escorial, exterior view (Ill. 197)

This chief monument of High Renaissance architecture in Spain forms a large rectangle. The Escorial,[21] larger than **Versailles, is exceeded in size only by such buildings as the Parliament Building and Westminster in London. The church,** on a central plan, dominates the complex, which includes a monastery, a royal palace, a mausoleum, a library, and an art gallery. Compared with the church, the adjoining palace is of modest size. In its day the Escorial was looked upon as the eighth wonder of the world. It is surrounded by a continuous wall; in France and England palaces are usually open. The Escorial, in the severe Italian style of Vignola, expressed the somber religious fervor of Philip II. It became the burial place of Charles V, of the Hapsburgs, and of the Bourbons. The Spaniards refer to this cold academic style as the style without ornament, the *estilo desornamentado*; of all Spanish styles it is the least Spanish.

The Escorial stands at the opening of Spain's golden century, which extended from 1560 to the end of the seventeenth century, with Cervantes and Calderón in literature, Murillo and Velázquez in painting, and others in sculpture and music. The Plateresque (*platero,* silversmith) style [p. 184] of the Early Renaissance, from c. 1480 on, spread to palaces and other secular buildings in Santiago, Burgos, Salamanca, Valladolid, Segovia, Toledo, Zaragoza, Valencia, and Seville.

John Thorpe: *plan and elevation of house (Ill. 198)*

During the first half of the sixteenth century the Italian palace was receiving its final form, and France was turning the medieval château into the more open palace. Blois was followed by Chambord [p. 249] and Fontainebleau.

246

During the Elizabethan (Queen Elizabeth I, 1558–1603) and Jacobean (King James I, 1603–1625) periods, the English manor house in the country [p. 251] corresponds to the Italian palace in the city. Italian palaces have enclosed courts; English manor courts are open. Mullioned windows and high roofs continue the Gothic. The imported Renaissance style appears in entablatures between stories, in balustrades at the eaves, and in the elaboration of the entrances. Rooms have individual fireplaces; broad, paneled walls; oak staircases; and corridors that provide direct access to rooms. In this type of house we have the beginnings of the modern home.

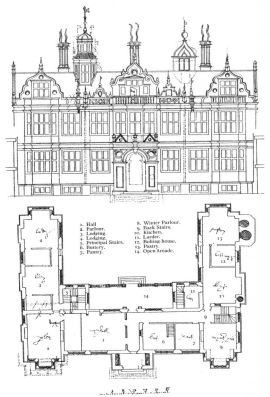

1. Hall
2. Parlour.
3. Lodging.
4. Lodging.
5. Principal Stairs.
6. Buttery.
7. Pantry.
8. Winter Parlour.
9. Back Stairs.
10. Kitchen.
11. Larder.
12. Bolting house.
13. Pastry.
14. Open Arcade.

Ill. 198 John Thorpe: plan and elevation of sixteenth-century English house. Soane Museum, London. *After Gotch (1901)*

Oak panels, Hôtel de Ville (Ill. 199)

During the second decade of the sixteenth century the Renaissance style became general in Belgium. The northern provinces of the then united Netherlands—the Holland of today—began to erect Renaissance buildings toward the middle of the century. From the elaborate portal of the council chamber of the city hall this panel (one of twenty-eight) by a native Flemish carver, is in the best Florentine tradition. The panels show variety of invention; each one is a masterpiece of vigor and good taste. All acanthus foliage is basically the same and yet is capable of a surprising variety.

Gable from former meat market, Haarlem (Ill. 200)

A Dutch national style expressed itself in brick and cut-stone buildings. The gable from the facade with a mullion window is in the Gothic tradition of steep roofs. Italian Renaissance pediments, pilasters, and Ionic capitals have been thoroughly merged. Horizontal cornices are balanced by vertical vase-shaped pinnacles; scrolls fill in the setbacks. The Gothic here touches the Baroque, with little that could be called Renaissance. This style is vigorous and consistent, though quite different from the Italian, to which it owes the details.

Danzig arsenal, detail (Ill. 201)

Northern Germany and the Baltic regions received the Renaissance style through the Netherlands. The arsenal (Zeughaus) in Danzig, designed by an architect from Malines (Mechelen), is in the typical brick and cut-stone Netherlandish style, with stair towers at the corners (not shown in illustration). The portals are heavily carved, and the gables show scroll and "strap" ornamentation common to the Baroque style, found in all countries. The finest example of this North German Renaissance is the City Hall in Bremen.

Southern Germany and Austria took over North Italian Renaissance forms. Artists like Holbein and Peter Vischer (sculptor) pioneered the Renaissance in Germany. The Fuggers, merchants in Augsburg as well as rulers of local states, advanced the style in their own cities. Perhaps the best-known example is the Preller House in Nuremberg, with

Ill. 199 Flemish wood-carved oak panels from the Hôtel de Ville at Oudenaarde, by Peter van Schelden (1531). *After L'art pour tous*

Ill. 200 Gable from former meat market in Haarlem, by Lieven de Key (1602–1603). *After Hartmann (1911)*

the narrow street facade, divided horizontally by stories, showing a high, steep gable.

Portico of Town Hall, Cologne (Ill. 202)

The two-story entrance arcade was added to Cologne's Town Hall in an Italianate style that reached Germany from the Netherlands. It is exceptional in that it is basically classic, elaborated with carved reliefs, panels, and medallions that the other countries received from northern Italy. In proportion and details there is an all-prevailing delicacy, closer to the worker in metal than to the builder in stone. This elegant structure is twice removed from the vigor of ancient Rome that inspired Palladio in his basilica at Vicenza. Even two roughly contemporary Renaissance buildings that make use of the same motif, arcades using the orders, arrive at individual solutions; they speak the same Renaissance language but each in his own local accent.

Ill. 201 Arsenal at Danzig (1603–1605), detail by Anthony van Obbergen. *After T. Roger Smith (1890)*

Ill. 202 Portico of Town Hall of Cologne (c. 1560–1570). *Cologne Tourist Office*

Fredericksberg Castle (Ill. 203)

Denmark received the Renaissance late, through Netherlandish influence. During the long reign of King Christian IV (1588–1648), the arts advanced. Fredericksberg is the most important architectural monument of the period, located on three islands connected by bridges. The main structure of the wings includes an open court *(court d'honneur)*. In the handling of the masses the design is most effective, the large tower relating well to the smaller stair towers. Two open galleries are a feature of the central structure. The ornamentation, in the scrolled gable ends and the massive entrance portal, is noteworthy in its reticence. Several builders are named, but no chief architect; it is believed that the basic idea was furnished by King Christian himself.

Italian majolica plate (Ill. 204)

Majolica, the most colorful variety of European pottery [p. 252], was made for use at the table and for display and decoration. It is named after the island of Majolica (or Majorca), from which a Spanish tin enamelware with luster decoration was imported into Italy. Italian majolica

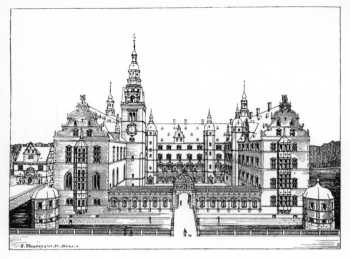

Ill. 203 Fredericksberg Castle (1602–1625). *After S. Pickersgill (1895) and Hartmann (1911)*

painting is centered in a few places in Central Italy, including Faenza, and Deruta. From Faenza is derived faience, the French name for tin-glazed pottery.

The unfired majolica absorbs the moist colors like a blotter and permits no correction; the painter had to be sure of his design. So-called lustered wares were given additional decoration using metallic pigments to produce iridescent hues. When polished, the thin metallic films produce the luster.

The ornamental motifs were often derived from illustrated books or from loose woodcuts or engravings. The decorators are unknown unless the wares are signed. The large and heavy dishes from Deruta are outstanding in decorative effect; the design is bold and large in scale; only blue and yellow-brown are used. For balance and power and for variety, invention, and purity of line, this dish is among the finest. The Roman imperial name of Faustina appears on the banderole, which carries this inscription: *FAVSTINA PVLITA E BELLA* ("Faustina, refined and beautiful"). Presumably this is a reference to Faustina the Younger, wife of the emperor Marcus Aurelius and model of conjugal love and virtue.

Ill. 204 Italian majolica plate from Deruta, sixteenth century. *National Gallery of Art, Widener Collection*

Milanese helmet (Ill. 205)

The Renaissance armorer [p. 252] is here represented by an embossed helmet. The relief is hammered out of the metal. Made for display, such helmets were worn on festive occasions rather than in actual warfare. They represent armor-making in its most elaborate development. Such pieces are the result of collaboration of designer, armorer, and embosser with painters, sculptors, and architects who furnished the designs. Verrocchio and Leonardo made designs for fantastic helmets. The fusion of the fantastic with the structural is remarkable; the projecting front suggests a dolphin. When seen from the side, an animallike character is apparent in the eye and the gaping mouth. Helmets represent a survival from primitive masks once worn to inspire fear. Ornament has become a part of the helmet itself and is not a sculpturesque addition. Leaves and tendrils are adjusted to the curved surfaces, lines are precise, and the craftmanship is excellent.

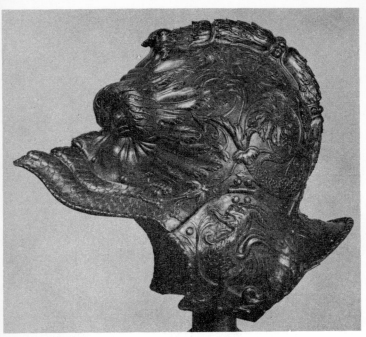

Ill. 205 Milanese helmet, about 1540. *National Gallery of Art, Widener Collection*

Silver-gilt ewer (Ill. 206)

Renaissance goldsmiths on occasion ranked with painters, sculptors, and architects. Nuremberg had its goldsmiths and Milan its armorers and workers in rock crystals, all working for the courts of Europe.

Such vessels were for ornament. Every part is elaborated; the body of the vessel and the spout, handle, and base retain a functional expression only in a general way. This ewer is as much sculpture as utensil. Leda and the swan on the lid is small sculpture; the reliefs on the sides symbolize the triumph of Time, Truth, Death and Fame. The scrolled handle is more ornamental than practical. All techniques—embossing, casting, and chasing—are combined. The total impression is one of magnificence and craftsmanship intended to impress. It was made for Emperor Rudolph II about 1603, when handicrafts were flourishing and before science and technology had opened new fields for creative endeavor.

Ill. 206 Silver-gilt ewer, signed by Christophoro Jamnitzer, h. c. 17 in., German, sixteenth century. *Kunsthistorisches Museum, Vienna*

X

Baroque and Rococo Art:
1600–1800

STYLISTIC CHANGES in art are often identified with the names of individual artists. Though one artist may influence another and contribute something toward a local school, it is the exceptional individual who starts a trend that leads to a new style. The changing cultural background [p. 253] makes new demands upon the artist and presents him with opportunities for new solutions of traditional problems. Painting is the representative art of the Baroque: the best-known names of artists are those of painters like Velázquez and Goya, Rubens, Van Dyck and Rembrandt or Hogarth. In sculpture Bernini and Houdon could be placed in the same category. Technically oil painting achieved maturity but left some areas undeveloped. The masters of modern art explored aspects of painting not touched upon by the old masters. Painting placed man in the center of an idealistic or a realistic world. What painting encompassed of the visual world in such artists as Rubens and Rembrandt represents a kind of excellence that has not been equaled, largely because the objectives of one period appear destined not to be attempted in another. The concept that painting appeals to visual impressions more than to tangible forms also gave to sculpture and architecture a pictorial character. All countries participated in the Baroque, though in architecture Italy, Germany, and Spain produced the most characteristic examples. The Baroque originated in Italy, but the Rococo spread from France under Louis XV to other countries.

Church of Sta. Maria in Campitelli (Ill. 207)

The Baroque lost some of its enthusiasm for antiquity. Classical orders, no longer objects of veneration, were made into a system that could be taught. Published by the Italian architect Vignola as a treatise, the five orders had become a matter of rule. To take liberties with rules became an ambition with the more daring architects. Michelangelo's in-

Ill. 207. Church of Sta. Maria in Campitelli, Rome, by Carlo Rainaldi (1611–1692). *After Joseph (1912)*

Ill. 208 Lorenzo Bernini (1599–1680): The Rape of Proserpina.
After Seemann (1879)

novations, as in the design of the Medici stair-hall (Ill. 188),
were looked upon as welcome liberation. The self-confident
Baroque took the view that only its own style had any
validity, a point of view that became increasingly popular
with artists. In this facade the orders are placed one in
front of the other. Pediments, curved or broken, are fitted
into recesses. Only Corinthian columns are used, and for
emphasis, they stand on pedestals. Huge scrolls fill in the
corners at the second-story level; at the very top a central
cartouche cuts across the cornice. By crowding every motif
upon the facade as if it were a picture, the Baroque proclaimed its revolt against the traditions of antiquity.

Bernini: *The Rape of Proserpina (Ill. 208)*

During the Baroque period Rome replaced Florence as
the artistic center of Italy. Bernini became the dominating
personality and with his pupils made Rome over from a
Renaissance into a Baroque city. Bologna's *Rape of the
Sabine Women* (Ill. 153) inspired the youthful Bernini, whose
most celebrated work is *The Ecstasy of St. Teresa* [Fig.
187]. Each emphasizes the front view, like a picture, in
one plane rather than as a group that exists in depth. Here

the main lines in both figures extend in breadth, stressing horizontals or diagonals. A fleeting moment of action is made permanent, though sculpture is best suited to express repose. The uplifted arm and raised knee of Proserpina suggest a graceful posture rather than a fierce struggle, as in a Pollaiuolo nude [Ill. 117]. Except for the academic painter, the Baroque pursued its own objectives and no longer depended on the Renaissance, which sixteenth-century Mannerism and Naturalism had already abandoned [p. 230].

Carracci: *Jupiter Receives Juno (Ill. 209)*

The Carracci—Lodovico (1555–1619), Agostino (1557–1602), and Annibale (1560–1609)—were the founders of the Academic phase of Baroque painting [p. 230] in Bologna. It was their belief that every problem of painting had been solved by the great masters of the High Renaissance. To combine the best from each painter was their ambition, which was not always adhered to in performance, as their style actually constituted a new phase of the Baroque. Annibale decorated the vaulted ceiling of Cardinal Farnese's Roman palace, his greatest work. A series of framed paintings above the cornice is divided by painted herms and seated figures in white and gold to give an illusion of stucco and marble sculpture. What looks like carving and sculpture, above the real architectural cornice, is painted, like the framed picture of Jupiter gazing at Juno. Even these voluminously draped figures are sculpturesque. In Michelangelo's Sistine ceiling the architectural background is separated from the figures; here they overlap. A thick maze of figures, fruit garlands, shells, moldings, and cartouches completely deceives the eye. What Carracci began was carried to even greater extravagance by Cortona and Pozzo, who added figures in flight against a seemingly open sky [p. 258, Fig. 189].

Reni: *Apollo and the Hours (Ill. 210)*

Lodovico Carracci's pupil Guido Reni is best known for his *Aurora*. In Greek mythology, the sun god, Apollo, drives his chariot across the heavens, bringing with him daylight. He is led by Aurora, goddess of dawn, and accompanied by the dancing figures of the "Hours." Aurora, scattering flowers, leads the way, followed by a torch-bearing cupid. This is indeed the grace and poise of the idealizing style of

Raphael [Fig. 149]. Apollo with ease controls the reins of the onrushing horses, his flying mantle revealing a well-proportioned body. One figure in full back view is contrasted with another in full front view. They join hands in such a way that the arrangement of arms and legs brings out subtle repetitions of lines and angles. The figures, youthful and calm in expression, reflect the classic spirit. Each one is modeled individually to suggest roundness, as if illuminated by a light falling on them from above. Warm yellow and orange hues of dawn contrast with the cool blues and greens of the portion of the earth still enveloped in night. The rays of the rising sun fall on Aurora and the horses, and the glow makes Apollo's head and right shoulder stand out in relief.

Magnasco: *The Baptism of Christ (Ill. 211)*

The Genoese painter Magnasco represents a transitional stage in the development of painting. What had been traditionally represented as a quiet scene by the banks of the Jordan is imbued with a sense of agitated fervor. This restless turbulence derives from Tintoretto. His technique of

Ill. 209 Annibale Carracci: Jupiter Receives Juno, ceiling decoration on the theme The Loves of the Gods, begun c. 1597, Farnese Palace, Rome. *Alinari*

Ill. 210 Guido Reni: Apollo and the Hours, or Aurora (1610), ceiling painting, fresco, Rospigliosi Palace, Rome. *Alinari*

strokes and spots seemed novel in comparison with the traditional style of smooth surfaces and exacting detail [p. 259]. Suggestions of this fleeting manner of isolated touches reappear in the eighteenth-century Venetian painter

Ill. 211 Alessandro Magnasco (c. 1667–1749): The Baptism of Christ. *National Gallery of Art*

Guardi [p. 260]. This style, as yet individual with the painter, anticipates the Rococo.

Ill. 212 Giambattista Piranesi (1720–1778): Prisons (*carceri*), No. 7, etching. *National Gallery of Art, Rosenwald Collection*

Piranesi: *Prisons, No. 7 (Ill. 212)*

Piranesi specialized in large etchings of the ancient Roman ruins. His lifework is enormous, consisting of many volumes, reprinted many times. After the plates were worn down by many impressions, the prints became excessively black. The earlier, more desirable prints, like this one, are still light.[22] The plates of his *Prison Scenes,* in the early issues, have an imaginative quality showing his inventive genius at his best [p. 259].

Church of Monastery Melk, upper facade (Ill. 213)

The Baroque in Germany and Austria [p. 260] is based on the Italian, in this case on Vignola and Giacomo della Porta's chief monument, the Church of Jesus (Il Gesù). The differences are in the towers; vigorous in profile, they terminate in vase-shaped cupolas. Below the cupola the corners, like a narrow facade in their own right, terminate in mighty scrolls supporting flaming vase-shaped finials. The entablature, which in Renaissance architecture continues uninterrupted, in the Baroque forms double recesses at the pilasters. Sculpture in freestanding figures, each one clothed in a mass of swaying drapery, stands out in sharp contrast against the flat wall or is silhouetted against the sky. Throughout southern Germany and Austria there are Baroque churches, even in small towns; these Baroque churches give the countryside its character, just as the Gothic churches left their stamp on rural England and the château style marks the Loire district of France.

Palace at Würzburg, stair-hall (Ill. 214)

Not only churches but also palaces of the largest dimensions, characterize the German Baroque. The absolute rulers of the numerous German states, inspired by the shining example of Louis XIV of France, maintained their prestige by their building activities. Architecture became a part of the education of every young prince and a matter of concern for ambassadors. Architects, employed by the courts, had supervision of the planning of great formal gardens, court festivals, public displays of fireworks, and even the opera. The princes of the Church were also great builders. Würzburg Palace was designed for the Prince-Bishop of Speier. Its interiors, like this stair-hall, are among the most sumptuous in

Ill. 213 Church of Monastery Melk (Austria) by Jacob Prand-
tauer (d. 1727), upper stories of facade. *Österreichische Licht-
bildstelle, Vienna*

Europe. Architecture, sculpture, and painting in the ceiling
decoration of Tiepolo [p. 259] combine to create a
magnificent effect. The use of light plays a part; every

sculptural accent is set off against a plain surface or is silhouetted to bring out its profile. Grandeur is matched by clarity, and there is no sense of oppressive decoration.

Ill. 214 Palace At Würzburg (Bavaria, stair-hall by Balthasar Neumann, construction 1737–1744; paintings by Tiepolo, 1765–1775. *Leo Gundermann*

Ill. 215 Zwinger Palace (1711–1722), Dresden, by Matthäus Pöppelmann. *Bundesbildstelle, Bonn*

Zwinger Palace (Ill. 215)

In the central pavilion, architecture and sculpture achieve an unprecedented fusion. No single part stands out by itself but is closely related to adjoining parts. Pilasters and entablatures merge with carved floral ornament, massive cartouches, and freestanding figures. Here is one of the ultimate achievements of the Baroque in any country. Separate buildings are connected through lower one-story enclosed arcaded terraces planned around an open court. In its day the court was used for tournaments and festivals.

Wrought-iron gate, Erbach Monastery (Ill. 216)

Ornamental wrought iron had been associated with European architecture since the Gothic period. During the Baroque wrought iron reached a culmination of great splendor. The designer of this gate was called to the Würzburg court from the imperial workshop in Vienna. The German craft derived inspiration from the engraved plates of Jean Bérain used in a French publication, itself derived from the Renaissance of the *loggie* of the Vatican. In this gate there is little left of the original Italian sources. Though based on acanthus foliage, the motifs have been freely developed in the exuberant spirit of the Baroque. Wrought iron for grilles was replaced by cast iron in the nineteenth century and has since practically gone out of use for architectural ornament.

Ill. 216 Wrought-iron gate of Erbach Monastery, Würzburg, c. 1750, by Johann Georg Oegg. *After F. Bruckmann (1922)*

Ill. 217 Paul Frank: writing master's model sheet (c. 1600). *German National Museum, Nuremberg*

Frank: *writing master's model sheet (Ill. 217)*

Illuminated manuscripts receded with the invention of printing, but as reading and writing became more popular there were writing masters to instruct in penmanship. For important documents, a basic legibility was developed into "beautiful writing" known as calligraphy. As an art form, calligraphy encouraged ornamental pen flourishes, for which experienced penmen produced the copy books, using pens of several widths. After writing with pens gave way to the typewriter, penmanship lost its importance. Calligraphy as a minor art is today the specialty of a few.

Ribera: *portal of Hospicio de Madrid (Ill. 218)*

Ill. 218 Portal of Hospicio de Madrid, by Pedro Ribera (after 1722). *Mas, Barcelona*

Vásquez: *sacristy of the Cartuja (Ill. 219)*

The full flowering of the Baroque began with José Churriguera (1650–1723), the Michelangelo of Spain. The churrigueresque style received its name from its founder. His chief work is the City Hall of Salamanca. Even more fantastic is the facade of the Hospicio Provincial by Churriguera's pupil Pedro Ribera. As was common since the Renaissance, in Spain as elsewhere, architecture was largely a matter of decorating exteriors and also interiors with no essential changes in structure or plan. What was left of Renaissance entablatures, herms, scrolls, and consoles was changed in proportion and in the relationship of one to the other. These changes should not be thought of as distortions, for each style has merits of its own. The carved detail is vigorous and the total effect is massive, overflowing its frames. Compared with this wild burst, the Dresden Zwinger is delicate and Italian Baroque almost a model of restraint. For exuberant vitality the churrigueresque style is in a class of its own; there are no European parallels outside of Spain. Its nearest relatives are the wood-carved pulpits in Belgian

Ill. 219 Sacristy of the Cartuja, Granada, by Manuel Vásquez (1727–1760). *Mas, Barcelona*

Ill. 220 Velázquez: The Surrender at Breda, 1635–1636. Prado, Madrid. *Alinari*

churches [p. 264]. It has always shocked the timid and the purists, but others glory in it.

In the Cartuja sacristy at Granada the detail is crisper and is filled with a nervous energy. It constitutes an original variation of the same spirit.

Velázquez: *The Surrender at Breda (Ill. 220)*

The besieged fortress town of Breda in North Brabant surrendered to the Spanish general Spinola after a staunch resistance of twelve months. The victorious Spanish general had granted honorable terms to the captured garrison. The ceremony of the delivery of the keys is the subject of Velázquez' painting [p. 262].

We note (1) the chivalrous attitude of Spinola advancing to meet the Flemish governor; (2) a suggestion of a vast crowd, Flemish on the left, Spanish on the right; (3) the interest centered on the two chief figures contrasting against the light background of the Flemish troops filing past; (4) contrasts of light and dark—the light full-face figure on the left with the dark profile to the right; (5) a suggestion of force in the solid wall of lances; (6) warm hues in the foreground against a blue-green background; (7) an atmospheric distance; (8) the aristocratic elegance of the Spanish officers contrasted with the sturdy Flemish; (9) differences of costume, wide and baggy on the part of the Flemish, trim and neat on the part of the Spaniards; the use of lace in collars and cuffs and of silk scarves, broad-brimmed hats, muskets, and halberds.

Ill. 221 Bartolommé Murillo: The Virgin of the Immaculate Conception. Prado, Madrid. *After Seemann (1879)*

Murillo: *The Virgin of the Immaculate Conception (Ill. 221)*

Murillo as a painter of religious subjects made his finest contribution in his large altarpieces showing the Virgin on a crescent surrounded by angels holding lilies as they emerge from clouds. The combination of white and blue (mantle) against a luminous background is effective seen from a distance. In their proper setting above the altar in a church, Murillo's paintings of the Virgin served as a focal point upon which to concentrate the feelings of religious enthusiasm. Murillo was eminently successful to that end. Today Murillo's sentiment is often objected to, but this does not impair the artistic significance of his work.

Goya: *The Shooting of the Madrid Patriots (Ill. 222)*

Goya [p. 262], a century after Velázquez, followed in his style. He also admitted influences from Rembrandt and from nature and is a forerunner of Impressionism. Technically his emphasis is on brushwork; modeling with definite outlines is abandoned until revived by the French classicists. He is interested in figures and portraits; landscapes are used occasionally as backgrounds. In his *Majas on a Balcony* (Metropolitan) the conventional type of composition gives way to the impressionistic manner of suggesting a section cut from a larger composition. Goya belonged to no school of painting; he developed his own style after early influences from foreign styles. In the selection of his topics Goya was sensitive to the challenges of his day; he was a representative of the general revolutionary spirit. Color—yellow and white in the center, red from pools of blood, a dull-gray sky—is used to emphasize the brutality of the event.

Goya: *Why? from The Disasters of War (Ill. 223)*

Goya denounced vice, ignorance, hypocrisy, and cruelty in all levels of society. As a satirist, he used realism as well as allegory, but he also included in his etchings scenes of tenderness, motherhood, and love. His disgust with the degradation of man at his worst is given graphic expression in this etching of a hanging scene, and is underscored by the title *Why?* In another print, showing the torturing of prisoners, Goya's caption is *Security Does Not Require Torture.* Another title is *What Cruelty.* To highlight a representation of a heap of corpses, the title is *For This You*

Ill. 222 Goya: The Shooting of the Madrid Patriots. *Prado, Madrid*

Were Born. What Goya thought about individuals comes out through comparisons with animals, which he includes to bring out the satire. A man looks into a mirror and sees a monkey; a woman sees herself in a mirror as a serpent coiled about a scythe; there are cat-men and frog-men; and the ignorant man becomes an ass, a quack, or a parrot.

Goya expresses what is of basic human significance. The way in which he achieves his results makes him one of the great etchers of the world. In his etching *Men Flying with Great Wings* he makes man's ability to fly seem plausible. Compared with all winged angels in religious painting, Goya's flying men seem convincingly realistic.

Rubens: *Cimon Finding Iphigenia (Ill. 224)*

Rubens based his art on Titian and the Venetian mode of painting. He spent eight years in Italy, was court painter to the Duke of Mantua, worked in Madrid, and settled in Antwerp. To the extent that he depended on assistants— Frans Snyders for fruit and flowers and Jan Wildens for animals—painting was the result of collaboration with others [p. 263].

This painting represents a scene from Boccaccio's *The*

Ill. 223 Goya: etching No. 32 from The Disasters of War: Why? (Por que?). *National Gallery of Art, Rosenwald Collection*

Decameron. Cimon, uncouth and unlettered, would not take to learning. But once he beheld Iphigenia all this was miraculously changed. As a result of love, he began to learn the letters, improved his speech, became accomplished in song, and mastered the fine points of riding and martial exercises.

The setting is in the land of fable. Iphigenia, reclining with eyes half open, is painted in pearly flesh tints varying from pink and yellow to cool blue and green. Her outstretched arm is enveloped in a delicate haze, and glistening lights build up from a silvery tone that is pronounced in the diaphanous veil. Draperies are cool beside the flesh tints of Iphigenia, red and orange beside the ruddier tints of her companions. The figures form a glowing center of light within a darker tonality that frames it on all sides. Shadow and half-tone on the reclining figures melt together in a large passage of light.

On the left water pours from a dolphin's mouth in a sculptured group. The arched back of Cimon on the right keeps our attention from straying out of the picture. The contours of his body, angular, strong, and masculine, stand in contrast to all this suffused femininity. At the level of his knees we get a glimpse into the distant landscape.

275

Ill. 224 Rubens: Cimon Finding Iphigenia. Kunsthistorisches Museum, Vienna. *Photograph, National Gallery of Art*

Rubens: *Henri IV Receives the Portrait (Ill. 225)*

This large painting is one of twenty-one painted for the decoration of the Luxembourg Palace in Paris. They now occupy a sumptuous gallery in the Louvre, perhaps the most overwhelming display of painting to be found anywhere.[23] The subjects represent episodes from the life of the queen. Rubens furnished the designs and finished the paintings, for which his pupils did the underpainting. In this scene history and mythology are mingled in the exaggerated manner of the Baroque. The king in rapture gazes upon a portrait of Marie de' Medici, held before him by winged genii.[24] Jupiter and Juno with clasped hands are seated on a cloud bank above. By their presence they raise an incident to a level of celestial magnificence. The god of war is the proper patron for a king; Mars places his hand on the king's arm, as putti play with the god's armor and shield. Juno's peacocks and the eagle of Jupiter are beside the gods. This is the period when Richelieu laid the foundation for the absolute monarchy of Louis XIV. Here is a supreme example of art placed in the service of royalty. Such an expression of luxury must have contributed to the prestige of the court.

Ill. 225 Rubens: Henri IV Receives the Portrait of Marie de' Medici. Louvre. *Archives Photographiques*

Van Dyck: *William II of Nassau and Orange (Ill. 226)*

Van Dyck became the portrait painter of royalty and aristocracy; he also painted religious subjects. He collaborated in his youth with Rubens, his most gifted pupil; his style in such paintings is indistinguishable from that of Rubens. In this portrait his own style is clearly indicated; refinement is combined with firmness and solidity. Textures are differentiated in the soft hair against the metallic armor; thick cloth in the doublet stands out against the fluffy shirt sleeves. The background, emphatic in its plainness and smoothness, forces attention on the figure. To avoid monotony the dark right side is pleasantly relieved by the view into the landscape.

Ill. 226 Anthony van Dyck (1599–1641): William II of Nassau and Orange. *National Gallery of Art, Mellon Collection*

Ill. 227 Rembrandt: Joseph Accused by Potiphar's Wife. *National Gallery of Art, Mellon Collection*

Rembrandt: *Joseph Accused by Potiphar's Wife (Ill. 227)*

The seven northern provinces of the Netherlands proclaimed their independence from Spain in 1579 (Union of Utrecht). After the conclusion of the Thirty Years' War in 1648 the Republic of the United Provinces obtained recognition of its independence from Spain and the Empire. Holland, as a republic, had no royal courts and aristocratic patrons. With no palaces to decorate, the larger public, municipalities and corporations, furnished painters with commissions for large oil paintings. Franz Hals painted such canvases as the *Archers of St. George* (1627, Haarlem Museum) and Rembrandt his *Anatomy Lesson* (1632, The Hague Museum) [p. 268], *The Syndics* (1661–1662, Rijksmuseum), and *Night Watch* [pp. 268–69]. Holland, now Protestant, had no need for altarpieces or paintings dealing with the lives of the saints, but religious subjects were not completely abandoned. Rembrandt continued as a painter and etcher of stories from the Bible, often interpreted in a personal manner. He also painted biblical subjects heretofore not commonly represented, as this incident from the story of Joseph [p. 269].

Ill. 228 Rembrandt: Christ at Emmaus, etching. *National Gallery of Art, Rosenwald Collection*

Ill. 229 Rembrandt: The Three Trees, etching. *National Gallery of Art, Rosenwald Collection*

Rembrandt: *Christ at Emmaus (Ill. 228)*

This etching represents the moment when Christ is recognized by the two disciples and the innkeeper. The intense illumination flattens modeling; shadows vanish, and the scene is unified. The light, emanating from Christ, fills the alcove, and all shadows are under the table in a single streak of darkness. Both disciples are individualized; each responds in his own way to the miracle. The technique is simple—open lines in parallel diagonals and crosshatching in the darker shadows [p. 267, Ill. 121].

Rembrandt: *The Three Trees (Ill. 229)*

Rembrandt's greatest landscape etching, *The Three Trees*, represents the country after a rain as the storm retreats before a flood of sunlight. Trees are damp and clouds are drifting off; the sky behind the dark, silhouetted trees has cleared so that the trees once more cast shadows. Note the breeze turning the branches and the light along the contours of the trees. A farm wagon is seen behind the trees on the right, and road and shrubbery at the end of the bluff stand

Ill. 230 Rembrandt: pen-and-ink drawing. *National Gallery of Art*

out in full sunlight. As we look over the flat countryside the misty distance is streaked with cloud shadows, producing a spectacle of light and shade and transparent atmosphere. Rembrandt was also a sensitive designer. The trees as a group contribute to the general spaciousness; if the trees were enlarged, something of the spatial effect would be lost.

Rembrandt: *pen-and-ink drawing (Ill. 230)*

The scratch and dash with which Rembrandt conjures up this figure, leisurely seated on a chair and flooded with light, is instantaneous in its effect. In the loosest possible way, violently and in places brutally, the penstrokes are made to express light and action. In the turn of the head and the cast of the features we sense the individuality of the person represented. The seemingly careless and free technique still retains definition in the features. Character is suggested in the way the mouth is touched in, yet there is no loss of spontaneity. Dürer in his drawing (Ill. 176) brings out form; Rembrandt aims at a broad contrast of light and shade.

Kalf: *Still Life (Ill. 231)*

In the first half of the seventeenth century, still life developed in Holland into an independent branch of painting. By the middle of the century this specialty had reached its full development [p. 267]. Here a few choice objects—goblets, a wineglass, a porcelain bowl, and fruit—are ar-

Ill. 231 Willem Kalf: Still Life. *National Gallery of Art, Chester Dale Collection*

ranged on the corner of a marble-top table in a studied relationship to contrast light and shade, texture, and shapes. The painter places the hard and shiny materials—marble, porcelain, and glass—next to the soft, dull texture of the Turkish rug. The general tonality is dark; a small section is in full light, but the brightest accent is the lemon, its yellow making a complementary color harmony with the blue of the bowl. The rind is rough, to imitate a real lemon, and creates the illusion that the actual form could be felt. Though Kalf was not a pupil of Rembrandt's, he was influenced by him.

De Hooch: *The Mother (Ill. 232)*

Of the painters of interiors, Pieter de Hooch invented a new type by giving a view from one room into another. In this mode of full visual effect, light comes in through

Ill. 232 Pieter de Hooch: The Mother. Berlin Museum. *Photograph, National Gallery of Art*

Ill. 233 Jan Steen: The World Upside Down. Picture Gallery, Vienna. *National Gallery of Art*

the open door, making the little girl stand out dark, fringed with reflected light. From the high window in the near room, light falls on the mother by the cradle and is caught by the folds of the bed curtain. Every object, like the warming pan, the candle on the table, or the chair in the distance, is painted in its proper value to denote the plane it occupies in space. De Hooch's emphasis on depth influenced his contemporary Vermeer.

Steen: *The World Upside Down (Ill. 233)*

Paintings of interiors include besides the genteel rooms of a De Hooch or a Vermeer another specialty that deals with groups of people, especially peasants. Adriaen Brouwer,[25] a Fleming by birth, and Adriaen van Ostade were peasant painters. Brouwer shows the peasant in taverns, drinking, smoking, and carousing; the peasant as tiller of the soil is foreign to the seventeenth century.

Jan Steen is interested in how people amuse themselves. Here is a lusty scene contrived with much invention to show how many things can go wrong. From left to right here is what happens: the keg is running out, a child plays with the family treasures, a dog on the table is eating the pie as the mistress is dozing, and for contrast a goose is perched on

285

the learned man who is reading. The interest is in action and expression and in accurate detail, but not in painting for the sake of visual truth. For vitality and zest in the way people behave, the Dutch and Flemish painters have never been surpassed.

Hogarth: *Shrimp Girl (Ill. 234)*

Hogarth set English painting on a course of its own [p. 270]. This portrait, fresh and vigorous in style, catches a fleeting expression in an unposed manner. The painting is brushed in with bold strokes that allow for no detail, recalling the style of Franz Hals. Hogarth's world fame is based on his satirical paintings, which derive their interest from telling gestures, facial expressions, and the invention of dramatic situations. Among his best known are his paintings for the *Rake's Progress* (Soane Museum), where the gambler lands in prison and in the insane asylum. The Dutch painters, as Jan Steen (Ill. 223), are objective; they represent facts without comment. Hogarth, though less grim, is closer to Goya. Even in his moralizing, story-telling paintings, Hogarth is vigorous in his technique. They attract as paintings, aside from all literary content. Hogarth engraved some of his own paintings, like *The Harlot's Progress,* but left *Marriage à la Mode* to others [Fig. 208].

Reynolds: *Lady Elizabeth Delmé and Her Children (Ill. 235)*

As a portraitist, Reynolds [p. 271] painted aristocratic ladies in a landscaped, parklike setting. We cannot judge the likenesses obtained in each case, but all look elegant and refined. Costumes are treated as thin drapery, tastefully varied, and sometimes allow dainty, slippered feet to protrude from under the gown. As one stands in front of a Reynolds painting it is easy to forget that his paintings may seem much alike. Color is lush and masses of shadow are luminous, mingled with mellow sunshine. The rusty foliage is exactly right to set off the pink cloak spread out in magnificent breadth, as if inspired by Michelangelo's *Madonna and Child* (Ill. 152). Lady Delmé looks dreamy, her children attractive; the bluish distance adds a sense of repose. We linger until we have explored all portions of the large canvas. One turns away reluctantly; it really does not matter where his inspiration came from.

Ill. 234 Hogarth (1697–1764): Shrimp Girl. *Photograph, National Gallery, London*

Ill. 235 Reynolds: Lady Elizabeth Delmé and Her Children. *National Gallery of Art, Mellon Collection*

Gainsborough: *Mrs. Richard Brinsley Sheridan (Ill. 236)*

Gainsborough painted portraits and landscapes, and is often compared with Reynolds. His style is also derived in part from others, particularly the Dutch masters and Van Dyck. These influences nevertheless are fused into a style that is more personal than that of Reynolds. In his youth he was a pupil of the French illustrator Gravelot. In this painting the foliage has the feathery treatment of the French Rococo painters; in comparison Reynolds is sturdy and robust. Mrs.

Ill. 236 Thomas Gainsborough (1727–1788): Mrs. Richard Brinsley Sheridan. *National Gallery of Art, Mellon Collection*

Sheridan's gown is all flimsy fluff, delicately ruffled, as if all might dissolve in atmosphere. There is no attempt at drapery, only loose brushwork and no sense of solid structure; hands are limp and arms shapeless. The background is subdued; the wide sky and broad view into the valley serve to set off her beautiful head. Her tousled hair and crinkly shawl seem designed to create lively movement to isolate her calm features. A vaporous artificiality about Gainsborough constitutes his own personal style.

Ill. 237 George Romney (1734–1802): Mrs. Davenport. *National Gallery of Art, Mellon Collection*

Romney: *Mrs. Davenport (Ill. 237)*

With little training and a two-year stay in Italy, Romney became an excellent draftsman. He is the third of the English school of portraitists, all able interpreters of feminine beauty and charm. Romney was at his best in this specialty. Here he added a touch of imperiousness, where ordinarily one would expect to find aloof dignity. The brushwork is particularly crisp and fresh in the opaque white on face, neck, and shoulders.

The English school of portraiture became widely known through mezzotint engravings reproducing the paintings. Prince Rupert introduced this technique of soft velvety tones into England; by 1700 it was developed. Among the mezzotint engravers, Thomas Watson produced the richest and most luminous of mezzotints in large prints, after paintings by Reynolds. Mezzotint never had a comparable development outside of England; engraving served the same purpose in France.

Jones: *Queen's House (Ill. 238)*

The Baroque in English architecture of the reign of James I expressed itself in cartouches and strapwork added to buildings that were basically Gothic [p. 272]. During the remainder of the seventeenth and the first quarter of the eighteenth century, Inigo Jones introduced into England the Italian Renaissance. This country villa of Queen Henrietta Maria, who was painted by Van Dyck [Fig. 199], has six freestanding columns in the projecting portico. The emphasis of a main floor above a ground floor is in the manner of Palladio. This restrained academic style depended on proportion and used the classic orders in the ancient Roman rather than the Italian Baroque manner. Jones brought this type of architecture back from Rome and Vicenza and from a study of

Ill. 238 Inigo Jones: Queen's House, Greenwich. *After Lübke*

Palladio's writings. Of his major projects as Crown surveyor —designs for the palace at Whitehall—only the Banqueting Hall was executed. It was later destroyed by fire.

Ill. 239 Sir Christopher Wren (1632–1723): Saint Paul's Cathedral, London, 1668–1710. *British Information Services*

Ill. 240 Wren: Tower of St. Mary Le Bow, London. *After Hartmann (1911)*

Wren: *Saint Paul's Cathedral (Ill. 239)*

Wren's [p. 272] masterpiece has a medieval type of plan, a nave and a long choir. There are transepts at the crossing, which is crowned by a dome. In length St. Paul's compares with Cologne Cathedral, but it is smaller in area than St. Peter's. The exterior is well composed; the western towers are related to the central dome, perhaps the finest in Europe. The facade, designed for external effect, is unrelated to the interior, as is common in the Renaissance style, but has great dignity.

Wren: *Tower of St. Mary Le Bow (Ill. 240)*

Wren, who has been called England's greatest architect, received no formal training in architecture. This was not unusual; the same was true of Perrault. Wren, a man of many talents, an inventor, a scholar with a large architectural library, got his training from his illustrated books and through travels in France. He was also favored by environment, as his father had dabbled in architectural design. After the great fire of London (1666) Wren was appointed to furnish designs for new buildings, which included parish churches. Wren is credited with having been the inventor of a Renaissance square tower forming the base for a pyramidal spire. In various ways he solved the transition from the square tower to the pyramidal spire by receding stages. The details are classical and include inverted consoles, as in St. Mary Le Bow.

Ill. 241 Claude Perrault: East Facade, Louvre (1688). *Archives Photographiques*

Perrault: *East Facade, Louvre (Ill. 241)*

The long reign of Louis XIV (1643–1715) gave French art a unity of expression. It was *le grand siècle*; though often criticized for artificiality, it produced masterpieces of art. France was the most populous and most powerful state in Europe. French taste and good manners were generally acknowledged. These qualities are also found in architecture —in the colonnade of the Louvre, the Dome of the Invalides, and the Palace and Garden of Versailles. The basic elements of classical architecture are here combined with a stately dignity that was novel. The main feature is the use of coupled columns in a single gigantic order (the columns are nearly forty feet high), recessed back of the wall of the ground floor. The end bays are particularly successful in the way the carved features are related to the plain wall surfaces.

Lebrun (decorator): *Hall of Mirrors (Ill. 242)*

This is Lebrun's [p. 273] most important surviving work at Versailles. The gilded frames of the ceiling paintings and the trophies over the cornice are in wood or stucco. The extensive paintings of the ceiling that kept Lebrun occupied for a long time have received little attention. In one panel Louis XIV in a commanding position is surrounded by gods, heroes, and generals. The seventeen arched windows correspond to arched mirrors on the wall side. With light-colored walls, dark pilasters, and low-toned ceiling, this gallery is one of the most elegant in European architecture. Once the windows had white brocade curtains, and the hall was furnished with orange trees in silver vases, book cabinets, and silver chairs and tables, products of the Gobelin manufactory.

Soufflot: *Church of Sainte Geneviève (Ill. 243)*

Before the coming of Neo-Classicism, during the second half of the eighteenth century, architects had been content to apply classic details to facades. Following Winckelmann's appeal for "noble simplicity and quiet grandeur," architecture turned for inspiration to the classical monuments themselves rather than to the Baroque or Palladian adaptations. For the first time in France, Soufflot used a full-scale motif from the Roman Pantheon for a modern church. Corinthian columns rise to the full height of the facade. The crossing of the Greek cross plan is expressed on the exterior by a dome on a circular drum. To get the desired effect of "noble simplicity," the exterior is designed as a single story. The walls are so high that they conceal clerestory windows that admit light to the interior. This is an ingenious but also involved and deceptive solution of the practical problem of illuminat-

Ill. 242 Lebrun (decorator): Hall of Mirrors (Galérie de Glaces), 1680–1684, Versailles Palace. *French Government Tourist Office*

Ill. 243 Soufflot: Church of Sainte Geneviève (the Panthéon), 1759–1790, Paris. *Bulloz*

ing an interior, but produces an external effect of "quiet grandeur." Though the Pantheon has been called one of the finest of domed buildings, the interior hardly compares with the naves of Gothic cathedrals.

Clodion: *The Intoxication of Wine (Ill. 244)*

The third generation of French eighteenth-century sculptors includes Pajou, Clodion, and Houdon. They all lived into the nineteenth century. Clodion is the exponent of the light and frivolous Rococo spirit. His subjects are nymphs, satyrs, bacchantes, naiads, and putti, used for decorative reliefs, statuettes, and groups. The Bologna-Bernini tradition is carried a step further toward a loose and open contour, part pose, part dance. His modeling is realistic, and for small pieces terra-cotta is the preferred medium.

Ill. 244 Claude Michel, called Clodion: The Intoxication of Wine, terra-cotta. *Metropolitan Museum of Art, Altman Collection*

Houdon: *Voltaire (Ill. 245)*

The greatest sculptor of the eighteenth century was Houdon, who compares with the best sculptors of any period. Voltaire was a humanitarian who advocated tolerance and freedom of the human mind. Voltaire's capacity for ridicule, which he used lavishly, forced him to leave one country after another, driven out by the enmities his sharp tongue had

Ill. 245 Jean Antoine Houdon (1741–1828): Voltaire. *Giraudon*

Ill. 246 Nicolas Poussin (1594–1665): Shepherds of Arcady. Louvre. *Giraudon*

aroused. The last twenty years of his life he spent in Switzerland on Lake Geneva, on the borders of France. Here he published his writings, witty, cynical, and on occasion malicious. He was also accused of having a lofty humor and being possessed of avarice and duplicity.

Houdon seated Voltaire as on a throne, clad in a togalike garment, and imbued with grandeur. His head is alive and expressive of a vitality that comes from the mind, a reflection of everything that the name Voltaire suggests. There are few portrait statues so charged with personality. Of all the great sculptors, only Houdon had a Voltaire for his model.

Poussin: *Shepherds of Arcady (Ill. 246)*

We now turn to French painting and begin with Poussin, who did not participate in decorative painting but developed easel painting. He worked for the wealthy upper classes, including bankers who were forming their own private collections. Poussin [p. 275] took this subject from classical antiquity. Shepherds, wandering through the campagna, have halted at a tomb. One kneeling traces the inscription *Et in Arcadia ego* (I too was in Arcady). The second shepherd looks up to explain the meaning to the standing woman. The appeal is in the sentiment and the design. Figures, foliage,

mountain peaks, and clouds are placed in harmonious relationship. "Simplicity of expression gives this painting a
grandeur to assure it a place among the masterpieces of all
time" (Pierre Marcel).

Rigaud: *Louis XIV in Coronation Robes (Ill. 247)*

The claim to grandeur on the part of the "Sun King" is
here demonstrated by posture, costume, drapery, and costly
materials. The heavy coronation robe is given a massive
spread, piling up over the supporting arm. By contrast, feet
and right hand are dainty and introduce a note of elegance.
Free space surrounds the upper part of the figure, and the
head is slightly off the central axis. The figure appears towering as the eyes look down from great height. An expression
of disdain is suggested in the features. The lower lip, thrust
forward, is made to appear as the king's usual expression.
This single trait, more than any other, suggests aggression.
This portrait makes all too vivid the king's saying: *"L'état
c'est moi!" Ramesses II* (Turin) is more benign (Ill. 16).
Rigaud had to deal with this pomp, but he gave it force
and majesty. It seems fitting that French art also has a
Houdon with his *Voltaire*. It was given to the artist to take
the measure of the great as well as the mighty.

Mellan: *Delilah and Samson (Ill. 248)*

A leading school of portrait engraving flourished in the
seventeenth century in France. Using line, engraving expresses form and texture with great skill. As this art lacked
a personal style, it could be taught and passed on to others.
Nanteuil engraved the whole entourage of Louis XIV, forming a portrait series comparable to Clouet's series of drawings. The best portrait engraving was done by Nanteuil, but
others acquired the technique. Engraving does not have the
spontaneity of etching, but etched lines were combined with
engraved to produce light and textures. Mellan introduced
the swelling line in engraving. It is noticeable in the flesh
parts; the line increases in width toward the shaded side to
help bring out roundness.

Callot: *etching from The Italian Vagabonds (Ill. 249)*

Callot, of the early seventeenth century, used the swelling
line in etching. His subjects, from the life of the people he
observed on his travels, are close to the Le Nain brothers

Ill. 247 Hyacinthe Rigaud (1659–1743): Louis XIV in Coronation Robes. Louvre. *Giraudon*

[p. 276]. Callot is more dynamic; he also left a record of the horrors of the Thirty Years' War, which was going on during his lifetime. His plates are frequently small; his style is mannered and precise, but he describes his subjects realistically. He is a forerunner in etching of popular subjects that Chardin [p. 277] in painting took up a century later.

Si non amplexus gustaſſet Sanson amoris
Dalila non vires abripuiſſet ei.

C. Mellan G. pinx. et ſ.   Romæ Sup. pm.

Ill. 248 Claude Mellan: Delilah and Samson, engraving. *Metropolitan Museum of Art, Dick Fund, 1917*

Ill. 249 Jacques Callot (1592–1635): etching from The Italian Vagabonds. *Museum of Fine Arts, Boston*

Watteau: *Open-air Entertainment (Ill. 250)*

The absolutism in matters of art under Louis XIV brought on a reaction. Through the foundation of the Academy [p. 272] all artists gained in prestige, and some artists who received no official patronage from Versailles obtained commissions in Paris from the nobility and bourgeoisie. Painters turned to Rubens for inspiration as a revolt against Poussin. During the period from the death of Louis XIV to the ascendancy to the throne of Louis XV (regency, 1715–1723), there was a relaxation in social life away from ponderous artificiality toward ease and comfort. Furniture and interior decoration reflected this change in a lighter, more graceful style based on curved lines. This change favored Watteau,

Ill. 250 Watteau: Open-air Entertainment. *Dresden Gallery*

who became the founder of a truly French school of painting no longer dependent on Italian art. An original inspiration came from Rubens, but was merged with Watteau's early experience as an assistant to a designer for stage sets, theatrical costumes, and decorative paintings for Italian comedy. Through Watteau a theatrical unreality carried over into the style of his pupil Pater and his followers Lancret and Fragonard. In Watteau's paintings the figures retain a sense of structure and are distributed through space. One group is in the middle distance stretched out on the grass and there is a diminishing outlook beyond. The colors, rich and warm, are in the Rubens tradition [p. 276].

Boucher: *Madame Bergeret (Ill. 251)*

François Boucher (1703–1770) was the most versatile artist of the mid-eighteenth century. In addition to easel pictures he practiced etching and furnished designs for the decorative arts, for costumes and scenery for the opera; as director for the Gobelins he was responsible for tapestry design.

The Rococo style permeated all the arts; a fashionable

painter who turned to designing tapestries hardly changed his models. An English lady seen against the natural environment of a park still seems convincing to the modern eye; *Madame Bergeret* between a stone bench and a huge vase looks artificial. There are roses everywhere; the light blue of the dress, the dark-blue ribbon, and the pink roses carry out his favorite color scheme. The sheen of the silk of the

Ill. 251 Boucher: Madame Bergeret. *National Gallery of Art, Kress Collection*

full, heavy skirt is beyond compare. To compensate for all this extravagant commotion, the head is seen against an open background, free and detached. The ruffled sleeves, beribboned and beflowered, and the crinkly ruche around her neck lead the eye to the pretty face, which is a portrait, not a fashion plate.

Ill. 252 Fragonard (1732–1806): The Meeting. *The Frick Collection*

Ill. 253 Jean Michel Moreau le Jeune (1741–1814): Couchée de la Mariée, etching after a drawing by Pierre Antoine Baudouin (1723–1769). *National Gallery of Art, Widener Collection*

Fragonard: *The Meeting (Ill. 252)*

Fragonard represents the last generation of French Rococo painters, who concluded the style that Watteau had begun. A pupil of Boucher's, he was a favorite of Madame du Barry [26] and painted this panel, one of four, *The Progress of Love,* for her palace. In mock surprise the lover is held off by the lady. In the sculpture group a cupid seems to be clamoring for the arrows Venus won't let him have at this stage of Love's progress. The garden retreat, overgrown and secluded, is a perfect setting for a rendezvous.

Soft and silky, like the elegant costumes, the leafy background melts away as if Nature were adjusting and accommodating herself to the lovers. Combining daintiness with precision, the drawing of the figure is elaborate but also refined. Every motif—wall, vase, figure, twig, or massed foliage—is spaced with calculated effect to make all parts related, to keep the interest alive across the whole surface.

Le Jeune: *Couchée de la Mariée, etching (Ill. 253)*

Baudouin has been called frivolous; this etching illustrates the point. In the midst of all the welter of dress and drapery, the figures are firmly drawn, textures are differentiated, and flesh tints are expressed by the brilliance of the white paper.

307

Ill. 254 Gobelin tapestry, Spring, designed by Pierre F. Cozette. *National Gallery of Art, Widener Collection*

Cozette: *Spring, tapestry (Ill. 254)*

The decorative arts of the period of Louis XV—furniture, tapestries, porcelain, as well as sculpture and engravings—reflect lightness and gaiety. The light-colored tapestries find an echo in the floral decorations used on the coverings of upholstery, and in the playful spirit in Clodion's terra-cottas. In all materials—wood, terra-cotta, porcelains, bronze, and tapestry—lines undulate, surfaces curve and bend, modeling is soft, and colors are delicate. The eighteenth century tried to make tapestries look like paintings, even turning the borders into imitation frames. Note the contrast between the weighty, bronzelike outer border and the light, fanciful figures seated on clouds. Acanthus foliage lightly touches scrolls that form shelves for busts, from which festoons of flowers are tied to a medallion of cupids and floral wreaths, all modeled in light and shade.

A modern eye trained to simplicity may find these contrasts strained; these borders suggest imitation moldings, for eighteenth-century tapestries were designed for paneled walls. To relate tapestry to wall, the designer made the tapestry borders look like architectural moldings.

Console table and mirror (Ill. 255)

In the console table placed beneath a tall wall mirror (shown here in the lower part), scrolls and shell shapes are combined with acanthus leaves, flowers, and interlaced ribbons. The marble top curves out over the sides, legs, and front. Supporting a clock or porcelain vase or figure, such

Ill. 255 Console table and mirror, gilt wood, from the palace at Bruchsal, Germany, style of Louis XV. *After L'Art pour tous*

consoles formed part of the interior decoration of the paneled room. All countries, including Germany, participated in the Rococo style. The more reserved English Queen Anne and Chippendale styles never attempted the exuberance of continental Rococo furniture, but are also based on the curved line carved in the natural wood. The comparable style in the American colonies, as in Philadelphia, followed the English manner, with American variations (Ill. 353).

Upright secretary (Ill. 256)

Eighteenth-century marquetry furniture used veneers, thin sheets of imported wood glued to a structural frame, encas-

Ill. 256 Upright secretary, signed by Martin Carlin, with porcelain painted plaques, style of Louis XVI, 1775–1780. *Metropolitan Museum of Art, Gift of the Samuel H. Kress Foundation, 1958*

Ill. 257 Book cover, morocco leather, eighteenth-century, French.
National Gallery of Art, Widener Collection

ing it completely [Fig. 223]. It differs from the intarsia
of the Renaissance (Ill. 190), which is truly inlaid, as the
structural wood is left exposed except where the inlay is set
in. An important part of this marquetry furniture is the gilt
bronze so-called ormolu mounts. The ormolu mounts were
first modeled in the manner of sculpture, then cast in bronze;
finally the casts were perfected through chiseling. Elaborate
and costly furniture had been made before, but never had
furniture achieved such refinement and perfection of workmanship. This is particularly true of the Louis XVI pieces
inlaid with painted porcelain plaques.

The works of the great cabinetmakers of the period enjoyed the prestige accorded to sculpture and painting. The
best furniture makers worked for well-to-do Parisian society,
including the nobility and the court. New types of furniture
were developed, like secretaries and desks, varied in size and
shape according to use, and many were designed for women.

Book cover (Ill. 257)

The splendor of the gold and jeweled book covers [Fig.
78] of the early Middle Ages was never equaled in later
centuries. As books became more plentiful after the invention

311

of printing, the book covers became less elaborate. The Renaissance produced stately bindings of red morocco, gold-tooled and with crowned arms for kings or the princes of the Church. Among the last of these ornamental leather bindings are the eighteenth-century French books, in this case a book of the fables of La Fontaine. Front and back have a border in common, but each panel has its own design. Both are exceedingly elegant; the motifs are derived from sources other than those common to Rococo decoration. The craftsman, who did the tooling, was not necessarily the one who furnished the design.

XI

Modern Art in Europe:
1800–1950

THE AGE of the old masters came to an end with the seventeenth century. Such artists as Raphael, Titian, Michelangelo, Rembrandt, and others continued to enjoy an undiminished prestige during the nineteenth and twentieth centuries, but the nineteenth-century artist in Paris or London did not enjoy the same privileged position accorded to the artist of ancient Athens, of Renaissance Florence, or of the Baroque period.

Rubens was sent on diplomatic missions and Velázquez was on friendly terms with Philip IV [p. 261], but after the Napoleonic era there was no official recognition for those painters who are today accepted as the masters of modern art. Cézanne was the pioneer of modern painting, as Giotto had been of the late Gothic period. Today both artists are highly regarded, but the reception accorded to each painter in his own day was quite different: Giotto was kept busy working on large frescoes; Cézanne could not sell his modest-sized paintings.

The place of the artist in society declined during the nineteenth century, and fewer great names stand out. In music [27] the line of great composers carries over into the nineteenth century, which also produced some of our great novelists. Yet art during this period had popular support in amateur painting. Today the arts as creative, leisure-time activities are accessible to more people than ever before. But the professional painter is not held in the same high regard he enjoyed in these earlier periods. Amateurs today are not sharply separated from professionals. Formerly artists began their lifework in their teens. Though this is still true occasionally as in the case of Picasso, other well-known painters began painting late in life, as Van Gogh or Grandma Moses. Whatever the reason may be, in popular esteem painters trail behind composers and writers. There are no Nobel prizes for painters,[28] and the interpretation of art has not developed writers or critics who have the glamour of conductors of symphony orchestras. Since painting has been separated from religion, it has lost in social status but gained in individual appeal.

In addition to the reduced prestige of the artist, the last century and a half has revealed other differences that characterize modern, and particularly contemporary, art. Styles differ more by artists than by nationalities. Painting has come under the influence of science, and architecture is based on engineering. The contemporary painter resembles a laboratory research worker who aims at new discoveries, the architect a chairman of a board of specialists in various mechanical fields. Artists look upon themselves as pioneers and accept economic insecurity in the hope of gaining fame.

The nineteenth-century artist also had to take time off from painting to devote his talents to what would contribute to his income. Daumier was an illustrator who engaged in oil painting for his own satisfaction. Renoir began as a designer for porcelain before he devoted all his time to easel painting. With the advance of industry, artists of every kind worked for the practical needs of a growing economy. Today some are free-lance artists on contracts, others on a long-term employment status. Contemporary painting and the graphic arts are so diversified that they can hardly be spoken of as representing a unified expression aiming at common goals. Those who work for collectors hope to have their paintings exhibited in metropolitan centers and eventually to win recognition. It is this group that appears to contribute to the history of art. We say "appears" advisedly, for we do not know how the future will evaluate the painting of our day.

We should probably not speak of any work of art created since the end of World War II as being part of the history of art. What has been done since 1945 is contemporary and hardly part of history. When the art historian ventures too close to the present or tries to predict the future development of art, he is out of his field. At best he may be tolerated as a commentator on current events in art. We begin with painting, France being the most important country.

Ill. 258 Ingres: The Stamaty Family, drawing, 1818. *Louvre*

Ingres: *The Stamaty Family (Ill. 258)*

Ingres was a younger contemporary of David [p. 282], who based his style on line. This drawing represents friends of Ingres in Rome. They stand assembled to have their picture drawn as a few decades later they might have posed for a daguerreotype.

Heads and hands—the significant parts in portraiture—are emphasized. The smooth spinet contrasts with textures of cloth; ribbons and curls add liveliness. Lines are important;

315

there are practically no shadows. The influence of classical sculpture appears in unsuspected places, as in the father, who holds his hand in his vest as if it were a Roman toga.

Géricault: *drawing (Ill. 259)*

Géricault, also a contemporary of David's, caused a sensation with his painting of *Raft of the Medusa* [p. 283, Fig 226]; he was an early founder of the Romantic school. One of his passions was to ride and to draw horses; he introduced the racehorse as a subject for art. Smithies, stables, and circuses were his favorite abodes; this love of horses was deep-seated and probably went back to his early years. His study of horses after the living model was a novelty that attracted attention. His knowledge of the human figure was derived from Rubens, Michelangelo, and Caravaggio. The loose, sketchy drawing of this prancing horseman is in the Romantic spirit.

Ill. 259 Géricault: drawing. *Pierre Dubaut Collection, Paris*

Ill. 260 Corot: The Artist's Studio. *National Gallery of Art, Widener Collection*

Corot: *The Artist's Studio (Ill. 260)*

Corot, like Daumier and Millet, stands between Romanticism and Naturalism. He studied nature as well as the classical compositions of Claude and Poussin, but seems more modern than either. Corot usually discovered his motifs out-of-doors, but his work is not a literal transcription of nature. He restricts his hues to a few greens and emphasizes values that produce the soft atmospheric landscape for which he is known.

This painting of an interior looks informal, but upon study turns out to be a marvel of delicately balanced shapes, values, and colors. Every part is calculated; rectangles and triangles are carefully but unobtrusively fitted together. A green bodice is set against red hair; ribbons and reflected lights on face, hands, and mandolin relate the painting to Vermeer. A subtle color harmony is worked out between the warm-gray dado and the yellow-gray-green wall. This is a modern painting steeped in the qualities of the old masters.

Millet: *Departure for Work (Ill. 261)*

Millet [p. 285] painted and etched what were then considered commonplace subjects but that in the eyes of the painter were imbued with nobility. As a young peasant Millet went from his native Norman village to Paris, where he learned how to paint. To support himself he painted salable pictures in the Boucher manner he despised. When he could no longer stand it he returned to the farm in Barbizon. Millet became a much beloved painter; his attachment to the soil and his sympathy for the down-trodden peasant endeared him to many. The two figures silhouetted against the sky take on a monumental quality and the landscape is filled with light. Millet simplifies until he achieves large forms subjected to a single expression. He makes his peasants, with their bulky arms and large hands, seem important. The Dutch painters Brouwer and Jan Steen (Ill. 233) saw the peasant as a carousing figure often fighting and given to uproarious behavior. Millet reflects a new social consciousness that is not confined to art, though art served as a vehicle for its expression. Millet has been called sentimental, as if he owed his reputation solely to the appeal of his subject. Though his popularity depends in part on the fact that he makes peasants seem heroic, his style also shows the effects of working out-of-doors, as is true of Corot and other painters of the Barbizon school.

Daumier: *Crispin and Scapin (Ill. 262)*

Daumier, next to Goya, was the great caricaturist who criticized, in the men and manners of his day, what he felt was wrong with society. He drew cartoons by the thousands, mostly in crayon, but his paintings failed to equal the popularity of his cartoons. He painted to please himself and had no need to compromise for the sake of recognition. In this painting the footlights bring out the leering features of Crispin as he listens to Scapin's whisper. The painter seems to gloat over the expressions of these two popular characters of the French eighteenth-century stage.

Ill. 261 Millet: Departure for Work, etching. *National Gallery of Art, Rosenwald Collection*

Ill. 262 Daumier: Crispin and Scapin. *Louvre*

Ill. 263 Courbet: Stone Breakers, 1851, Dresden. *Staatliche Fotothek*

Courbet: *Stone Breakers (Ill. 263)*

Corot (b. 1796), Daumier (b. 1808), Millet (b. 1814), and Courbet (b. 1819) were contemporaries. They lived to the opening of the last quarter of the century. All have in common the fact that they turned away from subjects based on history [Fig. 224] or literature [Fig. 225] and selected their subjects from nature or the real world of their own environment. They still represented nature as having a certain permanency that could be recorded objectively, but they differed individually. Corot was romantic and Millet idealized, though his contemporaries thought him brutally realistic. The term Naturalism applies most to Courbet, who was a real peasant who painted. He was strong of body, muscular, all beef and brawn, thoroughly unintellectual. Millet, by comparison, was a sentimental dreamer. Though Courbet talked like a revolutionary and got himself into trouble with the government, he was not interested in the social problems of the worker. His realism is in his choice of subjects, in the torn vest of the man and the tattered shirt and trousers of the boy helper. One incident of the motion is recorded; arm, hand, and sledgehammer show more detail than the eye would be aware of, and color is still local color.

Courbet could not conceive of painting anything he had not seen. To paint like Raphael or Michelangelo something that existed only in the imagination made no sense to him. To speak of "soul" to Courbet brought on convulsions of laughter. He sought reality and truth, which to his contemporaries was truth "sought in the dirt of the street." Actually Courbet did not paint the dirt of the street; this was left to Dubuffet a century later (Ill. 298).

Before we continue with the second phase of French nineteenth-century Realism, Impressionism of the period 1875–1900, we turn to painting in England and Germany of the first half of the nineteenth century.

Turner: *Dogana and San Giorgio Maggiore (Ill. 264)*

John Constable, with John Crome (Old Crome), the founder of English landscape painting, selected his subjects from the flat countryside of East Anglia. His broad technique, at times showing the use of the palette knife, introduces a convincing feeling of sunlight falling through foliage. The Dutch painters like Hobbema separated branches and leaves silhouetted against the sky; Constable fused both with light and atmosphere. Houses, farm wagons, figures, horses, and clouds were painted as a total impression, not as isolated objects [p. 285, Fig. 228]. The term *plein air* was applied to this new style that revolutionized painting.

It was left to Turner to carry further this total impression that merges objects with the environment. In his later, mature style Turner painted those high and brilliant skies over glistening water with mists in the distance. Gondolas and the campanile of San Giorgio (Palladio's Church of San Giorgio Maggiore) reflect in the water, painted like a smooth sheet ever-changing through ripples of light and transparent shadow. Claude Lorrain had invented these effects; Turner stored his memory with close observations of the real scenes. Turner's early style was topographic and his middle period naturalistic; only his late style, here illustrated, was impressionistic [p. 285], though not as yet as objective as Monet's [Fig. 232].

Burne-Jones: *King Cophetua and the Beggar Maid (Ill. 265)*

The rise of the English landscape school coincided with the Industrial Revolution of the Victorian era. A prosperous middle class as well as an impoverished proletariat grew out of the new machine age. Towns and countryside exposed to mines, mills, and factories took on a new ugliness. The increased comforts of the home were expressed in ostentatious furnishings. A shoddy commercialism and a widespread degradation of taste were in part due to an ill use of the machine. The need to correct the exploitation of child labor found expression in Dickens; social reform and socialism became new forces in society.

A parallel reaction in art was the revolt of the Pre-Raphaelite group of painters (1848) such as John Madox Brown (b. 1821), Dante Gabriel Rossetti (b. 1828) and Burne-Jones. The movement was directed against the popular Victorian painters of the day, who were looked upon as the English imitators of the Italian painters that followed Raphael. These painters, like Landseer, Leighton, and Alma-Tadema, appealed through the topics they selected and the lifelikeness of their techniques. Edwin Landseer (1802–1873) painted animals with a portraitlike quality that makes fur seem real and the animal expression take on a human aspect. Landseer, the favorite artist of Queen Victoria, was made a member of the Royal Academy, was knighted, and was buried in St. Paul's Cathedral. His worldly success was in the

Ill. 264 Joseph Turner: Dogana and San Giorgio Maggiore. *National Gallery of Art, Widener Collection, 1942*

tradition of the great masters of the past. Lord Leighton (1830–1896), originally a sculptor, was equally popular as a painter of classical subjects; he cultivated the smooth surface. Lawrence Alma-Tadema (1836–1912) in the same style specialized in smooth marble and idealized classical nudes. His palatial home provided the marble pools that he used in his paintings. Among the successes of the period, reproductions of which have not entirely disappeared today, are such paintings as *Her Mother's Voice* (W. Q. Orchardson) and *The Doctor* (Luke Field). These and other favorites of the Victorian and Edwardian (Edward VII, reign 1901–1910) periods have been held in low esteem ever since the rise of the French Impressionists [p. 286]. This combination of photographic literalness and literary content became intolerable to the Pre-Raphaelites, who felt art should ever expand horizons and retain a sensitivity to the new ideals of a younger generation of artists. Burne-Jones, as in this medieval subject, returned to the Gothic for inspiration, to ideals of faith and love rather than power and wealth. King Cophetua marrying a beggar maid [29] gave prestige to poverty at a time when prosperity was popular. Burne-Jones adopted Botticelli as his idol and like Botticelli created a type for his female figures. His linear style, without strong contrasts of light and shade, is in the spirit of the Italian *quattrocento*; the vertical panel is a Gothic contribution.

Morris: *News from Nowhere, page 2 (Ill. 266)*

Burne-Jones met William Morris at Oxford when both were studying for the ministry. Burne-Jones instead became a painter to carry on a holy warfare against the ugliness of the age. When Morris set out to furnish his studio home in London (1851) and his house at Bexley Heath (1861), he became aware of the poor craftsmanship in furniture, textiles, and the applied arts generally. To initiate improvements he started his own firm. The artist had lost touch with everyday life. To restore art to all became part of the Morris doctrine. William Morris defined art as "The expression by man of his pleasure in labor." Honest craftsmanship rather than inspiration was basic to his artistic creed; thus art was linked to morality and social structure. In his return to medieval craftsmanship he rejected the machine as an evil thing. Without modern methods of mass production he could

Ill. 265 Edward Burne-Jones (1833–1898): King Cophetua and the Beggar Maid. *Tate Gallery, London*

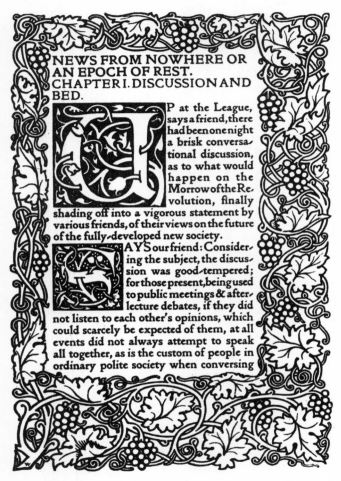

NEWS FROM NOWHERE OR AN EPOCH OF REST. CHAPTER I. DISCUSSION AND BED.

UP at the League, says a friend, there had been one night a brisk conversational discussion, as to what would happen on the Morrow of the Revolution, finally shading off into a vigorous statement by various friends, of their views on the future of the fully-developed new society.

SAYS our friend: Considering the subject, the discussion was good-tempered; for those present, being used to public meetings & after-lecture debates, if they did not listen to each other's opinions, which could scarcely be expected of them, at all events did not always attempt to speak all together, as is the custom of people in ordinary polite society when conversing

Ill. 266 William Morris (1834–1896): News from Nowhere, page 1, written and printed by Morris at the Kelmscott Press, 1892. *Victoria and Albert Museum*

produce only for the few who could afford to pay for hand-made objects. In his later speeches Morris did admit the necessity of man's learning to control the machine. Eventually artistic craftsmanship was improved through the arts-and-crafts movement, which spread to other countries and to the industrial arts in our own day. Walter Crane became his disciple and Ruskin was associated with him. England began the modern movement, but after the start the initiative passed to Belgium (Henry van de Velde), Austria (Otto Wagner) and the United States (Frank Lloyd Wright). Walter Gropius (b. 1883), founder of the Bauhaus School in Weimar, Germany, in 1919, continued into our own age what Morris had begun.

Morris was also a pioneer of modern printing; his private Kelmscott Press had a worldwide influence. His books of handmade paper became museum pieces, but their ornamental magnificence discouraged reading. They were protests against the mechanical book production of his day. In their striking effects of black backgrounds, ornamental borders, and massive initials, they are modern variations of early printed books (Ill. 107), themselves imitations of manuscripts. Type, ink, and paper constitute an organic unity, a conception that ever since has been recognized as a basic principle of good printing. In title pages and endpapers the principles of Morris were used for mass-produced books by J. M. Dent in Everyman's Library (1906). The care that the private presses had used for "fine" printing was applied to commercial printing in England (Nonesuch Press, 1923), in Germany (Ernst Poeschel, d. 1949), and in the United States (D. B. Updike and Bruce Rogers).

Beardsley: *The Death of Pierrot (Ill. 267)*

As an illustrator in black and white Beardsley produced perhaps the most distinguished designs of the century. His use of line in wide, sweeping curves; his placing of blacks to make the white seem expansive; and his ornamental patterns in costume create a sense of distinction. The flat decoration also retains a suggestion of depth. The chair drawn in perspective marks the foreground; Pierrot's head appears set back into space. Figures are elongated and heads small; a favorite Beardsley type of head seems to have been after his own image, with prominent cheekbones, firm mouth, and a projecting chin; Sandro Botticelli as drawn by Beardsley is made to look like Beardsley. Various influences merge—the Japanese Utamaro, Botticelli, the French characteristics of the illustrator Eisen, and Saint-Aubin—to create a style that is precious and original.

Ill. 267 Aubrey Beardsley (1872–1898): The Death of Pierrot. *From Arthur Symons,* The Art of Aubrey Beardsley *(1918)*

Friedrich: *Meadows at Greifswald (Ill. 268)*

German Baroque art of the seventeenth century was chiefly devoted to architecture (Ill. 215), sculpture [Fig. 192], and the decorative arts (Ill. 216). Painting existed as mural decoration or was dominated by foreign influence. There were no great artists of the stature of Dürer or Grünewald, or comparable to Hogarth or Watteau. Germany's contribution to European art owed more to Johann Winckelmann [p. 63], the founder of classical archaeology (1763), than to the eclectic painter Anton Mengs (1728–1779), whom Winckelmann patronized and praised.

Kaspar David Friedrich represents nineteenth-century Germany after the Napoleonic Wars. A North German from Greifswald on the Baltic coast, he painted his native landscape bathed in luminous mist. Nature is approached with solemnity, love, and a sense of wonder. Where figures are introduced, they convey to the spectator that they too are held under the spell of nature. This kind of landscape, unified by a veil of light and atmosphere, appears throughout European and American painting in the Barbizon as in the Hudson River school. This Romantic landscape is panoramic and takes in a sizable view. Though atmospheric, the shrubbery in the foreground and the horses in the meadow are still well defined. Drawing by contours is softened to denote distance, as in the medieval town silhouetted on the horizon.

Ill. 268 Kaspar David Friedrich (1774–1840): Meadows at Greifswald. *Kunsthalle, Hamburg*

Von Schwind: *Wedding Trip (Ill. 269)*

Schwind (b. in Vienna) is the representative painter of the German Romantic school, the painter of medieval sagas, of myths and fairy tales, as well as scenes from daily life. Schwind is as German as Hogarth is English or Jan Steen is Dutch. Color, the least part, is used as a final brightening up of an illustration that tells its own story. Schwind's subjects were unpolitical, unlike those of Daumier or even

Ill. 269 Moritz von Schwind (1804–1871): Wedding Trip. *Bavarian State Gallery, Munich*

Ill. 270 Alfred Rethel (1816–1859): Triumph of Death, woodcut, 1849. *After Bock, Hanfstaengl (1922)*

Courbet, who through their art let their conscience speak. The German romantic painters retreated to a safe past or to an innocuous present that offered no hazards. Here is the life of the small provincial town of the mid-nineteenth century. The innkeeper sees his guests off, and the storekeeper across the street makes sure to take in the event. Nostalgia contributes to the picture's appeal.

Rethel: *Triumph of Death (Ill. 270)*

Rethel was a painter of historical subjects but is best known for his drawings, reproduced in woodcut. The Revolution of 1848 became the subject for a series on the "Dance of Death" in the Holbein tradition. It is his reaction to events he did not approve of; only Death wins in the end, as he rides across the barricades. The towering skeleton, grinning, looks down upon the dying man surrounded by corpses. The open technique of parallel lines creates space, distance, and clarity. His scene is one of tragic relaxation rather than horror. Goya does not let us off as easy as Rethel, whose technique is as calm and composed as Goya's is realistic.

During the second half of the nineteenth century Germany had more state-supported art academies than any other coun-

Ill. 271 K. Arnold: Der Rassemensch (1924), drawing for the Munich illustrated magazine Simplicissimus. *Fackelträger-Verlag, Hanover*

try. The professors of art in these schools were highly regarded. They trained many artists, few of whom attained any historical significance. The inspiration came from England through Constable and from Belgium and France through painters who attained international fame. Adolph Menzel (1815–1905) was the leader of the realists in such paintings as the interior of steel mills. During the eighties German painting, with Max Liebermann (b. 1847), came under the influence of the French Impressionists. Fritz von Uhde, figure painter, applied a modern technique to religious subjects. Christ seated on a chair in a contemporary German village interior greets the schoolchildren, who shake hands with him. A third group could be labeled idealists, like Böcklin [Fig. 230, p. 285], a Swiss by birth, from Basel. The most original painter of the group, Max Klinger (1857–1920), was hardly touched by Impressionism. He achieved distinction as sculptor, painter, mural decorator, and particularly etcher. Klinger is thoughtful and imaginative; in the eyes of a contemporary French critic (S. Reinach) he is cultivated, eccentric, but "possessed of a robust talent."

Arnold: *Der Rassemensch (Ill. 271)*

German cartoonists of the early twentieth century through their satirical drawings for the well-known Munich *Simplicissimus* carried on a merciless warfare against their own reactionaries and militarists. The swastika, used nine times over, characterizes the man as the early adherent of National Socialism in the days after World War I but before Hitler's rise to power. The German label *Rassemensch* means superman but is here used to denote ironic contempt, not racism. The monocle was almost the emblem of the haughty aristocrat. In a more tragic vein, Käthe Kollwitz [p. 291, Ill. 125] became widely known through her lithographs denouncing war.

Masereel: *The Strike (Ill. 272)*

A social consciousness reflecting a general sympathy for the oppressed found expression in art in all countries. Masereel was the Belgian parallel of Käthe Kollwitz. Here the single figure of the factory owner, identified by the high hat, is opposed by the pleading crowd.

Ill. 272 Frans Masereel: The Strike, wood engraving. *From Carl Zigrosser*, Six Centuries of Fine Prints (1937)

Ill. 273 Johan Barthold Jongkind (1819–1891): Holland Canal, near Rotterdam, etching. *National Gallery of Art, Rosenwald Collection*

Jongkind: *Holland Canal (Ill. 273)*

The last quarter of the nineteenth century was dominated by Impressionism. Color became important and individual form, under the influence of light and as part of the total impression, was lost in a pattern of colored areas. The impressionistic technique went beyond Courbet, who was still concerned with static effects. Impressionism studied momentary effects in nature as they occur through the action of light. It was developed by French painters and adopted by painters in other countries. Early trends in the direction of Impressionism occurred in Spain under Goya and in Holland in the paintings and etchings of the Dutch artist Jongkind. The French Impressionists acknowledged a debt to this Dutch master. Jongkind in this etching carries on a tradition from Rembrandt in the loose, sketchy line. Foliage and windmill combine into a mass of dark against heavy clouds in a bright sky; the total effect is one of brilliant illumination.

The favorite painter of nineteenth-century Holland was Joseph Israels (1824–1911), the "Dutch Millet." His "tonal" painting is based on Rembrandt; his subjects from the life of the fishers and sailors are represented in shadowy interiors and imbued with melancholy. In *Alone in the World* (Rijksmuseum) every device is used to create a sense of sadness and emptiness. Israels expanded painting toward literature, but through pictorial means, as his style does not readily translate into words. Without Rembrandt there would have been no Israels. But subsequent development turned away from mood painting.[30]

Manet: *The Skating Rink (Ill. 274)*

The term Impressionism [pp. 286–88] came into the art vocabulary when Manet exhibited a *Sunrise at Sea* at the Salon des Refusées and labeled it "one impression." A critic then called the exhibition *"Salon des Impressionistes."* "Simultaneous vision" was thereby substituted for "consecutive vision," as illustrated in Van Eyck (Ill. 120). For Manet light became the most important part in any picture. Note here the contrast of lighter against darker shapes, which replaces the rounded modeling of academic painting. Brush-strokes left in the raw as they touch the canvas are a direct influence from Hals, whom Manet copied. On the left a figure projects into the picture, cut off by the frame. By selecting a section from the crowd and by painting this section with a quick handling of the brush, the painter gets a lively, unposed effect. Manet was an elegant Parisian gentleman who would wear a Prince Albert and top hat. Groomed and cultured, he was a man of the world who moved in high society.

Degas: *Rehearsal on Stage (Ill. 275)*

Degas did not represent the ballet dancers at their graceful best, but working hard at rehearsal [p. 287], in individual postures, in side view, from the back, or standing on the sidelines awaiting their turns. One is yawning with hands clasped behind her head, another is cut off by the frame, and another stoops with her ballet skirt in back fluttering above her head. A bass viol projects into the picture, the sets look drab, but the flesh tints are warm and the stage floor a glistening green. Two men lounge in chairs; the footlights reflect from fluffy skirts as the baldheaded dancing master beats time. The figures are spaced to suggest a quickly changing scene. The drawing is perfect in outstretched arms, bony elbows, and precisely placed feet performing steps that had to be practiced.

Artists as persons differ as much as individuals in any group and have come from as many different backgrounds.

Ill. 274 Edouard Manet: The Skating Rink. *National Gallery of Art*

Degas was the son of a banker, and like Manet, was born in Paris. He was a royalist and a chauvinist and wanted to keep his paintings out of the hands of English and American collectors. During the last thirty years of his life he lived as a recluse in a fifth-floor apartment in Montmartre, refusing to show or sell his pictures. One painting that he did sell for "£20, changed hands for £17,500, the highest paid for the work of a living artist" (Underwood, 1936).

Renoir: *The Luncheon of the Boating Party (Ill. 276)*

Renoir was a friend of Monet and exhibited with the Impressionists. He defended the impressionistic creed when the word was still used as an expression of contempt. Like the Impressionists, he painted outdoors, took note of violet shadows, and mixed ultramarine and carmine to obtain depth in places where the old-style painters would have used black. Renoir subscribed to no system, neither to Manet's flatness nor to Monet's impressions. He wished to be thought of as being in the Watteau-Ingres tradition. Renoir, more than any other of the Impressionists, integrated into a personal style past traditions with the achievements of his own day.

This is an informal gathering in which actions of the individual are important even though there is no obvious suggestion of any story. What a lively time these young people are having is seen in the expressive gazes, the studied indifference of some, and the spontaneous behavior of others. Animation and relaxation, facial expression, and a subtle relationship between persons merge in the lush surface

Ill. 275 Edgar Degas: Rehearsal on Stage, pastel. *Metropolitan Museum of Art*

qualities, thereby avoiding concentration on the figure. The play of color, reflected light, and brushwork give a close-knit unity to the group so that no details are allowed to detach themselves. This is simultaneous vision achieved by an exercise of the will. One must look at the visual world through half-closed eyes to achieve a comparable fusion. Manet's figures exist as foils to demonstrate visual impression; Renoir's are individual human beings who are intensely alive. Renoir's style suggests a mingling of contributions from Frans Hals and Watteau.

Bouguereau: *The Virgin as Consoler (Ill. 277)*

The vital, forward-looking trends of French painting were represented by such painters as Courbet (Naturalism) and Manet (Impressionism), Renoir and others, but academic trends also continued. The academic painters enjoyed a considerable reputation at a time when Courbet and Manet were kept out of the Salon exhibitions. They differ chiefly in subject matter; what, not how, they painted was important; to

Ill. 276 Auguste Renoir: The Luncheon of the Boating Party.
Phillips Memorial Collection, Washington, D.C.

Ill. 277 Adolphe William Bouguereau (1825–1905): The Virgin as Consoler. Musée de Luxembourg. *Archives Photographiques*

revolutionize painting was not the aim of the academic painter. Principles handed down from the past were elaborated through increased technical skill and through the right models. In a new kind of historical painting it was no longer acceptable to represent the past in a contemporary environment as had been customary since the Renaissance. Gérôme, going beyond the classicizing figures of David, painted realistically modeled figures in archaeologically plausible settings. Meissonier (1815–1891) was the celebrated

painter of soldiers and battle pictures. His demands for
realism were so exacting that the saddles for his horsemen
had to show the signs of having been in actual use. Neuville's
battle pictures have few equals in other countries. They are
painstakingly accurate; compared to Goya they are fresh and
colorful and full of action but lack the emotional depth of
Goya. Neuville together with Detaille painted large circular
panoramic battles of the Franco-Prussian War (1882). From
a round central platform raised above the ground level one
would look out into a vast landscape, giving one the illusion
of standing in the midst of the battle itself.[31] Though
painted, the deception was made possible by a stretch of real
foreground that blended imperceptibly into the painted dis-

Ill. 278 Anders Leonard Zorn (1860–1920): Wet, etching. *National Gallery of Art, Gift of Walter Bogert*

tance that contained all the action. Panoramas, a form of entertainment, were popular in all countries including the United States. They finally disappeared in the first decade of the twentieth century, when the first moving pictures appeared. Today our natural-history habitat groups carry on this tradition.

Beautiful models served Bouguereau well. The consoling Virgin and the distressed mother are at their best. The charming infant, uncomfortably stretched out amidst roses, is in the grand manner. Superficiality is characteristic of other academic painters of the century, however realistic they were meant to appear. Bouguereau's extraordinary skill is noted in such details as the drawing of the hands.

Zorn: *Wet (Ill. 278)*

Scandinavian painters during the second half of the nineteenth century developed styles of their own. The earlier painters studied in Germany, the later ones in Paris, where they absorbed the teachings of Impressionism. To study in Paris became the ambition of painters everywhere. Returned to their homelands, the foreign students reflected not Paris but the flavor of their own countries. This was particularly true of Zorn. Local color and Swedish types, whether they are peasants or representatives of the upper classes, give to his paintings a Swedish character. Strong color, a vigor of form, and brilliant sunlight fill his canvases. His etchings are also strikingly individual. Using a simple parallel stroke, he modulates his technique to express the softness of flesh as well as the transparency of water on sunlit rocks.

Hill: *Tree Falling into the Sea (Ill. 279)*

At the time the Norwegian Edvard Munch was developing an expressionistic style, Hill in Sweden was following his own visions. During the last half of his life, living quietly at Lund, he produced black-chalk drawings reminiscent of Van Gogh. Having succumbed to mental illness, as a harmless eccentric his art was no longer taken seriously. Abandoning his earlier Impressionism, developed while studying in France, he turned to imaginative subjects in which his inner conflicts found a forceful artistic expression.[32]

Ill. 279 Carl Frederik Hill (1849–1911): Tree Falling into the Sea, black chalk. *After Erik Blomberg (1949)*

Munch: *The Cry (Ill. 280)*

The Norwegian artist Munch began as an Impressionist in the manner of Pissarro but developed his own expressionistic style. His emphasis is on expressing the basic facts of life that have a strong emotional link, like love and death. There are no distracting details; in this print simplification is carried to such lengths that nature is brought under the spell of the hysterical outcry, without furnishing a clue as to a possible cause. The distorted figure is all head, the body almost a part of a great, lonely emptiness. Often the figure faces the onlooker, as in Munch's painting of a little girl standing helpless and grief-stricken as she turns her back on the deathbed of her mother (*The Dead Mother*, Bremen). Munch makes Bouguereau seem pretentious and shallow.

The Swiss painter Ferdinand Hodler (1853–1918), an idealist, created imaginative figure compositions that have no literary content but a meaning in terms of symbolism and linear rhythm. His style, like Munch's, is outside the Naturalism and Impressionism of his day. Hodler's monumental fresco *Wilhelm Tell,* a figure symbolic of the Swiss will to freedom, marks with other frescoes a new trend toward monumentality without the literary elements of the Pre-Raphaelites. Italy's contribution to a modern style is related to Impressionism. Giovanni Segantini (1858–1899) applied the neo-impressionistic technique [p. 289] to the Alpine scene, giving the landscape the transparent clarity of atmosphere. A trend away from historical and literary subjects

Ill. 280 Edvard Munch (b. 1863): The Cry, lithograph. *National Gallery of Art, Rosenwald Collection*

was common to painting in all countries. The Spanish parallels are Joaquín Sorolla y Bastida (b. 1863), commonly called Sorolla, and Ignacio Zuloaga (b. 1870); both had an international audience. Sorolla is remembered for the fluent breadth in his brushwork, particularly in beach and bathing scenes; Zuloaga links up with Goya. Though popular in their day, they had no important followers. Cézanne [p. 288] and the Post-Impressionists stand in the main line of development. Impressionism became part of the Western tradition and for a brief period influenced painters in all countries.

Cézanne: *The Bathers (Ill. 281)*

Monet aimed to transfer to canvas objectively the appearance of an object as observed under a particular illumination. Cézanne started a new trend away from appearance toward abstraction and eventual unrecognizability.

Ill. 281 Paul Cézanne (1839–1906): The Bathers. *Philadelphia Museum of Art*

In this concept a painted landscape need not look real but must compose, and details must be related. Order is a basic principle; in this painting the design is based on triangles. The trees lean toward the center to produce triangles, repeated in the two groups of bathers. Torsos, legs, and arms are parallel to the inclined lines of the trees. Figures and tree trunks have form and are defined by contours. There is no merging of shapes as in a Monet landscape [Fig. 232], and figures are grouped in compact masses. In a Renoir (Ill. 276), solids and voids surge back and forth and keep the surface in movement. A Cézanne painting has repose; foliage, tree trunks, heads, and limbs are of the same substance but have no individuality as structural trees or anatomical figures. In place of the joyous humanity of Renoir we have what has been well termed the integrity of an oil painting. The detail is distorted, so it cannot be isolated and receive detached attention. Instead, every line and color patch is related to adjoining lines and patches, all contributing to the unity of the total canvas.

Gauguin: *Christ on the Cross (Ill. 282)*

In this woodcut Gauguin [p. 289] combines the crucified Christ with non-Christian symbols that might have been suggested to him by Oceanic motifs. From whatever emotional conflicts within himself Gauguin sought to escape by his flight to Tahiti, he probably found release through his much-sought-after "rebirth" in art. Calm and tranquillity are suggested by his oil paintings. Gauguin had sought a haven of refuge among the children of nature; here the symbols of a peaceful and primitive way of life are combined with Christianity. The design could be conceived of as a reconciliation of past with present or as an expression of revolt. Actually the symbols of his new home completely encircle the figure, which is absorbed in the total pattern. The design suggests an emotional background involving the artist. For a more positive interpretation, some expression from Gauguin himself would be necessary.

Picasso: *Seated Woman (Ill. 283)*

Picasso, the greatest of contemporary artists, is also the most versatile. His mural *Guernica* [p. 290, Fig. 241] represents one phase of his work (1937), Cubism another. Picasso rejects literary interpretation [p. 290], and none is here attempted. Even without color (dark browns) the

Ill. 282 Paul Gauguin: Christ on the Cross, woodcut. *Metropolitan Museum of Art, Dick Fund, 1929*

interest is essentially in design, an extraordinarily bold and varied mingling of lines, shapes, and textures, compactly interwoven. Vigorous curves sweep down from top to bottom, integrating with the few straight lines. Mild contrasts in uneven edges on the upper corners are combined with thin lines and are followed by sharp edges and thick, massive strokes. What is particularly exciting is a vital freshness. Things happen in unusual ways never seen before in this combination. The painting continues to convey an exhilaration that does not become stale with familiarity. As in other great works of art, every part seems right in its place, one never questions that anything could be changed to advantage, there is a place for every detail. What may seem

Ill. 283 Pablo Picasso: Seated Woman (1926–1927). *Museum of Modern Art*

hesitant in Cézanne is here carried through to a convincing finality.

Picasso: *Nude Seated (Ill. 284)*

Light envelops the massive figure seated in repose. With ease the contours describe form, lightly but firmly, without effort or hesitation, and with the greatest economy. Much is left out, details hardly exist, but the features suggest a classic marble come to life. Rarely has so much been said with so little.

Ill. 284 Picasso: Nude Seated, lithograph. *National Gallery of Art, Rosenwald Collection*

Schmidt-Rottluff: *Man Reading (Ill. 285)*

The early twentieth century brought with it a reaction against Impressionism, which no longer satisfied the younger generation. Once a style was accepted and available to all who would be followers, if it had no fresh potentialities to offer it lost its appeal to more dynamic artists. Western art during the last century and a half has ever been seeking new goals. After the visible world, past and present, had exhausted subject matter, the subject became unimportant. Art thereafter re-created the external world in obedience to the inner promptings of the artist. The German Expressionists were of this type. They imbued their motifs with a force that seemed like violence and with a simplicity that made conventional forms sharp and angular. These seated figures are childlike in drawing—large heads, strongly marked features, small hands—and without regard for perspective. In a search for a new-style child art, the geometric designs of the Neolithic

Ill. 285 Karl Schmidt-Rottluff (b. 1884): Man Reading. *National Gallery of Art, Rosenwald Collection*

period [Ill. 13–15] and Melanesian wood carving furnished inspiration. What these sources had to offer seemed to parallel what the Expressionists were groping for, each artist in his own way. The brutal strength of Schmidt-Rottluff's woodcuts is matched in his paintings by bold and glowing primary colors worked into broad surfaces.

Ill. 286 Franz Marc (1880–1916): Reconciliation, woodcut illustration of a poem, *Reconciliation,* by Else Lasker-Schuler. *After
Brandt, Kröner (1923)*

Marc: *Reconciliation (Ill. 286)*

Franz Marc became the expressionistic interpreter of animals; his blue and red horses have become generally familiar
through reproductions. The irrational mystical element in the
expressionistic creed, as expressed in words, is indicated by
Marc's desire "to represent the animal in the way the animal
senses itself."

In this case the painter found a topic in poetry. Expressionists were avid readers. Realistic elements here combine
with abstraction. After a lovers' quarrel, suggested in the
poem, love reunites the couple. Kneeling, she wards off the
retreating spirit of discord as a black devil still hovers over
the dog, a symbol of humility. The moon and stars shed
their light through the night; the rainbow, a symbol of reconciliation, begins to form as rays from above descend
upon the figures. Abstraction with elements of realism illustrates the lines of the poem.

Ill. 287 Ernst Barlach (1870–1938): Agony in the Garden, wood-cut. *National Gallery of Art, Rosenwald Collection*

Barlach: *Agony in the Garden (Ill. 287)*

The basic reorientation that modern art has undergone began well before 1900, and revolts have continued ever since. An often repeated explanation relates this search for new styles to the times we are living in. How can there be a unified style in a world that is complex and disjointed? The Middle Ages gave the artist faith, the Renaissance brought him personal fame, the Baroque still afforded him economic security. After the French Revolution the artist was free to shift for himself. Though it is true that art reflects environment, more is involved to account for individual differences in painting from realism to abstraction.

Architecture achieved a worldwide unity during the same period, but it is the easel painter who drives on to impress his individual personality. A more basic reason may be the freeing of the individual to become a creator in his own right and no longer simply to glorify an all-powerful Creator.

Standing alone in the universe, the artist is conscious of his capacity for creation that can result in monuments to proclaim his individuality and give added meaning to life. Modern art has a fervor that was once the province of religion. At the same time, religious subjects, when freely selected by the artist, are imbued with a new intensity not known since Grünewald.

In Barlach, agony is heartfelt and is concentrated on this kneeling Christ, who is isolated from the sleepers. Barlach may be called an Expressionist, and Expressionism was a spiritual reaction against the material world. It felt itself related to Munch as well as to the French Post-Impressionists, Van Gogh and Gauguin, and the contemporary Fauvism of Matisse. The artists' organizations the Bridge (1905) and the Blue Rider (1911) existed officially only a few years, but their influence spread. It receded during World War I and was officially suppressed as "decadent" by Hitler. Some Expressionists worked independently of groups, like Oskar Kokoschka, Max Beckmann (Ill. 294), and George Grosz [p. 291, Ill. 124].

Matisse: *Odalisque Seated (Ill. 288)*

Modern movements in painting and sculpture have one common element, the belief on the part of the artist that line, form, color, and texture have in themselves expressive powers. They not only reproduce realistically an image of what the eye sees but also convey moods and suggest feeling. Painting may convey tension or relaxation but does not arouse specific emotions [33] like fear, hate, love, envy, and others. Through a story that is represented, feelings may be linked to a painting through association. This is called illustration, which depends on Naturalism. The term imitation, or photographic, is often used in a derogatory sense. To identify himself with his own period the painter of the twentieth century has been adding to the artistic vocabulary of the past new forms of his own invention. The usual explanation is that the painter felt the urge to "revitalize" painting, because painting had lost its vitality. This assumed need on the part of painting that had to be revolutionized is not wholly convincing. It is the artist who desires new styles; the public is satisfied with the old styles it is accustomed to. Some modern artists also depend on the intuitive sensitivity of the observer, without drastic innovations.

Matisse [p. 292] in this lithograph suggests relaxation in pose and expression, but an element of tension is felt in the contours, in the long curves struck in with swift, determined strokes. The floral pattern in the dress and the small ruffles along the edge convey a sense of easy, careless abandon. In a seemingly effortless performance we are made aware of the control of the artist, here in a sense of breadth in the allover design brought out by the pattern of the wall and of flesh tone contrasted to costume. The wrist supporting the head, though not anatomically correct, is not disturbing in

Ill. 288 Henri Matisse (1860–1954): Odalisque Seated, lithograph. *National Gallery of Art, Rosenwald Collection*

this context. An emphasis on anatomy might have set up an uncomfortable attraction to the detriment of the total design. Matisse did not participate in Cubism; there is simplification, but abstraction is not involved. The art of Matisse is emotionally neutral, and color functions to enhance ornamental pattern [back cover].

Derain: *The Old Bridge (Ill. 289)*

Derain was influenced by mosaics and by Cézanne when he painted this canvas in his mature, but not his last, period. The sharp definition by contours in large, almost geometric shapes is carried into the distance and into the massed trees on either side. In the spirit of Cézanne no portion of the unified picture surface is permitted to become a separate element. There is linear, but no aerial, perspective; a generalized treatment, eliminating all detail, holds the picture together.

Ill. 289 André Derain (1880–1954): The Old Bridge. *National Gallery of Art, Chester Dale Collection*

Ill. 290 Georges Rouault (1871–1958): Christ Mocked by Soldiers. *Museum of Modern Art*

Rouault: *Christ Mocked by Soldiers (Ill. 290)*

Rouault was at one time a member of the Fauves [p. 292] and a fellow student of Matisse under the enlightened Gustave Moreau.[34] Rouault's experience as a painter of glass gave his later religious paintings a suggestion of stained glass in the use of black and a few strong colors, including red. But medieval stained glass uses black for details in well-shaped brushstrokes. The medieval painter, secure in his faith, aimed at fine craftsmanship. Had Rouault continued in this tradition, he would have been an academic drafts-man, imitating a historical style. But Rouault forced his technique in the manner of German Expressionists. Through broad smears and uncouth profiles he gives his soldiers a brutality that contrasts to the calm head and emaciated body of Christ.

Modigliani: *Woman with Red Hair (Ill. 291)*

The painters and sculptors of the twentieth century who have been in the forefront of the battle of modern art are known as the School of Paris. This includes, besides Frenchmen, also painters born in Spain (Picasso, Miró), Italy (Modigliani), Germany (Arp), England (Gill), Holland (Mondrian), Greece (Spyropoulos), Russia (Kandinsky), the Scandinavian countries, the Americas, and elsewhere in the world. Related to the School of Paris of the period before World War I were the German Expressionists and the Italian Futurists Carra, Boccioni, and Russolo and Severini. The Futurists aimed to indicate the passage of time by placing events on the canvas one beside the other, which is basically an illogical procedure. Objects were severed and recombined to give partial views; it was a disguised Naturalism, which took suggestions from Cubism, in such topics as that entitled *Bal Tabarin,* a surging mass of figures and curving dresses on the floor of the well-known Parisian dance hall, or *The Noise of the Street Penetrates the House.*

Modigliani's [p. 294] languid women also reflect Parisian influence but constitute an individual style of the painter.

Chagall: *I and the Village (Ill. 292)*

Chagall was closer to the German Expressionists than to the School of Paris. Two of the toy houses have toppled over like the farmer's wife, who has also broken loose. The egg-doughnut eye of the cow is threaded to the stitched-in eye of the profile man, who is the "I" of the title. A hand holds up a little, fluffy, treelike bouquet to tempt the cow. Nothing is exactly what it seems to be. A strongly accented pattern of curves and straight lines attracts to itself as much attention as the objects themselves. They are no more real than cut and stuffed Christmas-tree decorations. The real world is all but gone, but the images are still fully recognizable. The step to complete obliteration of recognizable objects was taken about the same time by another Russian, Kandinsky [p. 291, Fig. 240].

Ill. 291 Amedeo Modigliani: Woman with Red Hair. *National Gallery of Art, Chester Dale Collection*

Ill. 292 Marc Chagall (b. 1887): I and the Village (1911). *Museum of Modern Art*

Mondrian: *Composition 2 (Ill. 293)*

Kandinsky's world of form and space was made into a flat geometric design by this Dutch artist. Not only are there no images, but no volumes or textures or any other marks that could relate to the activity of a painter using a brush—mechanical straight lines, black on white, a few horizontals and verticals cutting out a single square and remainders of rec-

tangles filled in with a few bright colors. This is as close to
nothingness as one can get; by comparison, the spheres,
cones, and cylinders of Cézanne suggest a wealth of complexity. And yet this icy intellectualism, bereft of images
and emotion, has an appeal by its purity and restraint. In
other compositions Mondrian produces a maze or network
of crossing lines, occasionally slanting or curved. Daubs of
color, lighter or darker, and transparent, produce a mottled
surface. Kandinsky and Mondrian during the first two decades of the twentieth century achieved through complete
elimination of pictures [35] the extremes to which painting
could go. What followed in the period from about 1925 to
1945, the end of World War II, were ingenious modifications of what the early decades had produced. Some artists
followed the Expressionists, others the Abstractionists.

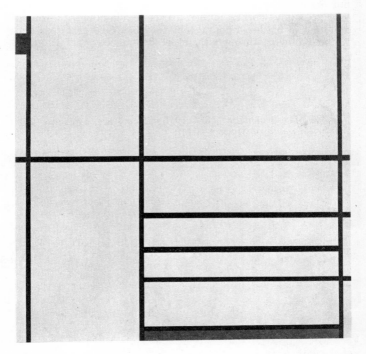

Ill. 293 Piet Mondrian (1872–1944): Composition 2. *Museum of
Modern Art*

Beckmann: *Departure, triptych (Ill. 294)*

The period from about 1925 to 1945 may be illustrated by paintings of Beckmann's, Chirico's and Miró's. In this not strictly chronological order they represent aspects of expressionistic, surrealistic, and fantastic trends. Beckmann's style derives from German Expressionism [p. 292]. Like Picasso's *Guernica* mural [p. 290, Fig. 241], *Departure* is a free creation, a sensitive artist's reaction against war as it had intruded itself into his own life.

Beckmann and Picasso differ from the battle painters of the nineteenth century, who illustrated events that had become part of history and with which the artists were not personally involved. All countries participating in both world wars had artists at the front who produced competent illustrations. Manet and Pissarro painted no war pictures, but instead went to England during the Franco-Prussian War to study Turner. Other artists in all countries fought and died in battle. A courageous few, like George Grosz and Käthe Kollwitz, through their art denounced war.

Ill. 294 Max Beckmann (1884–1950): Departure, triptych (1932–1935). *Museum of Modern Art*

Ill. 295 Giorgio di Chirico (b. 1888): Conversation Among the Ruins. *National Gallery of Art, Chester Dale Collection*

Di Chirico: *Conversation Among the Ruins (Ill. 295)*

Here is a kind of unreal realism—two massive figures seated on a platform with a view through a stage-set door into a hilly landscape that might suggest Greece. The man has classic features, the woman wears a classic costume of which the skirt has the solidity of a fluted column; the tablecloth repeats the marblelike flutes. The door is both fiercely real and unsubstantially unreal; the floorboards, hard as nails, are paper-thin; shadows are scribbles and perspective is distorted. But the intentional inconsistencies conform to a pattern. Without naturalistic illumination, the picture is glaring in its brightness. In the ruin of a house a serious conversation is going on. The scene is gaunt and barren and there is a frightening loneliness. In this rarefied, unreal world, the tawdry setting clashes with the well-dressed persons. It is like returning to a place in a dream where details are not clearly remembered. Here too specific detail has been suppressed to focus on the mood; as in Picasso's *Guernica* we get the sense of calamity without obvious realism.

Miró: *Carnival of Harlequin (Ill. 296)*

Surrealism [pp. 294–95] and the dream are said to have liberated Miró or given him the courage to develop a style of his own with some of the fantasy of a child. Miró is playful and spontaneous but controlled; the variety brings with it surprises in spots and lines that are made to appear as if they were the personal invention of the artist. No one

Ill. 296 Joan Miró (b. 1893): Carnival of Harlequin (1924–1925). *The Albright-Knox Art Gallery, Contemporary Art Collection*

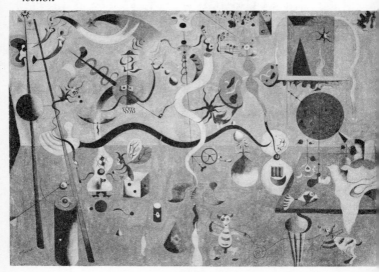

painting represents all aspects of Miró's style, but any one is recognizable as Miró. His earlier style is still concerned with objects that suggest influences from Matisse or from Cubism. What follows after 1925 is more or less in the manner of our illustration. Flat backgrounds, as here, dull, greenish-gray above, dull red-purple below, set off blues and blacks. What is here light is white in the original; there are stars, starfish, wings, cylinders, thin stringlike lines, and birds or animallike creatures, but hardly any wholly human suggestions; all wiggle or float. They cross before or behind one another, there is no space, but all seem to enjoy just keeping in motion or even standing still. Words are inadequate to name these precisely delineated creatures. Miró also produced murals (Cincinnati, Terrace Hilton Hotel), for which his decorative, joyful fantasy is admirably suited.

Spyropoulos: *oil, no title (Ill. 297)*

After 1945 painting entered a phase marked by a variety of individual styles. Though the term abstraction is commonly used to apply to contemporary painters of the last two decades, a pictorial element may be present, often distorted or concealed.

Ill. 297 Jean Spyropoulos (b. 1912): oil (no title). *Privately owned*

Spyropoulos is a contemporary Greek artist. His paintings tell no story, but neither do they shock or bewilder. The immediate appeal is one of an all-captivating profusion. There is brilliance and sparkle, variety in the use of pigment, and a sense that every surface and each stroke in shape, contour, and emphasis is as it must be. Skill of performance and a wealth of detail encourage study. His canvases reveal themselves slowly; with all the freshness and spontaneity that is obvious at first glance, familiarity makes one aware of the breadth of appeal. Opaque pigment (in the central spot of white) fuses with semitransparencies that turn soft and vaporous. Massive blacks, ragged in outline, turn to gray and become glowing and diaphanous. Black, white, and warm yellow ocher with touches of red constitute the simple color scheme. These paintings retain their interest in reproductions, but for the details, which contain some of the finest passages, one must see the originals.

Dubuffet: *Door with Couch Grass (Ill. 298)*

The painter Jean Dubuffet, Paris-born, has created an international sensation in the period since 1945. He is prolific, unpredictable, constantly changing his style, and a thoroughgoing artistic revolutionary. Spiritually, but not stylistically, Dubuffet is related to Courbet, Cézanne, and German Expressionism. He too advances an artistic creed against all tradition and established beliefs, including art.

Dubuffet is against ideas, logic, reason, Western culture, analysis, the written language, and beauty in objects or persons. However absurd his creed may seem, it supports his own style.

In Dubuffet's painting only the surface of the canvas is important; there is no depth. The pigment, thick and tangible, has substance that makes the surface uneven, or the canvas is soaked in paint to make canvas and pigment one. To base an impression on only one illustration is hazardous for an appreciation of Dubuffet's significance as an artist. As a revolt against what has been accepted as significant subject matter for art, Dubuffet paints an old door showing wood grain spotted with couch grass. Where the ground might be expected to be, the earth is seemingly cut, revealing a delicate maze of crystalline textures, an infinite variety of shapes like pebbles and snowflakes. In this painting the color is chocolate, warm and earthlike.

What traditional art heretofore has ignored, like the ground we walk on, for Dubuffet opens up a new realm for painting. Critics of Courbet's style spoke metaphorically of his style as having sought realism in the dirt of the street. Dubuffet made dirt, now called soil, the subject matter of a painting. He idealized the concept by delineating the earth as an intricate conglomeration of small shapes carefully defined to convey a sense of sparkle and radiance. In this guise

Ill. 298 Jean Dubuffet: (b. 1901) Door with Couch Grass (1957). *The Solomon R. Guggenheim Museum*

radiant earth may be interpreted as the symbol for the lovable mother. In a series of grotesque caricatures of women (*corps de dame*) the mother, hateful and feared, may be symbolized.[36]

Dubuffet seems to have invented his own style with little influence from others. That art depends for motivation on the unconscious is apparent in Dubuffet as in other artists. A combination of cultural factors appears to have favored contemporary trends in art. They are (1) freedom of choice on the part of the artist, (2) the stage of development of painting, (3) a desire for self-expression, self-importance, dignity, and immortality on the part of the artist, and (4) a familiarity with certain aspects of psychoanalytic literature. All play a part in explaining modern art.[37]

Appel: *Two Large Heads (Ill. 299)*

The paintings of Karel Appel, a contemporary Dutch painter, resist easy comprehension. They have been called paintings of "fire and blood" or "carnal devastation."[38] On first acquaintance they shock by their ragged brush smears of dark red against blue backgrounds. It is not clear whether this chaos is volcanic or cosmic or bears a relation to some

Ill. 299 Karel Appel (b. 1921): Two Large Heads (1960). *The Solomon R. Guggenheim Museum*

other source. As one studies the shapes at leisure and in detail, images appear, suggested resemblances from the human, animal, and plant worlds. Much vagueness remains, and discovery of what seems to be significant takes place gradually; meanings increase and eventually the canvas becomes alive. What first appears to be formless and vehement begins to look calculated and less ferocious, but a total impression of spontaneity remains. As in Rorschach's inkblot test, the observer reads into the painting interpretations that are personal.

Hayter: *Death by Water (Ill. 300)*

This engraving is a richly textured swirl of thin and thick lines, closely spaced, all following a downward movement. Noting the title, the clutching hand above, and the flapping hand below, we realize a man is drowning. Breathing, swallowing, and sinking are hinted at, but only rhythmic curves, descending in long lines or webbed areas, are clearly stated. Here the abstraction disguises the brutal reality.

Hayter, an Englishman living in Paris, is the most influential modern printmaker. His technical innovations have developed printmaking to the point that it parallels painting as a medium to express space and texture. Hayter's *Atelier 17* of the 1930's has revitalized the graphic arts of our time. He has taught artists of all countries and gives technical advice to the leading artists of the School of Paris.

Low: *Egregious Impostor, cartoon (Ill. 301)*

The political cartoon has been developed during the last two decades by a few outstanding artists to a place of preeminence. Compared to painters and printmakers there are few cartoonists of first rank; among them was the Englishman Low. As artists and as molders of public opinion they have received less than their due recognition. They interpret in drawings the day-by-day events in the world, international affairs and local politics. In no other contemporary art can the giants of the profession be so easily distinguished from lesser talents. No other group combines a talent for illustration with a comparable power to express ideas that are of importance to everybody. Hollow bombast and supreme derision are here contrasted with extraordinary persuasion.

From contemporary painting we now turn to sculpture beginning with Neo-Classicism.

Ill. 300 Stanley William Hayter (b. 1901): Death by Water, engraving. *National Gallery of Art, Rosenwald Collection*

Ill. 301 David Low: Egregious Impostor, cartoon. *From The Nation, February 12, 1944*

Canova: *The Three Graces (Ill. 302)*

The Italian Canova, the Dane Thorwaldsen, and the Englishman Flaxman represent Neo-Classicism in sculpture, which brought the Bernini tradition to an end. In Canova the softness of Praxiteles is combined with the grace of the Rococo. His contemporaries looked upon Canova not only as a great sculptor, but as the greatest of all time. His marble group of the winged Amor embracing the reclining Psyche is one of his most attractive. Canova represented Napoleon standing nude as a Greek-like Achilles, and Napoleon's sister Pauline Bonaparte seminude, reclining Venus-like on a couch in a stately pose. Canova's imitative style did not exclude originality in his composition. Actually his classicism was removed from Greek sculpture. What he imagined he was imitating hardly existed in either Greek or Roman sculpture.

These Graces,[39] fondly inclined one to the other with hair loosely tied in knots, are classic in their calm features but would be hard to match in classic sculpture in the way Canova unites them.

Ill. 302 Antonio Canova (1757–1822): The Three Graces, original in Leningrad. *After Seemann (1879)*

Thorwaldsen: *The Graces (Ill. 303)*

Thorwaldsen, a Dane from Copenhagen, may be taken as the representative sculptor of Neo-Classicism. Modern critics praise him for his reliefs of *Night* and *Day* and condemn him for almost everything else. His weaknesses are pointed out, but what his contemporaries appreciated is left unsaid.

How the nineteenth century felt about Thorwaldsen a generation after his death stands out in what Wilhelm Lübke, professor of art history in Stuttgart, wrote about him. Lübke pointed out that Thorwaldsen brought to fruition what Canova had aspired to, antiquity revived to a new life. An endless number of works, in the words of Lübke, demonstrate the nobility and chastity of the best of the Greek period, a clarity and perfection of form not equaled since the days of Greece. No words are necessary to explain the

Ill. 303 Bertel Thorwaldsen (1770–1844): The Graces. *After Lübke (1870)*

difference between Thorwaldsen's and Canova's Graces. Thorwaldsen's advance is demonstrated in a greater nobility of form, a purity of sentiment, an unintentional element expressed in its own repose.

We note here a clear statement of the Neo-Classic ideal that the period sought as a concept of the Greek ideal. What Lübke criticizes in Canova is the fact that heads are turned, indicating an expression of playful concern of one Grace for the other. For Thorwaldsen, all that was unseemly. His goddesses act with restraint; they keep their heads under control; they can afford to be nude because they are divine, naïvely innocent, like Adam and Eve before the Fall.

In the estimate of the nineteenth century the colossal statue of Christ in the Church of Our Lady in Copenhagen was the final triumph that fused classical beauty of form with a Christian content.

Other branches of nineteenth-century sculpture, devoted

to non-classical subjects of history and contemporary life, were thought to benefit from the newly discovered laws of classical art that cleansed sculpture from the influences of the Baroque and Rococo. The aloofness of Neo-Classicism from actuality was modified by a new realism that eventually flowered in the French school of sculpture. In Rude's well-known large relief from the Arc de Triomphe in Paris, *Departure of the Volunteers* (1837), a drive and passion recall the fervor of the French Revolution.

Carpeaux: *Neapolitan Fisher Boy (Ill. 304)*

From the second quarter of the nineteenth century on figure sculpture adhered more closely to the model than in any previous period. This meant contemporary uniforms for statues of generals and contemporary costumes for poets or men of learning who were commemorated by figures or busts, often with subsidiary figures to form a group. Major military heroes were represented on horseback and important sculpture was applied to architecture, mostly in public buildings. Except for public monuments the sculptor selected his own subjects and hoped for a purchaser when shown at exhibitions.

Carpeaux reintroduced into sculpture action and facial expression, as in this boy holding a shell to his ear. His elegant craftsmanship and smooth surface are here closer to the spirit of Bouguereau than to Courbet. Realism meant finding the right model and then adhering to it without generalizing the details in the manner of Neo-Classicism.

Antoine L. Barye (1795–1875) enlarged the subject matter of sculpture by specializing in animals, especially in small bronzes. Often two animals are in combat, a lion with a serpent or a tiger devouring a crocodile. The live animals were studied in the zoos and larger groups were placed outside in public parks. The sculptural adornment of the cities still made sense when people took walks for recreation and streets and squares were also used as marketplaces.[40]

Daumier: *Le Stupide, bronze (Ill. 305)*

Painting was the leading art during the nineteenth century, but painters like Daumier, Degas, and Renoir also produced small-scale expressive sculpture. Small bronzes by Daumier excel in a fantastic distortion that is expressionistic beyond anything else produced in his day. As a development out of his own style, it marks a step beyond his graphic work. This

Ill. 304 Jean B. Carpeaux (1827–1875): Neapolitan Fisher Boy.
National Gallery of Art

placid monster is like a regression to an earlier, prehuman stage, a complete absence of intellect, and a denial of what differentiates man from the beasts. Leonardo in his caricature is the impassioned recorder, Daumier the devastating critic who expresses contempt, tempered with compassion.

Rodin: *The Age of Bronze (Ill. 306)*

Realism in sculpture became Impressionism blended with Romanticism in Rodin [p. 295, Fig. 242], the outstanding sculptor of the nineteenth century, who worked in bronze and marble. The living quality he imparted to the surface brought on the accusation that he had made a cast after the model. Rodin replied by pointing out variations introduced for artistic reasons. An arm is not only a rendering of muscles but also a study of ridges and hollows, a more rough than polished surface treatment.

What is called romantic in Rodin is an emotional element. Man at the dawn of civilization clutches his head and raises a hand. Thus poised, representing mankind, he suggests a dimly seen future, symbolizing man's awakened intellect. This is an imaginative concept, probably not a literary interpretation. The idea of a Bronze Age, implying man's forging ahead through the making of superior tools and weapons, may not have received verbal expression before Rodin expressed this idea in clay to be cast in bronze. One of his public monuments in bronze, *The Burghers of Calais,* is a loose

Ill. 305 Honoré Daumier (d. 1879): Le Stupide, bronze. *National Gallery of Art, Rosenwald Collection*

Ill. 306 Auguste Rodin (1840–1917): The Age of Bronze, bronze. *National Gallery of Art, Gift of Mrs. John F. Simpson, 1942*

group of life-size figures. Six men delivered as hostages in 1347 to England in the Hundred Years' War were doomed to die. Each reveals his feelings. Despair, fear, resignation, and firm determination are recorded in action and facial expression. Through Rodin as a teacher, France influenced sculpture in other countries.

Other French sculptors, particularly Bartholomé and Maillol, developed their own styles. Bartholomé in his *Monument to the Dead* in Père Lachaise cemetery in Paris created an impressive memorial. It developed out of a personal monument to his wife, but enlarged is dedicated to the nameless dead. There are no references to religious beliefs; men and women enter the portal together as others approach from either side.

Ill. 307 Aristide Maillol (1861–1944): Daphnis and Chloe, woodcut printed in red. *National Gallery of Art, Rosenwald Collection*

Maillol: *Daphnis and Chloe (Ill. 307)*

Maillol began as a painter but turned to sculpture, inspired by archaic Greek sculpture. He worked on a modest scale, using female models that are devoid of any but a formal content [Fig. 244]. With Maillol, sculpture has overcome the realistic and impressionistic orientation. Whatever inspiration came from archaic sculpture produced no neo-archaic style, as there had been a Neo-Classicism. The sculptor's interest in the figure is here carried on in his graphic work, suggesting the massive breadth of his sculpture.

Sculptors born in the last quarter of the nineteenth century who were not French, abandoning the Rodin tradition, developed further Maillol's emphasis on form. Among those who achieved international recognition are Milles (Swedish), Brancusi (Romanian), Lehmbruck (German), Arp (Alsatian), and Lipchitz (Lithuanian-Polish). Milles begins with simplification; something close to abstraction is reached in Lipchitz and in the Swiss sculptor Giacometti (b. 1901). Paris was their artistic home, wherever they were born or in whatever country they became established. These sculptors worked for an international clientele.

Milles: *Aloe Memorial Fountain (Ill. 308)*

Simplified but not yet abstract form found a monumental expression in fountains. The Swedish sculptor Milles erected them in Sweden [p. 296] and the United States. They form broadly based accents in urban settings or in landscaped parks. The effect is one of a total impression of numerous figures united by the play of jets of water. Here, the *Meeting of the Waters* suggests in the two standing figures the joining above St. Louis of the Mississippi and the Missouri. Whereas equestrian statues appear to have come to an end, fountains are continued in the twentieth century.

Ill. 308 Carl Milles (1875–1955): Aloe [41] Memorial Fountain, bronze, St. Louis. *St. Louis Chamber of Commerce*

Lehmbruck: *Kneeling Woman (Ill. 309)*

Lehmbruck combined Maillol's static composure with elongated proportions and a suggestion of gentle submission and tender resignation [p. 296]. During a comparatively short life Lehmbruck created between thirty and forty statues, all variations of standing, kneeling, or sitting postures of the same type. The statues are life-size and exist in casts in various museums.

Ill. 309 Wilhelm Lehmbruck (1881–1919): Kneeling Woman (1911), cast stone.

Ill. 310 Constantin Brancusi (1876–1957): Mlle. Pogany (1928–1929), marble. *Philadelphia Museum of Art, Louise and Walter Arensberg Collection*

Brancusi: *Mlle. Pogany (Ill. 310)*

The Romanian sculptor Brancusi went through an academic training, was influenced in Paris by Rodin, and in 1913 produced *Mlle. Pogany* in bronze. In this later version, in marble, geometrical simplification is carried to a completely consistent form. Abandoning his Parisian training, Brancusi looked to other inspirations. The nearest to this work are certain Greek Cycladic marble heads. The artistic climate of the first decade of the twentieth century was congenial to non-European influences, as African and Far Eastern. Some such inspiration may account for these curves and ovals in rounded and polished surfaces. Brancusi sculpture appeals as much to the sense of touch as of sight.[42]

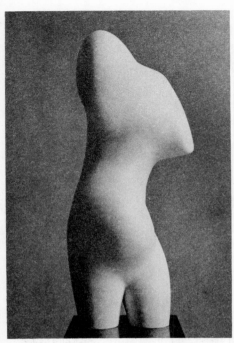

Ill. 311 Jean Arp (b. 1887): Torso (1953), marble. *Smith College Museum of Art*

Sculpture is often modeled in clay by the sculptor, the carving in marble being left to others. Brancusi's work was carved directly. Thereafter Moore and Modigliani, who was also a sculptor, following Brancusi, also turned to direct carving. In the early twenties Brancusi's *Bird in Space*, a sleek and elegant bronze extending to 54 inches, was not recognized as a work of art by customs officials, who tried to collect duty, claiming it to be but a piece of metal. It took a court decision, supported by art critics, to get the piece admitted to the United States as art. Since then "streamlining" has become a common expression.

Arp: *Torso (Ill. 311)*

Brancusi's heads have a man-made mathematical precision. Moore's figures [Fig. 243] suggest they might have been refined out of materials on which nature had also left an imprint. The sculpture of Arp is abstract, but a quality of

380

living form is also retained. The parts that are made to fuse and glide together retain human suggestions. The forward stride of a figure is cactuslike, but is labeled *Bird Skeleton*. What may hint at a squatting torso is termed *Dream Animal*. *Torso* suggests a fragment worn smooth through the action of sand and water. The rounded forms and smooth surfaces are as touchable as they are visual. The shape of the block seems to have inspired the final form, which evolved as worked by the chisel, to acquire a universal appeal. Arp is to sculpture what Miró is to painting. Arp's world of fancy is based on the solid objects found in nature, to which he imparts new meanings. In addition to carving in the round, Arp has also produced abstract reliefs in wood, bronze, plaster, and paper construction, as well as graphic works, woodcuts, lithographs, and drypoints. Arp participated in the artistic revolt of the early part of the century in Munich and Zurich [pp. 291, 294].

Arp: *Abstract Black and White Paper Construction (Ill. 312)*

In all its simplicity, this fluid and soft shape has vitality and complexity. The ease and flow of its contours is stimulating; broad, bulbous shapes contrast with sharp blacks that

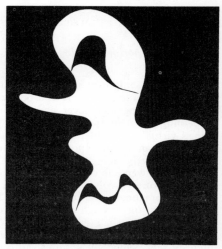

Ill. 312 Arp: Abstract Black and White Paper Construction. *University of Arizona, Gallagher III Memorial Collection*

thin out to nothing, and a faint suggestion of human and animal shapes adds living quality to the design. Rarely has so much vitalizing energy been expressed with such simple means. Here modern art is close to the Neolithic period [Ill. 1]; art links us to our past.

Lipchitz: *Sacrifice (Ill. 313)*

Twentieth-century sculpture is so complex that its variety of styles confuse until order is brought into a multiplicity of aims. Andrew C. Ritchie [43] has pointed out that Rodin considers the object in light, Maillol and Lehmbruck idealize, Brancusi and Arp purify, Lipchitz dissects, and Gabo constructs. Giacometti, Calder, and Lippold relate the object to the unconscious or represent older or newer tendencies. Lipchitz in a bronze entitled *Figure* creates a tower of rectangular sections, a symmetrical structure with penetrations you can see through. Here he retains the figure in repose, in others in movement or extreme agitation. Using themes like *Mother and Child, Prayer,* or *Sacrifice,* he distorts, elaborates, or expands his masses. His *Prayer* (1943) is agonizing distress. *Sacrifice* is a powerful mass about to strike. Both bronzes were modeled in the United States after the world-shaking events related to World War II. Through the potentials of modern sculpture, used symbolically, Lipchitz reacts to violence on the international scene by giving it a transmuted expression.

Giacometti: *Chariot (Ill. 314)*

Giacometti, a Swiss sculptor, added literally another dimension to sculpture, a suggestion of ever-growing, limitless height. In addition, there is a poignant expression of utter loneliness. Rising and never ending, the figure expands and is seemingly lost in space. As the eye reaches the head, the man is virtually separated from his base. The chariot, though also unsubstantial, has enough weight to make the threadlike man seem weightless, a reflection of the air- and space-minded mid-twentieth century.

Architecture involves utility, as a building serves the needs of practical, everyday living. The Industrial Revolution, brought on through advances in science and technology and a growing urban population, introduced new problems [p. 280]. During the nineteenth century the economic interests represented by administrators, lawyers, and realtors were often in conflict with the human interests represented

Ill. 313 Jacques Lipchitz (b. 1891): Sacrifice (1948), bronze, h.
49 in. *Albright-Knox Art Gallery, Buffalo*

by the architects. Even in basic planning, as far as it was
left to the architect, he was not a free agent. In the design
of public buildings, such as museums, theaters, churches, and
municipal buildings, he was overawed by the monuments of
the past. Roman, Greek, and Gothic architecture presented
the architect with ready-made styles, which he adapted to
the needs of the day. What today is commonly called imitation of a historical style was true chiefly of ornamental details. Actually each design still represented a new problem,
the solution of which involved creative activity. Famous
buildings like the Pantheon in Rome furnished the inspiration for the Pantheon in Paris, or the Propylaea in Athens

furnished the model for the Brandenburg gate in Berlin, but the modern structures are not copies of their prototypes.

The nineteenth century made its worst mistakes in unkempt factories and in large apartment blocks, which became urban slums. As old factories became uneconomical they were replaced by modern structures. Restoration of war-destroyed buildings in Europe and urban redevelopment in the United States are beginning to reduce slum areas in large cities.

Eclectic styles, oriented toward the past, dominated nineteenth-century architecture. But from the beginning there were also progressive architects who tried desperately to achieve independence. Among the best known were Soane and Paxton in England, Labrouste and Eiffel in France, Wagner and Messel and others in Germany and Austria. Forward-looking movements that constituted a revolt against traditionalism existed in architecture as in painting and sculpture. A few outstanding buildings must suffice to suggest the general development. A pioneer of the turn of the century related to Art Nouveau (Jugendstil) was Gaudi of Barcelona. This presentation of contemporary architecture will be amplified by an account of the American contribution (Chapter XII). The main styles are Classicism, Romanticism, Eclecticism, and Functionalism. They followed one another in the leading countries—Germany, England, France, and the United States, in that order—but they also overlap and run parallel courses. Thus the beginning of Functionalism goes back to the middle of the nineteenth century, though Eclecticism was then the prevailing style. Each style has its subdivisions, depending on which historical style was followed. Classicism means Greek or Roman (Brandenburg Gate), Romanticism means largely Gothic revival (House of Parliament), Eclecticism includes Renaissance and Baroque phases (Paris Opéra). Functionalism in the early twentieth century emphasized expression of purpose and construction and materials, excluded historic ornament, but retained in exteriors the concept that a facade had to have a base and a crowning feature. The international style of the mid-twentieth century minimizes form, brings out spatial relations, and seeks beauty in surface and material. A recent trend introduces color and form through painting and sculpture, which had long been absent until the modern style appeared to have achieved its maturity.

Ill. 314 Alberto Giacometti (b. 1901): Chariot (1950). *Museum of Modern Art*

Langhans: *Brandenburg Gate (Ill. 315)*

This monumental gate in the Neo-Classic style was inspired by the Propylaea of the Acropolis in Athens [p. 88; Ill. 59, no. 3]. The Roman Doric column was used with an attic and a suggested pediment, showing a measure of originality. The side wings were added some eighty years later, when the old city wall, to which the gate was linked originally, was removed. The attic is crowned by a classic-type quadriga in copper, with a Goddess of Victory by Gottfried Shadow, the best of the German sculptors of the Neo-Classic period.

The "Old Museum" in Berlin by Schinkel (1824), located on an island (or made land), that originally (before World War II) contained Berlin's museums, is raised above the ground colonnade of eighteen Ionic columns screening two stories. It was the first museum on the Continent that was planned as a museum. A broad staircase suggests that he who enters is raised to the higher level of art. In Paris, as a tribute to patriotism, Napoleon started the colossal Arc de Triomphe de l'Étoile (1806–1836) with its magnificent reliefs by Rude.

Ill. 315 Brandenburg Gate (1788–1791), Berlin. Langhans, Architect. *Lufthansa*

Ill. 316 House of Parliament (1840–1860), London. Barry, Architect. *British Information Services*

Barry: *House of Parliament, London (Ill. 316)*

In the second quarter of the nineteenth century, England began its Gothic revival. Gothic, accepted as the natural style for churches, had been only interrupted by the Renaissance influx of the Elizabethan and Jacobean periods [pp. 250–51]; in a sense it was still the national style of England.

Horace Walpole, author and amateur collector of curiosities (King William's spurs and Queen Mary's comb), had kept this interest alive in the eighteenth century through a debased kind of Gothic. Strawberry Hill (1753–1776) and Fontehill Abbey (1796–1814), spectacular and insincere showpieces, of which little remains, represent an early Age of Ignorance of Gothic architecture. This Age of Ignorance was followed by the Age of Plagiarism, represented by A. W. Pugin the Elder (1827), who nevertheless rendered a service through his accurately measured Gothic details. This was also the period (1820–1872) of various fantastic theories as to the origin of the Gothic. Pointed arches were declared to be due to intersection of round arches or inspired by interlacing of branches of trees or hands raised in prayer; or Gothic was Saracenic, brought to Spain by the Moors [p. 142].

The younger Pugin, author and architect, became the more famous and influential. His bias was that the Gothic was socially and morally superior; his own Gothic buildings neglected structure and showed a profusion of ornament and wiry moldings. Literary influences through Sir Walter Scott also contributed to the Gothic revival.

The final culmination was the House of Parliament, which had become necessary when the Old Palace of Westminster was destroyed by fire. It too excited much criticism, but critics agreed on the excellence of the riverfront location. It was also a practical solution to a complex planning problem. Portions of the old structure had to be accommodated to the new building. The perpendicular Gothic was chosen and a fierce battle of styles (1838–1872) began, the House of Parliament aiding the Gothicists against the Classicists. Criticisms were as follows: Thousands of square feet of carving were used for woodwork, iron, encaustic tile, painted glass, by men trained to copy; the result was dead and mechanical. The Gothic style was carried through with a vengeance, complete in every detail, down to the inkpots and umbrella stands (Sir Kenneth Clark). Because the style was Gothic it was wrong, the Classic should have been used (Hamilton).

Ruskin, writing in the finest English style, advocated Italian forms, bands of red and yellow brick, disks of marble, billet moldings and voussoirs of arches in color. He laid the foundation for what has been called the "Streaky Bacon Style." Ruskin, author of *The Stones of Venice*, had a university education and had studied botany, geology, and particularly Venetian architecture. He was a good draftsman but did not know construction, and he mixed aesthetics and ethics. Architects considered Ruskin a vain and uninformed enthusiast, absurd and irrational.

Paxton: *Crystal Palace (Ill. 317)*

Bridges rather than buildings were the forerunners for the use of structural steel in building. Railroad viaducts of great height, built of stone, spanned deep valleys, particularly in the Alps. In their boldness and elegance they rivaled the finest engineering work of the past. They were built by technically trained engineers whose names have usually not been handed down to posterity.

The great triumph of the mid-nineteenth century was the Crystal Palace, of iron and glass, built for the First World's Fair, 1851, in Hyde Park, London. It was the largest pre-

Ill. 317 Crystal Palace (1851), London. Paxton, Architect. *Smith College Museum of Art*

fabricated and demountable structure of standardized parts ever built (main area 1,848 by 408 ft.), and was reerected in changed form at Sydenham (1852–1854). It rose in three steps with flat roofs and a higher barrel-vaulted transept constructed of arched trusses. Some slight "capitals," part of the cast-iron shafts, were too minor to detract from the basic functional concept. Color was used, an all-over light blue with red and yellow for girders and columns. Paxton, who is credited with the building, was neither an architect nor

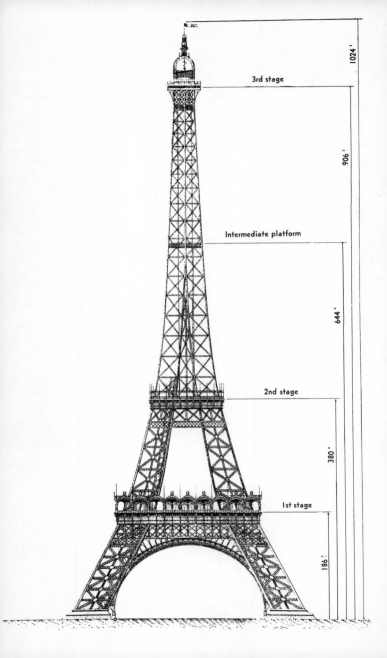

3rd stage

Intermediate platform

2nd stage

1st stage

1024'

906'

644'

380'

186'

an engineer, but a horticulturist in touch with engineers and engineering contractors who supported his project. The name "Crystal Palace" came from *Punch*.

The great achievements of nineteenth-century structures remained practically anonymous, as the great steel-constructed halls such as the Halles des Machines of the Paris Exhibition of 1889. The name of the designer, the engineer Cottancin, is not generally known. "With a height of 150 ft., a length of 1,400 ft., and a span of 385 ft., it must have conveyed an unprecedented feeling of space and weightlessness" (Pevsner, 1936). It was taken down in 1910. One architect, Henri Labrouste, used exposed iron shafts for the reading room of the Bibliothèque Ste. Geneviève in Paris. Labrouste was an architect; of the engineers, only Eiffel became famous.

Eiffel: *Eiffel Tower (Ill. 318)*

From a broad quadrangular base this iron tower rises in a fine sweeping curve to a height of 1,000 ft. There had been inspiration for such a tower in earlier projects on paper, but no actual precedent. The Eiffel firm had erected high piers for bridges that proved that even higher towers in iron construction were possible. Criticism against the proposed tower came from those who felt that the tower would belittle such monuments as Notre Dame, the Arc de Triomphe, and others. The broad base and four separate corner columns, which joined above the second platform, gave stability. The open spaces below the platforms and the curve of the legs were responsible for its structural soundness as well as its beauty. Its essential purpose was to demonstrate to the world the scientific, technical, and artistic achievements of the French Republic. The elevators, installed by Otis, an American firm, contributed their share to the success of the tower at the opening of the Fair, May, 1889 (Robert M. Vogel, 1961).

A belated appreciation has come to the works of the nineteenth-century engineers in our own day. At the same time it has become fashionable to belittle the eclectic styles as uninspired. As often happens, the sons berate the fathers but stand in admiration before the works of the grandfathers.

Ill. 318 Eiffel Tower, Paris, 1889. Gustave Eiffel, Architect. *Illustration: Smithsonian Institution*

Ill. 319 Grand Stairs, Paris Opéra (1861-1874). Garnier, Architect.
French Government Tourist Office

Garnier: *Grand Stairs, Paris Opéra (Ill. 319)*

Eclecticism and expression of use unite successfully in the Paris Opéra. The eighteenth century had taken over the concept of the princely stage of the Renaissance. The nineteenth admitted the general public to its theaters and opera houses, but the horseshoe plan of the auditorium still favored the boxholders. In the Paris Opéra more space was allowed for the foyers and grand staircases than for the auditorium itself. Parisians of the Second Republic under Napoleon III required a luxurious setting for the social side of operagoing. Scenery and stage sets had likewise developed such elaboration as to require a large stage of great height. Each section, stage, auditorium, and grand staircase, is expressed on the exterior and is revealed when seen from the sides. Admittedly every architectural motif of the Renaissance and Baroque, lavishly combined with sculpture, is here recapitulated with a total effect of elegance and splendor.

Gaudi: *Casa Mila (Ill. 320)*

The real innovations of a modern style were the iron bridges, railroad stations, exhibition halls, and steamships. Auguste Perret in 1903 designed the first reinforced-concrete construction, an apartment house in Paris (Rue

Franklin). Utility alone controlled these productions; decoration played no part. These works came into existence without benefit of artists. When the young architects around 1900 called for a new style, they did not think of iron bridges, but of a style comparable to the great styles of the past. But only a new style of ornament resulted, curvilinear and flamelike. Long, sweeping lines like ribbons curved around windows and doors, intertwined on walls, book covers, and stair railings. It was called Art Nouveau and began in Brussels in 1893 with Horta.[44] In the eighties Henry van de Velde had stressed the importance for architecture of form and structure; the inspiration had come from William Morris. Though function was expressed in chairs, the linear ornament was not related to the machine so admired by these innovators. It was largely surface decoration based on individual inventiveness. The German Jugendstil, named after the illustrated magazine *Jugend* (Youth), published in Munich, popularized the style. Art Nouveau was a transition to the modern style and marked a definite break with eclecticism.

Another departure from revival styles in architecture produced a highly individual expression in Barcelona, Spain. In Gaudi's apartment buildings curves take on a structural feel-

Ill. 320 Casa Mila (1905–1910), Barcelona. Antonio Gaudi (d. 1926), Architect. *Mas, Barcelona*

ing. Though based on modern techniques, architecture is given a sculptural expression, as if modeled in clay. Chimneys and stair towers on the roof are bottle-shaped with surfaces that are scooped out or spiral twisted. Each story is treated individually. Iron balconies luxuriate as if inspired by some fantastic vegetation. In spite of freely spaced openings unrelated to verticals, the total facade, in its mass effect, has the vigor of a product of nature, rooted to the ground it stands on. Gaudi's other works in Barcelona include the unfinished Sagrada Familia Church, more sculpture than architecture.

Gropius: *Bauhaus (Ill. 321)*

A truly modern architecture, as distinguished from Art Nouveau, came into being with the Turbo Factory in Berlin (1909) by Peter Behrens. Through the use of steel and glass, and without ornament, a monumental simplicity was attained. During the period between the two world wars, German architecture assumed the lead through the reorganized art school of Weimar, transferred to Dessau (1925). Here Walter Gropius created a practical laboratory of design based on a new concept. All the arts involved in building and home

Ill. 321 Bauhaus (c. 1925), Dessau, Germany. Walter Gropius, Architect.

furnishing were taught for the purpose of developing type forms for industrial productions. Gropius, the spiritual heir of Morris, for the first time related the handcrafts to industrial processes. With National Socialism the period ended and its leaders left Germany, Gropius himself settling in the United States.

Henceforth modern architecture took the position that the new forms are the inevitable products of the intellectual, social, and technical conditions of our age. On the practical side architecture concentrated on economical solutions to achieve the most utility with the least means at the lowest cost. Fabricated rather than natural materials were preferred, as they could be designed to meet specific needs. They were also of uniform quality and could be factory assembled to reduce cost. Standardization of parts used in quantity, already in common use in the manufacture of tools and machines, was expanded to building construction. Unnecessary variation in types of buildings was avoided by limiting them to a few types.

The materials are steel and concrete; loads are carried on inside steel columns that with floors and flat roofs constitute a steel structure. Walls are of glass held in by steel mullions to form curtain walls. In this shop building, the curtain walls rest on cantilever beams that project out from the main structure. Light floods the interior; a bridge across the street, mirrored in the glass wall, connects shops with classrooms and library. The vast space of floors is no longer obstructed by fixed bearing walls and can be subdivided by lightweight partitions that are movable as the changing uses of a building may dictate.

According to the nineteenth-century aesthete, each type of building should express its purpose—monumental (public building), inviting (railway station), gay (theater), etc. Actually this never quite happened, but the total heritage from the historic past was looked upon as a vocabulary to be used for expressive purposes. With Gropius architecture became truly functional, abandoning all intention of reflecting individuality. Neither use nor nationality need be indicated except as the practical requirement of each structure modified its plan and external appearance.

Modern architecture reflects basic human needs rather than specific aspirations. A spacious interior that could serve the needs of commerce, study, or recreation equally well would express structure. Thus schools may not look too different from factories. Modern architecture applies dignity to all human needs, and architects assume a social responsibility that aims at better living conditions for all. Architecture, like costume during the nineteenth century, now tends to establish a common level of adequacy for all men in one international style. Climate and basic regional differences rather than national or personal preferences on the part of the designer make for variations. Moreover, this has not resulted in monotony or uniformity.

Le Corbusier: *Maison de l'Unité d'Habitation (Ill. 322)*

This French architect of Swiss origin has contributed to a functional and international style but also has an individuality of his own. He became known as an advocate of Functionalism who called the attention of architects to the beauty of the airplane, automobile, and steamship. As a painter, associated with Cubism, he carried geometric shapes and the use of color into the design of houses. He is primarily (though not exclusively) a designer in the field of domestic architecture, both private homes and apartment buildings. His name is identified with the rectangular flat roof and box type of exterior. His buildings are raised on short columns, cantilevered at both ends, and provided with continuous ribbonlike windows, as in his Savoy house (Poissy-sur-Seine, 1929–1931). Proportions, color (blue and red), and fine textures of expensive materials contribute a decorative effect. Such houses were luxury products for wealthy clients.

This well-known apartment block was planned to house a community. It includes shops and community services and uses the flat roof for a playground and sun terrace. It was planned as one of several blocks to be widely spaced in a park. Though Le Corbusier coined the expression of a house being "a machine for living," his designs are by no means mechanical, but sensitive to purely artistic appeals. Modern interiors, light in color and open to sunshine and air, suggested to the people of the twenties and thirties the clinical atmosphere of hospitals. Compared with the overfurnished, cluttered rooms of the Victorian era, these practical furnishings, lean, shiny, and often of metal, seemed cold and unsentimental.

His earlier houses in their brilliant textures and rectangular shapes contrasted with nature. In the Church of Notre Dame du Haut (1955) in France, Le Corbusier introduced bulging mass and rounded, curving surfaces. The inspiration may have come from houses of fishermen on islands in the Mediterranean, representing an adjustment of architecture to environment.

The Scandinavian countries took to modernism in architecture after the Stockholm Exhibition of 1930, designed by Gunnar Asplund. With a whole section of town presented to the public, to compare with the picturesque manner of Ostberg's Town Hall (Stockholm, 1923), the more modern style was adopted. But the use of natural materials—wood, stone, brick—for buildings on a domestic scale resulted in a modified version. In designing housing for workers and fine furniture through methods of mass production, Sweden has set an example for other countries.

Finland, through Alvar Aalto, made important contributions through the use of reinforced concrete and timber. Aalto's work, like Frank Lloyd Wright's in the United States, demonstrates that modern architecture has the breadth that permits regional variations without compromising basic principles.

Ill. 322 Apartment building (Maison de l'Unité d'Habitation, 1947–1952), Marseilles. Le Corbusier (b. 1887), Architect. *M.R.U.*

Dierschke and Wildometz: *Kestner Museum (Ill. 323)*

Since the close of World War II the devastated countries of Europe have presented architects with unusual opportunities. Sections of towns have been rebuilt completely and individual buildings have been restored and modernized. This was in addition to new building that became necessary without direct relation to war damages, including such major works as Nervi's Sports Arena in Rome. Outside of Europe modern architecture has gained a foothold in South America, particularly in Brazil; in India; and in other countries.

The Kestner Museum has a peculiar interest because it shows one use of modern architecture not yet touched upon. It is not unusual to completely encase an old building that is old-fashioned in a new exterior to make it look like an up-to-date new building. Glass panes set in a concrete grid-iron wall in a rectangular plan produced a virtually all-glass screen around the old two-story building, which had lost its rear wing due to war damage. This new concrete glass box almost doubled the total area of the building and preserved the old front and rear elevations as part of the exhibit. The translucent glass panes filter the light, making blinds unnecessary. This method of encasing behind a glass or metal curtain whole facades that in their cluttered and restless design no longer suit the modern taste is gaining ground everywhere.

Ill. 323 Kestner Museum (renovation, 1958), Hannover. Werner Dierschke and Rudolf Wildometz, Architects.

XII

Art in the United States

The Red Indian was the first to arrive on the North American continent; his art has therefore first claim to the name American. Actually when we speak of American art we mean the art of those who have settled in the United States during the last three and a half centuries.

For almost half of the time span we are here considering, the populated eastern seaboard was a colony of England. During that period American culture was basically European. The new environment changed old habits, but it took time for differences to make themselves felt. The vastness of the country and its varying climates were reflected in art, and traits other than the purely English appeared. To climate and racial background we must add the temper of a new political system with its emphasis on freedom and equality of social status. Freedom of opportunity helped the amateur painter more than the artist aspiring to professional training. There were few art schools, and the artist turned to Europe for training and inspiration. The styles through which European art passed we find also in the United States. Europe, with its artistic heritage dating back to Greece, remained the spiritual fountainhead well into the twentieth century.

After the discovery of America, over a century passed before there were permanent English settlements in Virginia (Jamestown, 1607), Plymouth (1620), and Massachusetts Bay (1630). The Colonial period itself was almost as long as the national period that followed. The greater part of colonial art belongs to the eighteenth century. Colonial art, depending on Europe, is close to its European models. Painters like West and Copley are claimed by England as well as the

United States. Most of the works of art here discussed are of the national period. As the nation grew, the arts by the end of the nineteenth century had expanded through the whole country, but the first half of the twentieth century is here emphasized.

America was temporarily delayed in the pursuit of the arts, but the gap has been closing with the maturing of the country. As Western art is becoming world art, individual expression in art counts for more than national origin. Where the arts are linked to technology and science, as in architecture, city planning, and the industrial arts, they contribute to improved living conditions.

American architecture, like the architecture of Europe, remained retrospective during the nineteenth century until modern technology forced architecture into a contemporary pattern. Pioneers aiming toward a modern architecture existed in this country, as they existed in Europe. Frank Lloyd Wright was appreciated in Europe before he was recognized in the United States. Stone sculpture began early in the nineteenth century and won for itself official approval in the wake of the patriotic fervor of the day. Engraving on wood and metal and lithography began early and continue today, though reduced in scope. The political cartoon has developed since the nineteenth century and flourishes today. The graphic arts in various media enjoy a spectacular prominence in contemporary illustration; they are in constant focus. Photography began as a craft; today it rivals the printing press and is also practiced as an art. But painting everywhere has been the most flexible medium for artistic expression.

Reality seemed more important to American painters than ideas. Historical painting, for a time so prominent in Europe, was less important in America. An introspective approach also existed, as in Romantic painting, but was less general than Realism. Whether contemporary painting has come to the end of a cycle, is on the threshold of a new development, or is only going through a temporary change of style may be left for the future to determine.

Copley: *The Copley Family (Ill. 324)*

During the colonial period there was little painting, but by the time the most important colonial painter, John Singleton Copley, had painted his own family, American painting had caught up with England's. Drapery and landscape background are in the British tradition, as well as costumes and the stone pedestal. This artificial setting was something Eng-

Ill. 324 John Singleton Copley (1738–1815): The Copley Family (c. 1777). *National Gallery of Art, Purchase Fund, Andrew W Mellon Gift*

lish painting had taken over from Van Dyck, who helped to create the English portrait style.

Copley's style is part English and part American. The easy sweep in the folds of the orange-colored scarf of the little girl who looks at us with such determination is English, and so is the transparency of the sheer material contrasting with the heavier fabric of the blue skirt of the mother, seated in an upholstered armchair. The children are lively; they smile, lift their heads, and stretch out their hands. They are individualized in the way they express themselves, more so than is common in the traditional English portrait style. Particularly American is the emphasis on the heads—the strong, confident Copley and the forceful and rugged older man, his father-in-law.

Copley is the culmination of a long line of American colonial portraitists. Before Copley settled in London, he had painted portraits in America, all excellent character studies. The American public expected a convincing likeness, and that was best expressed by a painstaking rendering of features. Realism was as characteristic of early-American painting as diversity of styles is today.

Durand: *Kindred Spirits (Ill. 325)*

After independence had been won, the young nation began to take possession of the continent; this growth is reflected in painting. The early devotion to portraiture spread and kept many painters in business. Whatever else the painter selected to paint, he did to please himself, but for sales he had to compete in the open market. The best painters turned to incidents from daily life and to nature, like Durand and Bingham, who applied the European technique to American subjects.

By the mid-nineteenth century the eastern part of the United States had been brought under cultivation; the natural environment was no longer a threat. Man was impressed by nature's grandeur; Emerson wrote, "Nature is a language I wish to learn so that I may read the great book that is written in that tongue." Nature, formerly used as a background for portraits, here exists in its own right. Artists took time to study trees and foliage and to record every twig and leaf.

Durand's realism was romantic, intended to represent nature as wild and untamed, but the human element was also important. Durand painted this scene in memory of his friend and teacher the painter Thomas Cole, who stands to the left of William Cullen Bryant, the contemporary American poet. Illumination is a new acquisition, a delicate atmospheric tone combined with outline. Color is secondary; drawing is more important.

Like other nineteenth-century painters Durand made a living as an engraver of other men's paintings. These copper engravings were reproduced in popular journals and helped to make the landscape school of painting known.

Bingham: *Fur Traders Descending the Missouri (Ill. 326)*

This painting reflects the westward expansion of the country before there were transcontinental railroads. This was as yet unsettled country, inhabited by Indians. Bingham is the best of the painters of the frontier. As a boy he began by copying engravings, and then took lessons from Chester Harding, who did not have much training himself. At the age of twenty-six Bingham had a few months of art-school training at the Phildelphia Academy of Fine Arts; before that he had never seen an original painting.

Though Bingham had received little formal art-school training, he was by no means a primitive painter. He painted

Ill. 325 Asher Durand (1796–1886): Kindred Spirits (1849).
New York Public Library

the woodsmen and trappers who lived off the fur trade in the
Rocky Mountains and carried the pelts down the Missouri
River to sell in the St. Louis market. In this painting Bingham
expressed the solemn grandeur of the great river in its solitude and luminous smoky atmosphere.

During the second half of the nineteenth century, with
Whistler, Sargent, and Mary Cassatt, American painting took

Ill. 326 George Caleb Bingham (1811–1879): Fur Traders Descending the Missouri (c. 1849). *Metropolitan Museum of Art*

on a cosmopolitan character. French painting had progressed from one style to another. Classicism and Romanticism were being replaced by Impressionism when Whistler appeared in Paris. These American painters benefited from the liberating atmosphere of Paris, but each one was molded by influences of his own choosing.

Whistler: *The White Girl (Ill. 327)*

Whistler was the most original American painter, who influenced Europe as much as he was influenced by Europe. *The White Girl* caused a sensation in Paris in 1862. In this painting the full-length portrait reappeared in a new style that owed something to the sweeping lines of the Japanese woodcut. From Velázquez, Whistler took and adapted subtle harmonies of color, avoiding strong hues and replacing them with neutral tints, here silver-gray, and a near-white background. In place of individual modeling, undisturbed areas are separated by a few contours. Russet brown in the hair, dull blue in the rug, and grays are the only hues. Whistler emphasizes arrangement, color, and line for their decorative value; to get a likeness was only one of several aims. For storytelling, Whistler substituted color harmony; landscape paintings in which twilight became the subject matter rather than a literal transcription of nature were labeled "nocturnes." After the French Revolution artists had become self-conscious and rebellious because of lack of popular support. Whistler made "art for art's sake" a creed that became part of the artistic dogma of the age [p. 279].

Ill. 327 James A. McNeill Whistler (1834–1903): The White Girl (1862). *National Gallery of Art*

Sargent: *Repose (Ill. 328)*

This painting is a portrait in which the figure is engulfed in gray satin and dull gold; the head is but a small accent in the midst of precious fabrics. Light is shed over silk drapery that is convincingly painted with a glitter of high-lights and depth of shadow, a demonstration of skill and good taste.

Like Whistler, Sargent formed his style on that of Veláz-quez and expanded the technique of Frans Hals. He became the acknowledged practitioner of the slashing brushstroke; dexterity in handling the brush became his chief claim to fame. Sargent was born of American parents in Italy but spent much of his life in Paris and London. He shares with Whistler the distinction of having captured the attention of the international art world. As a brilliant technician he made American painting admired and respected. Sargent is not fashionable today but assumes his place in the history of painting.

Sargent based his style on the old masters. Homer [p. 302,

Ill. 328 John Singer Sargent (1856–1925): Repose (1911). *National Gallery of Art*

Ill. 329 Albert Pinkham Ryder (1847–1917): Toilers of the Sea (exhibited 1884). *Addison Gallery, Andover, Mass.*

Fig. 249], Eakins [p. 301], and Ryder [p. 301] were also exposed to European art, but developed their own styles. Eakins, in contrast to the self-taught Homer, is the scientific draftsman who studied all his life. Eakins' realism is less imaginative than Homer's; his subjects retain all the drabness of the original scene as in his painting *Max Schmitt in a Single Scull* (Metropolitan Museum of Art). The oarsman is ungainly; the river, the bridge, and the shore are as drab as only Eakins could represent them, but his skill as a draftsman is almost photographic. Today Eakins stands out as one of America's most honored painters.

Ryder: *Toilers of the Sea (Ill. 329)*

Ryder was another self-taught painter, a romantic visionary, as different from the robust Homer as from the exacting Eakins. Ryder had some art training but depended mostly on his imagination. Ryder's moonlit seascapes, painted around 1900, are still in the romantic nineteenth-century mood. In the midst of New York City he lived a lonely life. He worked with extreme slowness, and he wrote poems to accompany his paintings. *Toilers of the Sea* is an imaginative re-

Ill. 330 John Sloan (1871–1951): Sixth Avenue Elevated at Third Street (1928). *Whitney Museum of American Art*

creation of the sea, an arrangement of dark areas against a medium-light night sky. The surface is smooth, thick, and enamellike, with little color. At one time he painted decorative lacquer screens. Ryder was not typically American; he would have been an eccentric in any country. After he had been neglected for years, his rise to popularity brought on many forgeries. As there were not enough genuine Ryders available, the fakers imitated each other, so that Ryder's style has become obscured.

Sloan: *Sixth Avenue Elevated at Third Street (Ill. 330)*

John Sloan marks a departure for the first generation of twentieth-century painting. He was one of a group of eight younger painters, mostly of New York City, who took their subjects from city life [p. 303]. This painting shows the New York elevated railroad above a street scene with arc lamps and illuminated shop windows. Realism consists in the discovery of the life in the street as a new subject, but the impressionistic technique continues the brushwork of the Manet tradition.

Hopper: *Early Sunday Morning (Ill. 331)*

Hopper belongs to the second generation of this century. He too paints scenes of New York that bring out the loneliness of the big city. His paintings of streets or interiors convey a feeling of emptiness; the crowds have gone, or, as here, the city has not yet come to life. Hopper's realism differs from Sloan's. His is more imaginative and suggests a critical attitude toward the shabbiness of the street. At the same time, the painter gives his street an attraction gained from his handling of sunlight and shadow so that what is ugly in reality becomes poetically transformed.

Evergood: *Lily and the Sparrows (Ill. 332)*

With Evergood realism is tinged with fantasy; the realistic and imaginative merge but never combine to form an objective illustration. His paintings satirize, glorify, or in some illusive way comment on something observed or experienced. The waxen face of the little girl at a tenement window, looking up to the sparrows, is based on what the artist had observed while walking "under the old El between Sixth Street and West Broadway" (Bauer, 1960). The warm vermilion

Ill. 331 Edward Hopper (b. 1882): Early Sunday Morning. *Whitney Museum of American Art*

color of the sharp-edged wall, too thin to be convincing and of brick incredibly clean, enframes the smiling head to give a strange detachment to the scene.

Stieglitz: *From the Shelton, Looking Northward (Ill. 333)*

With the camera Stieglitz interpreted the massed sunlight and shadows as they momentarily became lodged between the steel and stone of the tall buildings of New York. In this

Ill. 332 Philip Evergood (b. 1902): Lily and the Sparrows (1939). *Whitney Museum of American Art*

Ill. 333 Alfred Stieglitz (1864–1946): From the Shelton, Looking Northward (1932), photograph. *National Gallery of Art*

late period all human elements are eliminated. Stieglitz was a perfectionist, often making a hundred or more prints from a single negative before selecting the one that satisfied him. This was not a matter of obtaining mechanically a perfect print from a technically perfect negative. Instead he sought the print "that would carry the irresistible emotional impact" (Doris Bry, 1958).

Among the several styles that existed side by side during the period between the two world wars, the so-called Ameri-

Ill. 334 Georgia O'Keeffe: (b. 1887) Black Hollyhock and Blue Larkspur. *Philadelphia Museum of Art*

can Scene painters [p. 304, Fig. 250] and the Precisionists (or Immaculates) [p. 303] stand out as groups that have something in common. Artists are individualists; the critics invent the labels and classify the styles. Georgia O'Keeffe and Charles Sheeler have been appropriately called "precisionists."

O'Keeffe: *Black Hollyhock and Blue Larkspur (Ill. 334)*

Here are flowers monumentalized to a grandeur and a sense of perfection that has no parallel in art or nature. A robust strength replaces delicacy, and yet the natural form is retained, full-blown and magnified. An element of unreality is also present, and a loving care in the way soft transitions are related to lush curves, sharp edges, and vaporous fadeouts. The eye wanders from the star-shaped corona of the hollyhock, enclosing a center like a floating bubble, to the undulating buds below, thinned out or rounded off. What look like familiar shapes subtly turn into strangely living forms, mingling but disconnected and no longer holding together as hollyhock and larkspur. Natural forms to an extent have become abstract and more dynamic than the shapes that originally inspired them.

Sheeler: *Incantation (Ill. 335)*

These geometric shapes of pipes, rods, tanks, and valves
speak a language not too dissimilar to the floral patterns of
Georgia O'Keeffe. Straight lines, angles, and large volumes
are contrasted with smaller, sharply accented shapes. The
magic of industry is lifted chantlike above the reality of
appearances into a superreality. But unlike surrealism, this is
a rational transformation of the visual world. It is a sober
and serious performance, and affirmation of, not a turning
away from, the facts of the modern world. Such artists as

Ill. 335 Charles Sheeler: (b. 1883) Incantation (1946). *Brooklyn
Museum*

O'Keeffe, Sheeler, Demuth (*My Egypt,* Whitney Museum of American Art), Spenser (*Wake of the Hurricane,* Walker Art Center), Lozowick in lithographs, and others, though aware of Cubism, created a new style that also had its cubes, cylinders, and spheres. The glorification of the spirit of the machine age rather than the theory of a Cézanne produced forms different from Picasso's individual inventions. These painters got their start in the twenties but continued to paint in their own styles even after World War II, when Abstract Expressionism began to take shape [p. 307]. This new American painting received worldwide attention in 1958, when an exhibition, organized by the Museum of Modern Art, was shown in eight European countries. An exchange exhibition between Moscow and New York made contemporary American painting known in the U.S.S.R.[45]

De Kooning: *Woman I (Ill. 336)*

De Kooning said "Art never seems to make me peaceful or pure. I always seem to be wrapped up in the melodrama of vulgarity . . . any kind of painting, any style of painting, to be painting at all, in fact, as a way of living today, it is exactly in its uselessness that it is free."[46]

Mental discomfort indeed shrieks from this canvas, suggesting that it functions as a kind of mental therapy for the painter.

In many canvases de Kooning has dealt with the subject Woman, literally destroying one canvas after another. The purpose of painting seems to have been its physical destruction. The sense of fury that emanates from this hideous image made an impression on European painting when exhibited at the Venice Biennale (1954). Willem de Kooning was born in Holland and now lives in New York.

Arshile Gorky (1905–1948) said the eye was made to cast a conducting wire between the most heterogeneous things, as in his painting *Agony.* This is perhaps an early example of painting that dealt specifically with the emotions, making emotions themselves the subject matter of painting.

Barnett Newman's painting *Adam,* about eight feet high, could be taken as a new beginning for art. Four vertical stripes, vermilion and maroon, seem to be Newman's reply to an earlier stripe pattern by Mondrian in which the rectangle is divided horizontally and vertically (Ill. 292). Newman takes issue with this kind of World War I geometry and substitutes his version (which he says has no geometry at all) in order to get rid of geometry. Newman, conversing

Ill. 336 Willem de Kooning (b. 1904): Woman I (1950–1952).
Museum of Modern Art

with Mondrian, aims for freedom from tradition and the
discovery of new principles. What they are he does not say;
artists rarely do. In traditional aesthetics this painting has
little meaning. Such paintings seem unimportant in the opinion
of those who say "Art divorced from life and human interests
is left with too little to communicate"; to others modern art
reveals a vast perspective of new possibilities. This may become clearer as we become oriented in the new styles.

Ill. 337 Franz Kline (1910–1962): Painting No. 7 (1952). *The Solomon R. Guggenheim Museum*

Kline: *Painting No. 7 (Ill. 337)*

Kline's paintings have the texture of paint smeared on in broad smudges that seem like defiant barriers. What the painter may be striving for is "emotional intensity" (*The New American Painting,* Tate Gallery, London, catalog, Museum of Modern Art, 1959). In the catalogs organized by the same museum for eight European countries, Kline is quoted as saying he wants to have "part of that noise," meaning presumably part of an active life. To attract attention is the aim of all art, but it is not usually stated in such outspoken language. What artists say about their work helps us to understand contemporary painting. Grace Hartigan *(Bathers)* says: "I want my canvases to resist . . . I don't want the spectator to walk into my canvas. I want an art that is not abstract and not realistic." Her canvas fulfills that demand; it resists recognition but invites exploration.

Robert Motherwell (b. 1915) wants to base his paintings, large canvases, on ethical concepts from which the aesthetic flows. He desires to venture everything for nothing—to renounce flattery. Other ethical values that painters respect are integrity, sensitivity, passion, dedication, sincerity. For Motherwell painting is a compensation for life's frustration. Without ethical consciousness a painter is only a decorator.

Pereira: *Drawing (Ill. 338)*

This artist is known for her abstractions based on geometry but aimed at spatial concepts. In this drawing we admire
the exuberance of the swinging line. Enough convincing anatomy is retained to give full play to the expression of movement and the incisive quality of line itself.

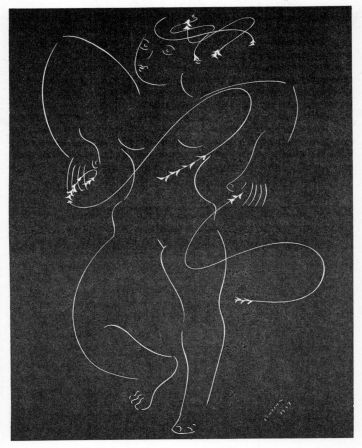

Ill. 338 I. Rice Pereira (b. 1907): Drawing (1957). *Barnett Aden
Gallery, Washington, D.C.*

Fels: *Price Control (Ill. 339)*

A sensuous quality of the medium, the feel of the woodcut, is perhaps the first attraction of this print, as well as the consistent character of the line itself. Beyond the basic appeal we grope for meaning hinted at by the title. A faintly human suggestion is part of an unstable contraption that is loosely mechanical. A peanutlike shape dangles out in front, but is

Ill. 339 C. P. Fels: Price Control, woodblock (c. 1944). *San Francisco Art Association*

Ill. 340 Misch Kohn: Processional, detail, wood engraving (c. 1956). *University of Illinois and the artist*

disconnected from the infirmly seated abstraction. From the dunce cap on top an angular motif projects, but it points back to the place of origin of the suspended shapes. A short plumb line at the rear suggests an uneasy attempt at control. The total impression as one seeks to link up the parts amounts to total frustration. If that be so, irony and bitter satire, but disguised, seem to be the intent. C. P. Fels is from California.

This design, in black and white, and those to follow are in a variety of styles, by artists from different backgrounds.

Kohn: *Processional (Ill. 340)*

About one sixth of a horizontal panel-shaped print is here reproduced. This intricate technique defies reduction so that only a small portion can approximate the effect of the whole print. Most of the effect of the parade, with its horsemen, here eludes us. Texture, brilliance, and a wealth of motifs combine to suggest figures, landscape, and sky. Realism in massive blacks is muffled and does not interfere with an involved and marvelous richness. The slashing whites of the sky create a sense of energy and vibration. A mosaic of small white dots against black produces a medium tone that tends to quiet the agitation. Vigor and technical competence link this print with the best traditions of wood engraving. The artist lives in Chicago and teaches at the Institute of Design at the Illinois Institute of Technology.

Tobey: *Space Ritual No. 7 (Ill. 341)*

This design depends for its appeal on an expression of spontaneity and freshness. And yet the spattered ink spots

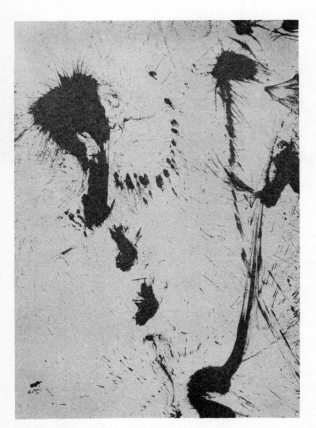

Ill. 341 Mark Tobey (b. 1890): Space Ritual No. 7, Sumi ink on Japanese paper (1957). *University of Illinois and Willard Gallery*

are not wholly accidental. Major accents are spaced and spatter is combined with marks produced through dragging ink across the paper. A delicate texture barely visible recedes from the foreground to suggest distance. This suggestion of depth is aided by the two streaks that cut across and under others; expansion and drift exist side by side. Through spatter, the American technique of painting by bodily action [p. 307] is combined with Orient-inspired inkbrush calligraphy.

Tobey, living in Seattle, Washington, studied in this country and in Shanghai under a Chinese artist. He is widely known in the United States and in Europe.

Lissim: *Marine Motif (Ill. 342)*

Here textures create ornamental effects according to a well-understood tradition for which there are masterpieces in many styles. Even where an artist works in a traditional mode, each new design is an adventure. Decorators like Lissim produce designs to be translated into color, cut in crystal, or applied to silver or porcelain. Paper designs, more akin

Ill. 342 Simon Lissim: Marine Motif (before 1958), design. *Courtesy of the artist*

to working drawings, are intermediate steps; the total design counts for more than the quality of the individual line. This is a magnificent pattern, held together by structural boundary lines.

Simon Lissim is known on two continents as a designer for porcelain; he teaches in the art department of City College, New York.

Pfeiffer: *Back Yards (Ill. 343)*

A modern emphasis on artistic concepts as the real content of art is also noted in black and white illustration, as in this linoleum cut, with its lights, darks, and textures. What is represented is incidental; composition establishes a bond among diverse subjects. Simplification in art has always been a means; in our own time it became an end in itself, and is so conceived by the artist. Hilde Pfeiffer, formerly in charge of a commercial-art studio, lives in Chicago.

Ill. 343 Hilde Pfeiffer: Back Yards, linoleum cut. *Privately owned*

Keeping a Watch on Man's New Moons (Ill. 344)

The nineteenth-century painter often added to his income by working for engravers. The twentieth century developed this sideline into a profession in its own right. Commercial art, advertising illustration, and photography absorb many of the graduates of art schools. Commercial art, as distinguished from the fine arts, has its own legitimate sphere. It tends to be conservative, but is affected by the innovations of modern painting. Occasionally, outstanding painters also serve advertisers without compromising with their art. The Container Corporation of America has used some striking advertisements in color in the modern manner. Here IBM suggests the use of a computer without depending on realism. As a result this advertisement stands out by virtue of its distinguished simplicity. It uses print and a line design in a combination that appeals to the imagination.

Herblock: cartoon (Ill. 345)

Art in its role of communicating ideas through dramatic shortcuts is here demonstrated. Many who followed the aftermath of the 1960 presidential election in the United States must have enjoyed seeing politics brought to their own doorsteps. Republican spokesmen, still hoping for victory, kept up a steady complaint hinting at illegal practices at the polls without actually insisting on taking steps that would settle the case one way or another (shown here by ballot box suggesting a recount). The cat at the open door on a wintry morning, unwilling to enter or go away, insists on being a nuisance. The immediate appeal of a cartoon is intended to carry conviction and to influence attitudes on the problem it raises. This cartoon is also a magnificent illustration [47] of a wintry morning with the cold blast streaming into the house through the open door [p.308, Ill. 129].

From painting and the graphic arts we turn to sculpture.

Powers: The Greek Slave (Ill. 346)

During the first half of the nineteenth century Neo-Classic sculpture had its American representatives in Horatio Greenough (1805–1852) and Hiram Powers. The statue of Greenough's Washington (Smithsonian Institution), seated Zeuslike in classic drapery, reflects a monumental effort of creating an image of heroic grandeur. Powers in his Greek

keeping a watch on man's new moons To trace an orbiting earth satellite as it hurtles through space, an IBM computer must match its capacity of over 250 million calculations a day against the tiny sphere's speed of 18,000 miles an hour. By processing data supplied by the satellite's radio, the computer pinpoints within a few miles the satellite's position days ahead, and predicts within seconds when it will pass over any point on earth . . . simultaneously keeping the same close watch on satellites launched previously. • Other IBM computers are performing tasks of similar difficulty for science and industry by handling mathematical chores which were impossible even yesterday, yielding information never before within man's reach. **IBM** ®

INTERNATIONAL BUSINESS MACHINES CORPORATION

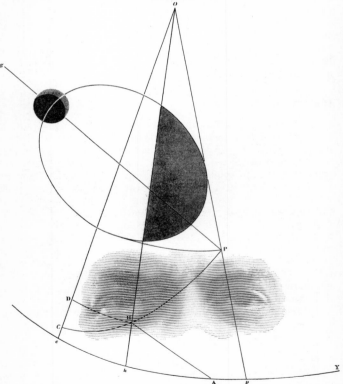

Ill. 344 Keeping a Watch on Man's New Moons, from an IBM (International Business Machines Corporation) advertisement. *IBM*

slave aspired to the grace of the *Venus dei Medici* [Ill. 48]. The daring of exhibiting nudity was revolutionary, but the sweetness and purity, properly certified by a delegation of ministers before the statue was exhibited, reassured the public. American sympathy for Greece since her war of liberation (1821–1829) also helped the effect, as iron chains against soft flesh produced pleasant shivers. This statue was shown at the Crystal Palace (Ill. 317) in London.

Ill. 345 Herblock (Herbert Block, b. 1909): cartoon, December 16, 1960. *Washington Post Company*

"I Don't Want In OR Out——I Just Want to Sit Here and Yowl"

Ill. 346 Hiram Powers (1805–1873): The Greek Slave (c. 1851). *Corcoran Gallery, Washington, D.C.*

Saint-Gaudens: *Adams Memorial (Ill. 347)*

Saint-Gaudens was the outstanding American sculptor of the second half of the nineteenth century. His bronze statue of Lincoln, in Chicago's Lincoln Park, is impressive. The tall, gaunt Lincoln is shown standing in front of an ornate chair. The plain base and the empty chair set a pattern of contrasts that the figure, with its bowed head, dominates. Vigor, sobriety, and distinguished elegance produce an arresting effect. All elements are calculated to give a sense of intimacy as well as grandeur. This is one of the great achievements of modern sculpture.

The Adams Memorial strikes a note of solemnity and brooding. Drapery is used with breadth and simplicity and contributes to the power and originality of the statue. Except for the architectural carving of the moldings of the background there is nothing to suggest a historical style.

For most of nineteenth-century American sculpture the reader should turn to Lorado Taft's (1860–1936) excellent ac-

Ill. 347 Augustus Saint-Gaudens (1848–1907): Adams Memorial (1891), Rock Creek Cemetery, Washington, D.C. *Brown Brothers*

count. With Taft, a representative sculptor in his own right, American sculpture turned for inspiration to Paris and away from Rome (since 1876). His *Solitude of the Soul* (Art Institute, Chicago) in the Rodin tradition is a work of distinction. Its symbolism was part of the Expressionism of the period, as legitimate for its day as Abstract Expressionism is for ours.

Ill. 348 Gaston Lachaise (1882–1935): Standing Woman (1932), bronze. *Museum of Modern Art*

Lachaise: *Standing Woman (Ill. 348)*

Whatever influences may have helped develop the style of Lachaise, they were not Italian, French, or American. Such massive rotundity, expansive in breadth but lightly posed and of proud bearing, goes beyond Maillol. The triumphant upsurge in posture, in its muscular strength, quite unfeminine, seems to declare this heroic female as the master of the universe. What the primitives could not have created, Michelangelo would not have dreamed of, and Rodin was not interested in, Lachaise has accomplished—a feminine Hercules dedicated to the perpetuation of mankind.

Lipton: *The Hero (Ill. 349)*

Lipton's *Hero* opens up into a burst of wild gesticulations beautifully related in sharp-edged points and disks. They rise in triumph on the left but also descend in modest resignation. A bundle of emotional gesturing forges ahead but retains a sense of orderly composure. The ups and downs, bends and sways, seem to conjure up faintly human touches. Such meanings read into the work were probably not consciously sought by the sculptor. However abstract, a work of art is meant to be communicated to an audience but need not confine the beholder to a narrow interpretation. We may discover it in a meaning of our own or see it in dehumanized form.

Gabo: *Linear Construction No. 2, Variation No. 1 (Ill. 350)*

With Gabo's constructions we have no other choice. This is pure form and shape to trap light in a delicate and scintillating web. Here is precision with transparency and glitter, creating form bounded by mists. Form originates out of the void, and in disappearing originates new shapes, a ceaseless wonder. Looked at from one side, effects appear; viewed from the opposite side, they seem to gain in strength, or else we have become more aware of what first escaped us. Gabo does for space and light with curved lines what Mondrian does in planes with straight lines.

Roszak: *Whaler of Nantucket (Ill. 351)*

Roszak has said that his sculpture is meant to suggest a primordial strife and struggle, brute forces that produce and destroy life (Ritchie p. 37). Though it is an abstract, one does not quite know of what it is abstracted—a living force emanates from this massive and yet sleek monster.

As modern art progressed, national characteristics tended to merge in general styles. Painting in the United States before World War II still reflected this country. The school of action painting, including Pollock and others, originated in the United States; but style no longer identifies an artist's citizenship. This is particularly true of architecture and sculpture. Some of our best-known sculptors were born outside the United States and may or may not have studied abroad. They were identified with this country after having settled here. Lachaise, Roszak, and Gabo are of this group. Other sculptors are native-born, like Alexander Calder, David

Ill 349 Seymour Lipton (b. 1903): The Hero (1958), nickel-silver, h. c. 7 ft. *Inland Steel Building, Chicago*

Ill. 350 Naum Gabo (b. 1890): Linear Construction No. 2, Variation No. 1. *Addison Gallery of American Art, Andover, Massachusetts*

Smith, Richard Lippold, and Seymour Lipton. What brings them together is the way they deal with form. When so considered, differences of country, birth, or residence become negligible. Twentieth-century sculptors, including Americans, could have been discussed as a group, forgetting nationality.

Ill. 351 Theodore Roszak (b. 1907): Whaler of Nantucket, steel.
Art Institute, Chicago

Lipton, Gabo, and Roszak have two things in common:
the human figure has been abandoned, Roszak retaining a
hint of a living thing; and all use metal in novel ways. No
longer dependent only on carving stone or modeling clay
for bronze casting, new metals are cast (Roszak), cut (Calder), or used as wires (Gabo) or rods (Smith) for linear and
spatial constructions. Art schools have added foundries to
their modeling rooms. As Michelangelo attacked marble
with hammer and chisel, so a modern sculptor applies his
blowtorch to metal.

Borglum: *heads of four American Presidents (Ill. 352)*

The preceding examples suggest the course of sculpture in
the United States to the extent that a few works can suggest
a trend. The two remaining works of sculpture here referred
to add little to the development of sculpture and are usually
omitted in histories of art. They are the Statue of Liberty
in New York Harbor and Mount Rushmore. These works are
of historical and patriotic importance and their social significance overshadows the artistic interest. Dedicated as we
are to advancing the artistic-aesthetic importance of art, we
may also accept some few works even though they may

stress, in their large bulk, social rather than artistic values, in the narrow sense of the word.

The Statue of Liberty by the Alsatian sculptor Bartholdi, one of the colossal statues of history (152 feet high on a pedestal nearly 150 feet high), was made in Paris and shipped in parts to New York. Here the copper plates were shaped by hammering into wooden patterns. This outer shell is supported by a steel framework designed by Gustave Eiffel, famed for his Eiffel Tower. A sense of the magnitude of the statue is gained from the dimensions of the arm holding the torch, which is 42 feet long and 12 feet in diameter at the point of greatest thickness. The Colossus of Rhodes [p. 78] was not as high, and it had only a staircase inside; the Statue of Liberty also has an elevator. The symbolic significance of the Statue of Liberty, of freedom and opportunity, is worldwide. Its profile looming out of the mist of New York Harbor has probably impressed more people than any other statue seen thereafter.

The heads of four presidents are blasted out of the granite of Mount Rushmore.[49] Each head measures about 60 feet from forehead to chin and is twice as high as the head of the great Sphinx [pp. 36–37]. Repeated blasting removed

Ill. 352 Gutzon Borglum (1871–1941): heads of George Washington, Thomas Jefferson, Theodore Roosevelt, and Abraham Lincoln, granite, Mount Rushmore, Black Hills, South Dakota, 1943. *National Park Service*

the rock within six inches of the final surface. The work was done by measuring, drilling, blasting; carving in the usual sense of the word did not enter in (Gilbert C. Fite, 1952). After the death of Gutzon Borglum, the sculptor who had made the model and supervised the work, his son Lincoln Borglum took over. The face of Theodore Roosevelt has never been completed because the funds, largely federal appropriations, ran out. The heads have not yet stood long enough to become as well-known as the Statue of Liberty. Both monuments are as much a triumph of modern technology as of art.

From sculpture, we turn to architecture. When the first settlers arrived in North America they brought with them the building habits of the mother country. Modified by climate and available building materials, the European style was continued in the New World. The Spanish colonies in Florida and New Mexico preceded the English on the Atlantic seaboard. The new nation grew out of the New England colonies, and the architectural history that started there is continuous and representative of much of the country. Architecture was essentially domestic, continuing the Gothic during the seventeenth century. With an abundance of wood, clapboards were used to cover the filled-in spaces between the timbers. The overhanging second stories had ornamental carved "drops" in the corners, and the windows small leaded casements. Steep roofs continued on one side into a lean-to on the ground floor.

During the eighteenth century the colonies had developed more nearly to the level of the mother country. Philadelphia compared favorably with most cities in England except London. The Classical style, now called Georgian, had been established, and a more comfortable mode of life followed the hardships of the formative period. Handsome facades show that the colonial builders just before the Revolution had made the details of the Classical style their own. Though the larger monumental structures were still absent, the town houses of the well-to-do merchants, less expansive than English manor houses, were furnished in excellent taste.

Chippendale furniture (Ill. 353)

In the years before the Revolution furniture and silver made in the colonies equaled Europe's standards in craftsmanship and good design. Furniture followed the English designs published by Chippendale. The more ornate types were simplified, the more exotic were avoided. Compared

Ill. 353 Chippendale furniture: highboy, chairs, tables. *Philadelphia Museum of Art*

with the carved and gilded French styles from Louis XIV through Louis XVI, carved but not gilded, and less pretentious mahogany reflected the democratic character of English society. American taste preferred restraint, but retained carved cabriole legs and pierced back splats. The chest on chest (highboy) with curved pedimented top ending in scrolls and with carved finials originated in the colonies. During the Colonial and Early Republican periods, cabinetmakers in Boston, New York, Philadelphia, Baltimore, Newport, and Annapolis developed specialties as to structure, carving, and marquetry inlay. American silver can be seen in various museums, including the Museum of Fine Arts in Boston, with its silver by Paul Revere. All large museums have collections of American decorative arts.

Outstanding among such museums is the Henry Francis du Pont Winterthur Museum (Delaware), which covers the period 1640–1840. Colonial Williamsburg (Virginia) is the most important preservation project; it includes restored and reconstructed public buildings, shops, taverns, houses, exhi-

Ill. 354 Independence Hall (south side, 1732–1759). Andrew Hamilton, Architect. Tower built 1749–1753; east and west wings, Supreme Court or Congress Hall, added 1782. *From* Freedom and Union, *July, 1947, and Iris Beatty, artist*

bition buildings, and furnishings. The Henry Ford Museum and Greenfield Village, Michigan, is a vast area containing many original historic structures, each a museum in itself. One of its main buildings is an architectural reproduction of the facade of Independence Hall at Philadelphia.

Hamilton: *Independence Hall (Ill. 354)*

Of public buildings built in the colonies before the Revolution, Independence Hall in Philadelphia is architecturally as well as historically the most important one. Old State House in Boston (1728) is the oldest and may have been designed in London (Tallmadge); Faneuil Hall in Boston (1741) is gaunt and awkward.

Independence Hall, built of brick, had a basic unity with its environment as it was when Philadelphia was built of brick. It has a domestic flavor in the central building, its wings recalling Southern manor houses like Westover with its dependencies. The larger scale and the addition of a tower, borrowed from the church, mark the public character of the building. The tower, set out in front, is loosely connected to the building by the cornice. Stone quoins, trims, and panels, used on the street side, were omitted on the park side to save expense. The designer was a lawyer by profession; architects of the period were likely to be amateurs. To complete the building took 27 years.

This drawing by Iris Beatty was published in 1947 and demonstrates the high level of magazine illustration in the mid-twentieth century. Without being a mechanical drawing it expresses the architecture and suggests the parklike setting. Foliage treated as a dark pattern against the sky is balanced by masses of trees receiving direct sunlight.

McBean: *St. Paul's chapel (Ill. 355)*

Colonial architecture was best in houses and in occasional public buildings like Independence Hall. Churches afforded opportunities for architectural design in basilicalike interiors and entrance porticoes as in St. Paul's. McComb added the steeple (1794) following Gibbs (design of St. Martin-in-the-Fields, published 1728). The design problem in the tower is in the transition from the square below to octagon above, from widely spaced columns to a closed grouping and a lengthening of proportion in the upper stories. The church is of stone in the English manner.

Thornton and Walter: *Capitol, Washington, D.C. (Ill. 356)*

The Early Republican period, between 1776 and 1820, produced a wealth of fine buildings in Salem (Massachusetts), Boston, New York, and Washington, often by designers who were not trained architects. Thomas Jefferson (1743–1826), an architect by avocation, designed his own house at Monticello, planned the University of Virginia, the state capitol, and various houses in Virginia. After achieving independence the young republic turned to antiquity for inspiration; Jefferson became the father of the Classical Revival in the United States. Washington selected Dr. William Thornton, born in the West Indies and educated in England, to design the new Capitol on a spot selected by L'Enfant, the creator of the plan for the city of Washington. After the Capitol was burned by the British (1814) it was rebuilt by Latrobe according to original designs. As it stands today, the Capitol is superior to the various competition drawings, which show the inex-

Ill. 355 St. Paul's Chapel, New York, 1764–1766. Thomas Mc-Bean, Architect. *Wurts Brothers*

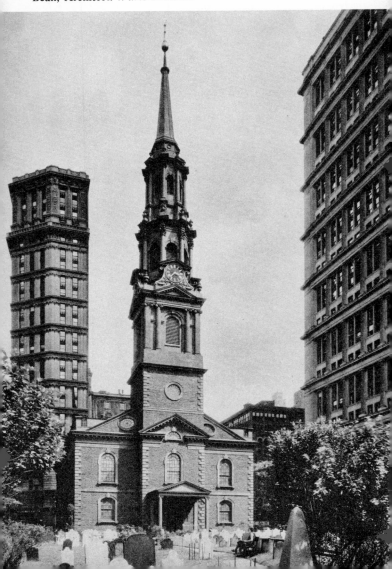

Ill. 356 Capitol, Washington, D.C., 1792–1802. William Thornton, Architect. Wings and dome, 1851–1865. Thomas V. Walter, Architect. *Smithsonian Institution*

perience and lack of training of the competitors. Bulfinch of Boston improved the design, and the painted cast-iron dome was added during the Civil War period. Because of its location on a hill, the total impression is only gradually revealed when approached from the wings, the broadly based dome holding the masses together. Thornton, Hallet, Latrobe, Bulfinch, and Walter all worked on the design. Various state capitols used the idea of a central dome, but hardly with the same success as in Washington. Latrobe worked on interior details. In an endeavor to achieve a purely American style, he designed the Indian corn capital for the Supreme Court stairway.

Renwick: *Smithsonian Institution (Ill. 357)*

A Gothic Revival paralleled the Greek Revival and was used by Richard Upjohn in Trinity Church. Ruskin's polychrome Gothic also left its mark in the United States.[50] Renwick's Smithsonian, more Romanesque than Gothic, combines arches, turrets, and towers with billet moldings and every other Romanesque detail. It is so picturesque that one

Ill. 357 Smithsonian Institution,
Washington, D.C., 1846.
James Renwick, Architect.

structure looks like a row of buildings that happened to be
connected. Certain parts, like the turrets here illustrated, are
as effective today as they must have appeared to the architect when he had the design on the drafting board. Having
stood for over a century, this building has become a historical monument.

Richardson: *Woburn Library (Ill. 358)*

Eclecticism, inspired by French Napoleonic Renaissance
and English Victorian Gothic, did away with the last of the
Greek Revival. After the Philadelphia Exposition of 1876 a
flood of new building followed the rapid growth of popula-

Ill. 358 Woburn Library, Massachusetts. H. H. Richardson (1838–
1886), Architect. *After Vogel (1910)*

tion. Paris became the center for young architects seeking instruction. Hunt designed the new mansions of the "Gilded Age" in Newport, New York, and North Carolina ("Biltmore"). Richardson, designing in the Romanesque style, became the country's outstanding architect. He used historic forms to new effects. Salamanca Cathedral is recalled in his Trinity Church in Boston (1872), of polychrome sandstone, which made him deservedly famous. His large public buildings, town houses, and libraries, low lying and wide arched, using dark stones to gain effects of texture, created a "Richardsonian" style. Unhappily, it was the poor imitations of the master's style, spreading west from Boston, that made the Romanesque known the country over.

Sullivan: *Wainwright Building (Ill. 359)*

Ill. 359 Wainwright Building (1890–1891), St. Louis, Missouri. Louis Sullivan (1856–1924), Architect. *From* The Idea of Louis Sullivan, *by John Szarkowski, University of Minnesota Press, 1956*

Ill. 360 Schlesinger-Meyer Building (now Carson, Pirie, Scott Department Store), Chicago (1899–1904), detail of ornament. Louis Sullivan, Architect. *From* The Idea of Louis Sullivan, *by John Szarkowski, University of Minnesota Press, 1956*

Sullivan: *Schlesinger-Meyer Building, detail (Ill. 360)*

A new school of Functionalism that arose in Chicago in the eighties aimed to give expression to the steel frame within masonry walls, which were no longer self-supporting. Stone was replaced by terra-cotta, which was given a surface pattern to suggest that it was used as a filling, not as a structural material. Continuous vertical piers of brick emphasize the height in contrast to the late-nineteenth-century tendency to disguise the height of commerical buildings. Tall buildings became desirable through a concentration of business in the downtown areas of the larger cities. Here the two lower floors are divided by a horizontal band, and the top ends in a projecting cornice. This style represents a revolutionary step away from the cast-iron columns on store fronts or the stone or terra-cotta columns used to disguise the steel-skeleton structure. Sullivan credits the idea of a steel frame structure to an architect named Buffington, who did not carry out the idea; how it originated, nobody knows.[51]

Sullivan also developed a very individual type of ornament carried out in metal in a dazzling profusion of intertwining and carving stems, leaves, buds, and scrolls. It is placed in front of glass, above the main entrance.

McKim, Mead and White: *University Club (Ill. 361)*

The conservative trend of American architecture is well represented by this firm. Whichever style, Italian Renaissance or Colonial, seemed best suited for a particular problem was selected. For this building the Florentine palace of the Early Renaissance furnished the inspiration. The reserve and dignity demanded for a private club was well expressed; originality in the choice of details was not the aim. Even though the vocabulary was familiar, the total design still had to be created. This resulted in a distinguished exterior in which proportion, refinement, and a contrast of plain areas against rustication, carved panels, and sculptured keystones play a part. The choice of a style, whether conventional or modern, does not determine the quality of the design.

Gilbert: *Woolworth Building (Ill. 362)*

The design of tall buildings in the United States has gone through perhaps four periods; we are now in the fifth. (1) The first stage, 1881–1890, used cast-iron and cage construction with masonry, with a maximum height of twelve stories. This was still the pre-skyscraper period, of which the Tribune Building in New York (1883), by Richard Hunt, is an example. (2) The second stage, 1884–1913, used a steel skeleton construction. The Chicago Home Insurance Build-

Ill. 361 University Club, New York. McKim (d. 1909), Mead and White (d. 1906), Architects. *Courtesy the architect*

ing by. Jenny (1884), since demolished and replaced, is an early example, the Woolworth Building a late example. Its soaring quality made the building a popular favorite in the years preceding World War I. (3) Between 1913 and 1926 the Classical style reached a climax; in 1916 the New York Building Zone Resolution was adopted; the American Radiator Building, New York (1924), represents this period. (4)

Ill. 362 Woolworth Building, New York (1913). Cass Gilbert (1859–1934), Architect.

Between 1926 and 1939 a trend toward simplicity started with Eliel Saarinen's second-prize design in the Chicago Tribune competition (1922). The Empire State Building, the Daily News Building (1930), and Rockefeller Center (1931–1932) date from this period. (5) Since the end of World War II our most recent period has started, in which a new technique and new materials give emphasis to glass, color, and reduction of any sense of bulk. The floor plans are the province of specialists who get the utmost utility out of every square foot of space.

The Woolworth Building is a compromise between Traditionalism and Functionalism. Gothic detail is suggested in the profiling of piers, in ornamental tracery, and in pinnacles and turrets where the roof and tower burst into a final termination. All this is a last echo of the Late Gothic. The Functional basis of the design is clearly stated in the verticals, which may be wide or narrow, for no structural reason, but because a varied play of light and shadow still has its attraction. Dormers and a steep roof conform to no Functional expression, but demonstrate that Gothic and modern together are not incompatible. Design no longer simulates stone masonry but frankly admits being lightweight terra-cotta. As a transitional stage, the Woolworth Building deserves its claim to distinction. Compared with the flamboyant Gothic of the Middle Ages, the early-twentieth-century variation is but a later and more attenuated form of Gothic.

Hood and Howells: *Daily News Building (Ill. 363)*

After the publication of Eliel Saarinen's Tribune Building design, skyscraper design emphasized rectangular masses, setbacks, and a final elimination of cornices and horizontal divisions. Thereafter the complete expression of the steel skeleton was no longer insisted upon; functionalism became one of several guiding principles; flexibility and universality became important.

Grand Foyer, Radio City Music Hall (Ill. 364)

This theater lobby illustrates the space-creating function of modern architecture. The great staircase, wide, ample, and inviting, adjusts itself unobtrusively to the interior as if absorbed by the space. The mural decoration on the end

Ill. 363 Daily News Building, New York (1930). Raymond Hood and J. M. Howells, Assoc., Architects. *Museum of Modern Art*

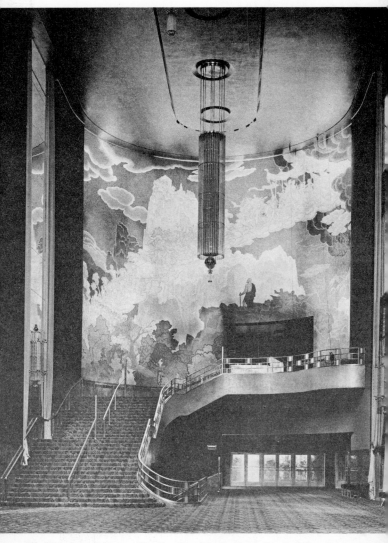

Ill. 364 Grand Foyer, Radio City Music Hall, Rockefeller Center, New York (1931–1932). Mural by Ezra Winter: Fountain of Youth. *Rockefeller Center*

wall adds to the spatial illusion, enhanced by the tall wall mirrors. The lighting fixtures, though large, seem more in evidence here than they are in reality when they are lighted. Baroque (Ill. 214) and nineteenth-century grand staircases (Ill. 319) were elaborated with space-filling decoration; modern stair-halls are self-effacing containers, sleek, empty, and waiting to be filled with crowds.

Mies van der Rohe: *Crown Hall (Ill. 365)*

Four widely spaced girders express uninterrupted open space on the interior; the roof is suspended from these girders. In external appearance and in the single interior space, universality is expressed. It is this universality that is especially emphasized by Mies van der Rohe. Though it was planned to serve as a drafting room for students, when it was nearing completion the Chicago fire inspector classified the school building as an industrial building and specified that as such it must have a sprinkler system. This illustrates the flexibility by which a building constructed for one use can be readily converted to another, one of the characteristics of modern architecture. Light, temporary partitions that bear no weight and are movable subdivide the space as the present use may require. The building is a steel and glass volume, finely proportioned, simple, and in scale to its use. The word "scale" as used here means that the building looks its size, as related to the human figure. A floating platform between main floor and basement allows for two broad, easy flights of steps. Transparent and opaque glass, two doors, venetian blinds, and the ceiling seen through the glass give variation and take the place of ornamentation. This latest trend, which matured after World War II but perpetuated earlier European trends, represents one of the aspects of architecture as an international style.

Harrison and Abramovitz: *Alcoa Building (Ill. 366)*

As the expression of the structural frame was gradually abandoned or modified, the exterior curtain wall could take on a variety of designs. Aluminum panels (6 by 12 ft.) one eighth of an inch thick have square windows punched out and fitted with aluminum frames. Between the windows the panels are stamped in a pattern of triangular facets for greater rigidity; a gunmetal gray is an integral part of the aluminum. The main entrance is fitted into the L-shaped plan as a separate four-and-a-half-story lobby of glass and

Ill. 365 Crown Hall, Illinois Institute of Technology (1956), Chicago. Mies van der Rohe (b. 1886), Architect. *Illinois Institute of Technology*

aluminum suspended from the building frame. To make cleaning possible from the inside, the windows are pivoted in the center so that the outside can be turned in. On entering the lobby, the visitor is impressed by a sense of spacious grandeur, made effective by planting, which draws the outside into the building itself.

Mies van der Rohe and Johnson: *Seagram Building (Ill. 367)*

The contemporary trend in tall buildings is shown at its best in the Seagram Building and Lever House (Skidmore, Owings and Merrill, Architects), almost opposite on Park Avenue. Both give over a portion of the site to a spacious approach, made attractive by landscaping, shrubs, and trees. The Seagram Building also has pools and fountains. The building setback allows space from which to see the building, an unprecedented innovation where land values are extremely costly. The metal-and-glass structure is here reduced so that total volume achieves the utmost with the least materials. This is a triumph of achieving the most through the least—glass, thin piers, and panels in a bronze color. A comparable effect is expressed through green in Lever House. The colored glass is heat and glare resistant. The panels, a few inches thick, the modern substitute for walls, fill in the space between the structural-steel pieces and are made of thin stainless steel, porcelain-enameled steel 3/8 inch thick, or

Ill. 366 Alcoa Building, Pittsburgh (1952). Harrison and Abramovitz, Architects. *Aluminum Company of America*

aluminum, usually painted. All materials are prefabricated (produced in factories) and assembled in the construction of the building. The use of natural materials, finished by the craftsman and cut and fitted to each building, has practically disappeared.

Many types of buildings are constructed of prefabricated parts selected from commercial catalogs but designed as individual structures by architects. Prefabricated houses are also on the increase. Engineering and industry have taken over the work of the craftsmen, but the architect remains the master designer and coordinator in charge of the total construction.

Eero Saarinen: *staircase (Ill. 368)*

In this staircase open risers of travertine rest on a central beam. To this single support the stairs are attached like vertebrae to a spine. The austerity and economy of modern architecture are here demonstrated in an open spaciousness that has replaced volume and mass. Steel and glass replace supporting masonry walls. The Technical Center—low-lying, horizontal laboratory, office, and shop buildings—is the outstanding accomplishment of industrial architecture. There are 25 buildings in a parklike setting of 155 acres of lawns, shrubs, and trees (over 13,000). Glazed bricks are used, a material that has hardly appeared in architecture since the late Babylonian period. They are blue above the windows in one building and yellow in another.

The curtain walls, visible in the distance, consist of greenish, glass windows in aluminum frames and porcelain-enameled metal panels two inches thick. This outer skin of porcelain-enameled steel is bonded to a honeycomb core filled with granular insulation.[52] Maximum flexibility and economy are obtained by using a five-foot module throughout the design, including furniture. This means all construction is based on multiples of five. Every unit, from window frames to ceiling panels, is prefabricated. The building is weatherproofed by using mechanical sealing gaskets developed for the windshields of automobiles. As in fifteenth-century Florence under Brunelleschi, so today engineering leads in architecture; details are technical rather than ornamental.

Ill. 367 Seagram Building, New York. Mies van der Rohe and Philip Johnson, Architects. *Ezra Stoller*

Ill. 368 General Motors Technical Center: staircase, Administration Building, Warren, Michigan. Eero Saarinen, Architect. *General Motors*

Harrison and Abramovitz: *church interior (Ill. 369)*

Since architecture has come to its maturity in a new, truly modern style, it has dared to link up again with past traditions. With new materials and new construction methods, something of the spirit of the Gothic interior is revived through the use of stained glass. Precast concrete panels (devised by Felix Samuely, an English structural engineer) form a monolithic structure. The glass is carried up in a continuous expanse from ground to ridge. Sides and roof merge and envelop, tentlike, the interior space. A massive lectern fits in with the boldness of the structural effect, with an incredibly slender cross rising to an impressive height. Austerity in the structure combines with decoration in the glass to produce an extraordinary effect.

Ill. 369 Interior, First Presbyterian Church (1958), Stamford, Connecticut. Harrison and Abramovitz, Architects. *Ezra Stoller*

Steel construction, Senate Office Building (Ill. 370)

The steel frame of a modern office building in its general appearance has not changed since it was first used. It is the design of the curtain walls, which fill in the open spaces, that determines the exterior appearance of the building after its completion.

Kahn: *National Bank of Detroit (Ill. 371)*

White Cherokee marble, stainless steel, and glass are used in the exterior curtain walls. The stainless-steel windows (pivoted for easy cleaning) are set in frames that above and below the window are porcelain-covered metal panels 2½ inches thick. Other varieties of black and veined marble as well as granite are used for floors and in lobbies and other places where their beauty contributes to the richness of the effect. The interior of this building, like those of the other buildings here presented, has an unostentatious splendor

Ill. 370 Steel construction, Senate Office Building, Washington, D.C. *Arthur Ellis, Washington Post Company*

Ill. 371 National Bank of Detroit, 1959. Albert Kahn, Architect.
National Bank of Detroit

that is overawing in its smooth and polished reticence.
Elaboration of form has been eliminated; color and texture
replace carving. The least visible features—electrical installa-
tions, heating, air-conditioning, and elevatoring—often absorb
one third of the cost of the building.

Wright: *Lucius Boomer House (Ill. 372)*

Modern architecture using prefabricated materials has given
us an international style. Buildings either are basically horizontal or vertical slabs used for factory, office, and apartment buildings or are lightweight metallic (Fuller) domes
for auditoriums. This "machine geometry" is also modified
by aesthetic principles and is less impersonal than its critics
admit. The personal contribution of the architect is most
apparent in regional styles that use the rough textures of
natural materials. Oblique lines replace the severe horizontals,

verticals, and right angles of the international style of the twenties. Frank Lloyd Wright was a leader who promoted in his designs for small houses a "humanistic" approach to architecture without abandoning the advantages gained by modern technology. Local stone is used in this house, made to fit into the stark desert background; the roof is featured; its overhangs cast shadows. Textures in wood and stone contribute to a sense that the man-made is not foreign to the natural environment. This house fits into the landscape as a chalet fits the Swiss mountains or a teahouse fits Japan.

Bank buildings in Washington, D.C. (Ill. 373)

The stylistic changes from Eclecticism around 1900 to Functionalism around 1950 are here illustrated in branch offices of a metropolitan bank. The same client followed the trend and demanded changes in design according to the prevailing styles of each period. In the earliest example (1), when the bank did not yet occupy the whole building, the six-story structure disguises height. Like the Classic order, a building also had to have a base, a main central portion corresponding to the column, and a crowning feature in the entablature. The main entrance is featured and treated independently. It includes suggestions from several historic styles. (2) Historic motifs are used to emphasize monumentality; a single colossal order dominates, but variety is

Ill. 372 Lucius Boomer House (now residence of the director, Phoenix Art Museum). Frank Lloyd Wright, Architect. *Phoenix Art Museum, Arizona*

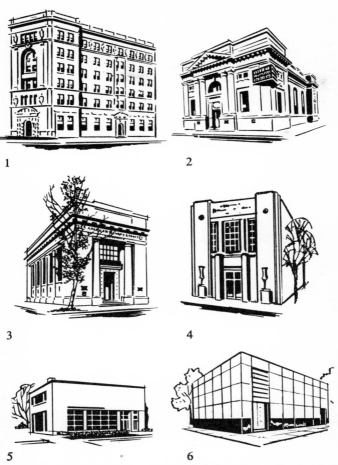

Ill. 373 Development of architectural design during the first half of the twentieth century: American Security and Trust Company buildings in Washington, D.C. (1) Central office, 1902. Appleton P. Clark Jr., Architect. (2) Northeast office, 1912. Same architect. (3) Southeast office, 1924. Same architect. (4) Uptown office, 1930. George Oakley Totten Jr., Architect. (5) Woodley Park office, 1949. Mills, Petticord and Associates, Architect. (6) "O" Street office, 1951. Irwin S. Porter and Sons, Architect. *American Security and Trust Company*

not abandoned. The entrance has a pediment, and projection and recession are carried into the side elevation. (3) When diversity no longer satisfied, what was monumental also had to be simple. (4) Architects of the thirties, tired of the Classic style, which was also expensive, tried the new simplicity featured by the more daring, progressive architects of Europe and the United States. Their example set a new trend. (5) By the middle of the century even this more subdued manner, with the emphasis on expression, was no longer economical. Buildings served only the needs of the first owner, but upon change of ownership interior remodeling became necessary. (6) During the last decade commercial buildings began to look like boxes, often depending on artificial illumination. Simplicity and the use of prefabricated materials made for utility rather than expression of interior arrangement or the temporary use to which a building was put. Today banks, libraries, museums, commerical buildings, or factories express essentially what they have in common as space-enclosing structures. The interiors are flexible and are easily adjusted to suit new uses.

Lincoln Center, model (Ill. 375)

Lincoln Center is culturally and architecturally the most important urban group of buildings in the United States of the mid-twentieth century. The arched facade of the Metropolitan Opera with its solid glass windows (90 ft. high), flanked by the Repertory Drama Theater, dominates the plaza. As never before, the performing arts are here united in monumental structures, designed in the contemporary modern style. Arched facades, glass windows, and flat roofs give the groups a unifying expression. The somewhat different character of the Juilliard School is given a more sober expression because it seems proper for an educational building not to compete with the severely grand manner of the major structures. A new flexibility underlies the design of the opera with its four stages, arranged to appear before the proscenium by push-button control. The boxes so typical of the traditional opera house have been eliminated. A "theater-in-the-round" effect is contained in the projecting stage of the repertory theater, but so constructed that the stage can be retracted to resemble the type of conventional proscenium theater. The total seating capacity of all auditoriums is estimated at 12,000.

Ill. 374 Plot plan of Lincoln Center, New York.

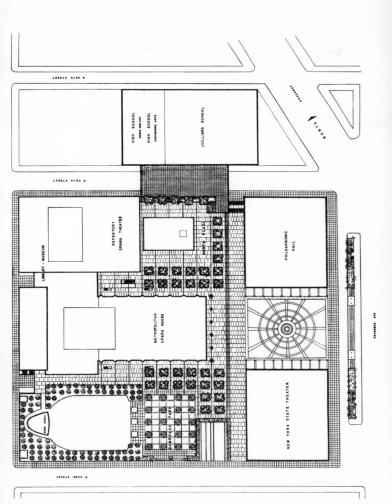

Plot plan of Lincoln Center (Ill. 374)

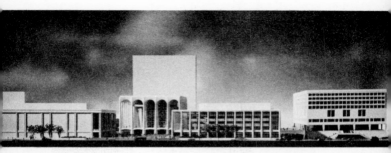

Ill. 375 Lincoln Center for the Performing Arts, Inc., model. Architects: Philharmonic Hall, Max Abramovitz; New York State Theater, Philip Johnson; Metropolitan Opera House, Wallace Harrison; Repertory Drama Theater, Eero Saarinen Associates; Library-Museum, Skidmore, Owings and Merrill; Juilliard School, Pietro Belluschi. *Lincoln Center*

Bronx-Whitestone Suspension Bridge (Ill. 376)

Bridge construction was in advance of architecture throughout the nineteenth century. In our own century bridge design of various types has maintained its lead, even though architecture has advanced. Cables in tension, attached to rigid frame towers (h. 377 ft.) support the load. By remaining clear of the roadbed, the curves remain free and unimpaired, which enhances the total effect. A magnificent slenderness gives this structure a distinction that is in the best tradition of the great bridges of the past.

Modern furniture (Ill. 377)

The human basis for design is carried into furniture. Chairs are comfortably formfitting, adapted to the curves of the body. Legs spread out to gain stability, and lightness makes chairs easily movable. Plywood, plastics, and metal can be molded into almost any shape, and great rigidity is possible in curved shapes. Airplane production was responsible for experimental research. Charles Eames in collabora-

Ill. 376 Bronx-Whitestone Suspension Bridge across East River (1939) Allston Dana, Engineer of Design; Aymar Embury II, Architect. *Wurts Brothers*

tion with Eero Saarinen experimented with new techniques and produced the twentieth-century chair, which in variation has become universal.

Ill. 377 Modern furniture, Museum of Modern Art. *Wurts Brothers*

Notes

1. With the completion of the Aswan Dam, Abu Simbel would be submerged; it is hoped the temple will be saved through UNESCO cooperation.
2. A 1961 re-creation of this occurred when the widow of the murdered former Premier Patrice Lumumba of the Congo raised her arms as she pleaded before the authorities.
3. Thomas Jefferson adapted the design to the Virginia state capitol.
4. "Pantheon" means temple to all gods, or all highest, suggesting the vaulted heavens.
5. Estimates as to the seating capacity of the Colosseum vary from 40,000 to 80,000.
6. According to Paul Graef (1888), as quoted by Karl Woermann (1922), 125 triumphal arches have been accounted for in all countries; there were 10 in Rome, 20 in the rest of Italy.
7. Scenes now visible only through binoculars could be seen at the time of the Renaissance from nearby housetops.
8. A comparable situation existed in early America when copies of Italian paintings were acquired for American houses.
9. In 1845 the vase was broken; the potter Josiah Wedgwood made ceramic copies finished by handwork; subsequent copies were cast from molds.
10. The Christian era was calculated by the monk Dionysius Exiguus in the sixth century after Christ. He placed the birth of Christ on December 25 in the year 753 of Rome and decided that 754 should be the first year of the Christian era.
11. Ninety-two pieces, painted red, were discovered on the island of Lewis in 1831.
12. Color reproductions fail to reproduce the coolness of tempera panels, and color transparencies turn the opaqueness of pigments into something resembling stained glass.
13. *See* Jacobus de Varagine, *The Golden Legend* (2 vols. New York: Longmans, Green & Co., Inc., 1941).
14. *See* Jacob Burckhardt, *The Civilization of the Renaissance in Italy* (New York: Harper, 1929), p. 531, note 43.
15. *See* Erwin O. Christensen, "Freud on Leonardo da Vinci," *The Psychoanalytic Review*, Vol. 31, No. 2, April, 1944.
16. *See* Erwin O. Christensen, "Basic Determinants in the Art of Andrea del Sarto," *The Psychoanalytic Review*, Vol. 29, No. 3, July, 1942.
17. *See* Erwin O. Christensen, "Infantile Sources of Artistic Interests

in the Neurosis of Marie Bashkirtseff," *The Psychoanalytic Review*, Vol. 30, No. 3, July, 1943.

18. *See* Erwin O. Christensen, *The Index of American Design* (New York: The Macmillan Company, 1950), p. 219.
19. The best-known work of Boethius (475–525), *Consolations of Philosophy*, is a fusion of Stoicism and Christianity, here meant to fortify those who are ill or distressed.
20. Bliss (1928), p. 141, quoting Richard Muther.
21. From *escoria,* slag, referring to a small iron mine where refuse was thrown out. The name was applied to the palace.
22. The dark prints are fairly common and are reasonably priced.
23. Hung at eye level, they can be seen, unlike Michelangelo's Sistine ceiling.
24. Perhaps the ancient "guardian angels" rather than Christian angels.
25. These specialist genre painters along with many seventeenth-century Dutch painters are well represented, outside the Rijksmuseum, in the Dresden Gallery.
26. Assigned to Madame du Barry rather than to Madame de Pompadour, as previously reported [p. 277].
27. For practical purposes, Western music did not until the eighteenth century produce works that are in repertoire today.
28. *The World Almanac* lists sixteen categories under *Awards,* but art and painting are not included.
29. Barefooted came the beggar maid
    Before the King Cophetua.
    In robe and crown the king stepped down
    To meet and greet her on her way.——Tennyson, *The Beggar Maid.*
30. The past is constantly being reevaluated, and some artists of the past come back to life after periods of neglect.
31. This deceptive characteristic has been carried to its ultimate triumph by the color motion pictures.
32. Erik Blomberg (*Carl Frederik Hill,* Stockholm, 1949) has given us a sympathetic study of this important modern artist, who has received a belated recognition.
33. The term emotion has meaning as a state of tension experienced by the artist during creative activity.
34. Moreau's house in Paris is now the Musée Gustave Moreau.
35. The fashionable but overworked term is "images."
36. The earth, a universal mother symbol, served his need for regression —in a dual aspect, lovable and hateful, desired but also rejected.
37. An analytical study by a psychoanalyst, an art historian, and the artist might reveal the motivation for which the art is but a symptom. This still does not make artists neurotic, although some artists may have been neurotic or more neurotic than other artists or laymen.
38. Julien Alvard, *Art International,* June 10, 1960.
39. The Graces—Euphrosyne, Aglaia and Thalia—were goddesses of the banquet, dance, and all social arts.
40. The public statues have become the forgotten relics of another era, sacrificed to the traffic that passes them by.
41. Named for late husband of Mrs. Louis P. Aloe, who started the movement for the fountain, dedicated in 1940.
42. Reproduction of small pieces that would retain the surface quality of the originals should open up a new world of art appreciation to the blind.
43. *See* Andrew Carnduff Ritchie, *Sculpture of the Twentieth Century* (New York: Museum of Modern Art, 1952).
44. No. 12 Rue de Turin, Brussels, by Victor Horta (1893).
45. For an impression of art in the U.S.S.R. the reader should turn to the catalog of the Moscow exhibition in New York.
46. *See* Museum of Modern Art, *The New American Painting* (New York: Museum of Modern Art, 1959), p. 52.

47. An objective attitude is difficult to maintain; we react to the idea and overlook the artistic means by which it is expressed.

48. Having admitted the Ramesses of Abu Simbel (Ill. 17), it would seem ungracious to leave out the presidents of Mount Rushmore.

49. Industrial Arts Building, Smithsonian Institution.

50. Edgar Kaufmann Jr., *Louis Sullivan and the Architecture of Free Enterprise*, 1956. The Chicago Home Insurance Building (1884) used a true skeleton form of construction (William B. Mundie, architect). The Tacoma Building (1887) in Chicago was the first building erected completely of skeleton construction. *Tallmadge* (1927)

51. To give insulation the panels are sprayed on the inside with a four-inch covering of perlite and sand.

Selected Bibliography

1. Prehistoric Art in Europe

Frobenius, Leo, and D. C. Fox. *Prehistoric Rock Pictures in Europe and Africa*. New York: Museum of Modern Art; London: George Allen & Unwin, Ltd., 1937.
Spearing, Herbert G. *The Childhood of Art*. 2nd rev. ed. New York: Henry Holt & Company, Inc.; London: Ernest Benn, Ltd., 1930.

2. Egyptian Art

Edwards, Iorwerth E. S. *The Pyramids of Egypt*. New York: Penguin Books, Inc., 1954.
Lange, Kurt, and M. Hirmer. *Egypt*. New York and London: Phaidon Press, 1956.
Smith, William Stevenson. *The Art and Architecture of Ancient Egypt*. New York: Penguin Books, Inc., 1958.

3. Near Eastern Art

Koldewey, Robert. *Excavations at Babylon*. New York and London: The Macmillan Company, 1914.

Schmidt, Erich F. *Persepolis*. 2 vols. Chicago: University of Chicago Press, 1953, 1957; London: Cambridge University Press, 1954, 1957.
Wooley, Sir C. L. *Ur of the Chaldees*. New York: Penguin Books, Inc., 1954.

4. Greek Art

Carpenter, Rhys. *The Esthetic Basis of Greek Art of the Fifth and Fourth Centuries B.C.* New York: Longmans, Green & Company, 1921.

Gardner, Ernest A. *A Handbook of Greek Sculpture.* 3rd ed. New York and London: The Macmillan Company, 1929.

Hege, Walter, and Gerhart Rodenwaldt. *Olympia.* New York: B. Westermann Co., Inc.; London: Sidgwick & Jackson, Ltd., 1936.

Lawrence, Arnold W. *Greek Architecture.* New York: Penguin Books, Inc., 1957.

Robertson, Martin. *Greek Painting.* New York: Skira, Inc., Publishers; London: A. Zwemmer, 1959.

5. Etruscan and Roman Art

Anderson, W. J., R. P. Spiers, and T. Ashby. *The Architecture of Ancient Rome.* New York: Charles Scribner's Sons, 1927.

Goldscheider, Ludwig. *Etruscan Sculpture.* New York: Oxford University Press; London: George Allen & Unwin, Ltd., 1941.

Richter, Gisela M. A. *Handbook of the Classical Collection.* New York: Metropolitan Museum of Art, 1930.

6. Early Christian and Byzantine Art

Anthony, Edgar W., *A History of Mosaics.* Boston: Porter Edward Sargent, 1935.

Talbot Rice, David. *Byzantine Art.* New York and London: Oxford University Press, 1935.

Whittemore, Thomas. *The Mosaics of St. Sophia at Istanbul.* London: Oxford University Press, 1933, 1936, 1942, 1952.

7. Early Medieval and Romanesque Art

De Wald, Ernest T. *The Illustrations of the Utrecht Psalter.* Princeton, N.J.: Princeton University Press; London: Oxford University Press, 1933.

Jacobus de Varagine. *The Golden Legend.* 2 vols. New York: Longmans, Green & Co., Inc., 1941.

Jameson, Anna B. Murphy. *Sacred and Legendary Art.* 2 vols. Boston: Houghton Mifflin Company, 1911.

Lethaby, William R. *Medieval Art.* New York: Charles Scribner's Sons, 1913.

Porter, A. Kingsley. *Medieval Architecture*. 2 vols. New York: Baker & Taylor Co., 1909.

Sullivan, Edward. *The Book of Kells*. 5th ed. New York: The Thomas Y. Crowell Co.; London: The Studio, Ltd., 1953.

8. Gothic Art

Adams, Henry. *Mont-Saint-Michel and Chartres*. New York: Doubleday & Company, Inc. (Anchor Books), 1959.

Holt, E. B. G. *Documentary History of Art*. New York: Doubleday & Company, Inc. (Anchor Books), 1957.

Karlinger, Hans. *Die Kunst der Gothik*. Berlin: Propyläen, 1927.

Mâle, Emile. *Religious Art from the Twelfth to the Eighteenth Century*. New York: Pantheon Books, 1949; London: Routledge & Kegan Paul, Ltd., 1950.

Villard de Honnecourt. *Sketchbook*. Edited by T. Bowie. Bloomington: Indiana University Press, 1959.

Von Simson, O. *The Gothic Cathedral*. New York: Pantheon Books; London: Routledge & Kegan Paul, Ltd., 1956.

9. Renaissance Art

Anderson, W. J. *The Architecture of the Renaissance in Italy*. New York: Charles Scribner's Sons, 1927.

Blunt, Anthony. *Art and Architecture of France, 1500–1700*. New York and London: Penguin Books, Inc., 1953.

Castiglione, Baldassare. *The Book of the Courtier*. Translated and edited by Friench Simpson. New York: Friedrich Ungar Publishing Company, 1959.

Cellini, Benvenuto. *Autobiography*. Translated by J. A. Symonds. New York: Modern Library, Inc., 1927.

Clark, Kenneth. *Leonardo da Vinci*. New York and London: Phaidon Press, 1954.

Dehio, Georg. *Geschichte der Deutschen Kunst*. 4 vols. Berlin: Gruyter, 1919–1934.

Dimier, Louis. *French Painting in the 16th Century*. New York: Charles Scribner's Sons, 1911.

Glück, Gustav. *Die Kunst der Renaissance in Deutschland, den Niederlanden, Frankreich*. Berlin: Propyläen, 1928.

Machiavelli, Niccolò. *The Prince*. New York and London: Oxford University Press, 1943; New York: The New American Library of World Literature, Inc. (Mentor Books), 1952.

Marle, Raimond van. *The Development of the Italian Schools of Painting*. 19 vols. The Hague: M. Nijhoff, 1923–1939.

Martin, Alfred von. *Sociology of the Renaissance*. New York: Oxford University Press; London: Routledge & Kegan Paul, Ltd., 1944.

Simpson, F. M. *A History of Architectural Development*. 3 vols. New York and London: Longmans, Green & Company, 1929.

Vasari, Giorgio. *The Lives of the Most Eminent Painters, Sculptors, and Architects*. New York: Random House, Inc. (Modern Library), 1959.

Waterhouse, Ellis K. *Painting in Britain 1530–1790*. New York and London: Penguin Books, Inc., 1953.

Wölfflin, Heinrich. *Principles of Art History*. New York: Dover Publications, 1950.

10. Baroque and Rococo Art

Bode, Wilhelm von. *Great Masters of Flemish and Dutch Painting*. London: Gerald Duckworth & Co., Ltd., 1909.

Fromentin, Eugène. *The Masters of Past Time: Dutch and Flemish Painting from Van Eyck to Rembrandt*. Translated by Andrew Boyle. New York and London: Phaidon Press, 1948.

Lucas, Louise E. *The Harvard List of Books on Art*. Cambridge, Mass.: Harvard University Press; London: Oxford University Press, 1952.

Sachs, Paul J. *The Pocket Book of Great Drawings*. New York: Pocket Books, Inc., 1951.

Seymour, Charles, Jr. *Masterpieces of Sculpture from the National Gallery of Art*. New York: Coward-McCann, Inc., 1949.

Wittkower, Rudolf. *Art and Architecture in Italy, 1600–1750*. New York and London: Penguin Books, Inc., 1958.

11. Modern Art in Europe

Barr, Alfred H. *Matisse, His Art and His Public*. New York: Museum of Modern Art, 1951.

———. *Picasso, Fifty Years of His Art*. New York: Museum of Modern Art, 1946.

Berger, Klaus, *Géricault and His Work*. Lawrence, Kans.: University of Kansas Press, 1955.

Cathelin, Jean. *Jean Arp*. New York: Grove Press, 1959.

Giedion, Sigfried. *Space, Time, and Architecture*. Cambridge, Mass.: Harvard University Press; London: Oxford University Press, 1941.

Johnson, Philip C. *Mies van der Rohe*. 2nd rev. ed. New York: Museum of Modern Art, 1954.

Kandinsky, Wassily. *Concerning the Spiritual in Art.* New York: Solomon R. Guggenheim Museum, 1950.

Le Corbusier. *Towards a New Architecture.* New York: Harcourt, Brace & Company, Inc., 1947.

Pevsner, Nikolaus. *Pioneers of Modern Design.* New York: Doubleday & Company, Inc., 1958.

Ragon, Michel. *Dubuffet.* New York: Grove Press, 1959.

Seymour, Charles, Jr. *Tradition and Experiment in Modern Sculpture.* Washington: American University Press, 1949.

Van Gogh, Vincent. *The Complete Letters.* 3 vols. Greenwich, Conn.: New York Graphic Society Publishers, Ltd.; London: Thames & Hudson, Ltd., 1958.

12. Art in the United States

Goodrich, Lloyd. *Winslow Homer.* New York: The Macmillan Company, 1944.

Gropius, Walter. *The New Architecture and the Bauhaus.* London: Faber & Faber, Ltd., 1935; New York: Museum of Modern Art, 1937.

Hitchcock, Henry Russell. *Architecture: Nineteenth and Twentieth Centuries.* New York: Penguin Books, Inc., 1958.

Hope, Henry R. *The Sculpture of Jacques Lipchitz.* New York: Museum of Modern Art, 1954.

Janis, Harriet and R. Blesh. *De Kooning.* New York: Grove Press, 1960.

Richardson, Edgar P. *Painting in America.* New York: The Thomas Y. Crowell Co., 1956.

Ritchie, Andrew C. *Sculpture of the Twentieth Century.* New York: Museum of Modern Art; London: Putnam & Co., Ltd., 1953.

Seitz, William C. *The Art of Assemblage.* New York: Museum of Modern Art, 1961.

Taft, Lorado. *History of American Sculpture.* Rev. ed. New York and London: The Macmillan Company, 1930.

————. *The New American Painting.* New York: Museum of Modern Art, 1959.

Index

Numbers in italics refer to illustrations